REVELATION THE GOOD NEWS

End of Days Timeline Revealed, Jubilee Edition

Bo Polny, Analyst of Time

CONTENTS

DEDICATION

This book is dedicated to God, the Father, Jesus, and the Holy Spirit. All GLORY goes to you! The timing outlined within this book is beyond any human possibilities, including my own. Without a doubt, it clearly illustrates you are God, the creator of all things, and you wrote the END from the beginning. Thank you for blessing me with wisdom and understanding, including the title "The Analyst of Time." You are the author and finisher of our faith. I love you!

To Sophia, my beautiful, loving wife, my rock here on earth, more precious than jewels. Thank you for your unwavering support and love throughout the years. Without you, there would be no book. You are the glue that brought and keeps everything together, and in the name of Jesus, you continually fill my life with His love and peace. May God continue to bless you always. I love you and our journey together, in His Glorious name!

To my mother and father. Thank you for your unconditional love and support in my younger years, and for guiding me to Jesus and His love.

To the Harvest Creek Publishing team. Your help was an answered prayer, giving life to this book. It brought me joy to witness everyone recognizing the incredible timing details revealed by God in Revelation and acknowledging it as the "Good News." I know God divinely put us together to publish His book, and it was all done in His perfect timing! God bless you all.

Finally, to our loyal, loving, and faithful followers around the world. We deeply appreciate your ongoing commitment to watch our interviews and podcasts, believe in the Lord's revelations, and offer your heartfelt prayers. I am grateful for your ongoing support and kind words over the years. May the Lord God Almighty continue to bless you all always!

JESUS ANSWERED...

"IT IS WRITTEN"

Christ admonishes us to discern **"THE SIGNS OF THE TIMES"** in which we live - Matthew 16:3
THE ISSACHAR ANOINTING: **"Men who understood the TIMES"** - 1 Chronicles 12:32

LUKE 4:12

PREFACE
The Issachar Anointing

> *From the tribe of Issachar, there were 200 leaders of the tribe with their relatives. All these men understood the signs of the times and knew the best course for Israel to take.*
>
> 1 Chronicles 12:32 NLT [Emphasis Added]

GOD IS EMPOWERING people with the Issachar anointing to comprehend the current times through discernment and knowledge. Issachars seek God's wisdom through the Word to know what needs to be done and how to act upon it. They grasp the signs of the times. Their goal is not just to understand, but to determine the best course of action.

Those with the Issachar anointing understand the chronological cycles of time. They understand how spiritual and political climates are connected, as well as the importance of timing. The current era allows us to choose between fear and faith. God is pouring out the Issachar anointing, granting kingdom discernment and knowledge for these times. An Issachar helps us understand the events going on and how we fit into a plan. God desires that we *run towards* Him, *not away* from the challenges of this world, so that we can bring others to the Kingdom as well.

The link between history and the present is more easily understood by those with the Issachar anointing. The Bible says, "You know how to interpret the weather signs in the sky, but you don't know how to interpret the signs of the times!" (Matthew 16:3 NLT)

Without knowledge of the past, charts and calculations could never yield precise predictions. As someone with this special gift from God, I believe that if you don't study history, you'll never know the future.

If you don't study history, you'll never know the future.

OPPORTUNITIES TO SEE GOD

This book provides the sensory opportunity to see what God has given me in terms of Revelation. I don't claim to be a prophet, for I have witnessed the modern-day prophets at work and have seen the fire come upon them. I do not have the same anointing that these prophets do. God uses everyone.

God has given me the anointed understanding of time. During my sleep, I often get a number, date, or a word. Then, I will pull up a scripture or a verse that corresponds exactly with what I am searching for. There is a yearning in me to calculate and review key dates where incredible biblical situations *have* happened and *will* happen.

Let's consider Daniel 2. The credit for interpreting Nebuchadnezzar's dream doesn't go to Daniel. It's clear that Daniel received the interpretation directly from God. And this dream was so critical to history because it foretold the next 2500 years. It was the foretelling of the end from the beginning. Again, if you don't study history, you'll never know the future.

There are critical time points in history that are foreshadowing what's going to happen here in America and around the world. Take the miracle at the Red Sea: Moses did not know what the Lord was going to do. But by faith, he took the Israelites to the edge of the sea. And God performed a miracle.

No person could have parted the waters or planned their way out of the situation. It was by God's hand and design. And we must believe in that same God today, who has a plan, who knows the end from the beginning, and who will perform miracles for us. He is the God of yesterday, today and tomorrow. He is a living God.

God is not caught off guard by any of this. He's still on the throne and still moving in this generation in the spiritual realm. He will fulfill His plans and purposes. Keep your divine perspective. Don't let what you see in the natural world sway you. Remain in the Word to maintain your spiritual vision.

While the world perceives it as a coincidence, believers see God's hand in every aspect. Look on the horizon and see Him. When you feel disheartened by God's seemingly slow pace, sharpen your spiritual senses to perceive His presence. Look for God's activity around you. There is nothing random on this Earth.

God wrote the end from the beginning, and He knows it. The only uncertainty is where you'll be—on what side—when the end comes. He gave us a choice to "choose this day" whom we will serve. The choice is yours to make. The rest is God's.

Bo Polny

Remember the former things, those of
long ago; I am God, and there is no other;
I am God, and there is none like me.
I make known the end from the beginning,
from ancient times, what is still to come.
I say, "My purpose will stand,
and I will do all that I please."

Isaiah 46:9-10 NIV

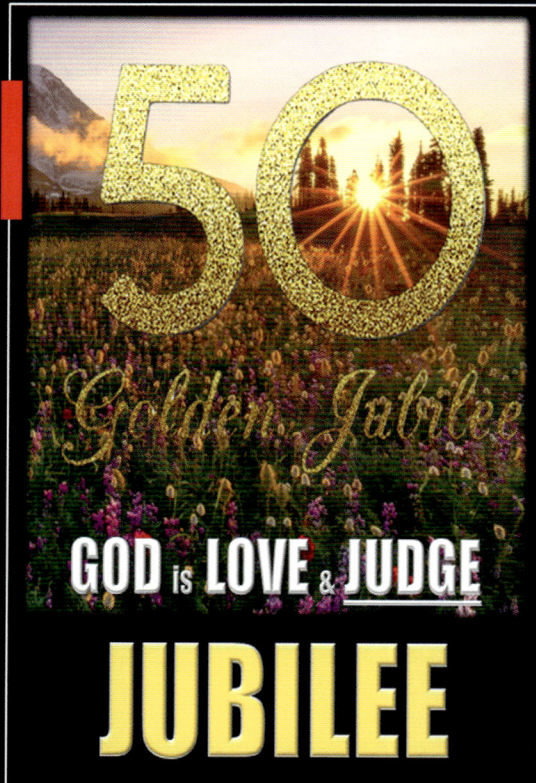

"The Spirit of the Lord God is upon me, because the Lord has anointed me to bring good news to the poor; he has sent me to comfort the brokenhearted, and to proclaim that captives will be released and prisoners will be freed; to Proclaim the **YEAR OF THE LORD'S FAVOR**, and **THE DAY OF VENGEANCE** of our God; to comfort all who mourn." - Isaiah 61:1-2

Jesus reads Isaiah 61, finishing with **"today this scripture is fulfilled"** ... announces He is Messiah!

Isaiah 61:1-2

YEAR OF THE LORD'S FAVOR ?

THE DAY OF VENGEANCE ?

"Vengeance is Mine, their foot shall slip in due time, for the day of their calamity is at hand and their fall shall come swiftly."
- Deuteronomy 32:35

Photo from The Chosen, Season 3, Episode 3

INTRODUCTION
The Good News

A MULTITUDE of books delve into theories and thoughts surrounding Christ's return and the events that precede His grand appearance. Prefixes such as *pre-*, *post-*, and *a-* are used by theologians to describe the millennial period when Jesus will return for His Church.

So why another book about Revelation? What makes this book different? Well, I'm glad you asked!

As end-time signs continue to unfold, people respond with fear. After all, the world is deteriorating before our eyes. Perversion, crime, anger, and abuse plague the earth, bringing tension and anxiety. Followers of the Faith wonder if things will ever get better instead of continuing to erode.

Like those scoffers mentioned in the Word over 2000 years ago, some may ask, "Where is this coming one?" that Jesus promised. Is He ever going to make things right again (2 Peter 3:3-4)? And so, we eagerly long for Christ's return to set the world right—to judge the living and the dead and to bring about the redemption of this mess.

But with that comes fear and angst about *how* and *when* that will happen. It is time to dispel misconceptions about the past, present, and future regarding the end days. There is much **good news** to be found in the days leading up to Christ's return. And as this book will emphasize throughout its pages, we know the *end* from the *beginning*.

FAITH VS. FEAR

When faced with their fears, individuals usually make a choice between: 1) Choosing to ignore the information or 2) being paralyzed by fear. However, ignoring the Truth won't change it; Jesus *is* coming back. The Bible says:

> *For the Lord himself will come down from heaven, with a loud command, with the voice of the archangel and with the trumpet call of God . . . we who are still alive and are left will be caught up together with them in the clouds to meet the Lord in the air. And so we will be with the Lord forever.*

1 Thessalonians 4:16-18 NIV

Being paralyzed in fear makes you unable to complete your purpose on earth. The world is full of fear because Satan is currently the prince of this world. His mission is to steal, kill, and destroy. He's a prince—the prince of darkness. However, the Lord is King. Not just *a* king. He's *the* King of kings.

Faith is the primary reason this book differs from the rest. Faith dispels fear. The Word says:

> *Blessed is he who does not see and yet believes.*
>
> John 20:29b NIV

While Satan brings destruction and death, God grants us a life of abundance. Satan is a liar; God is love, and perfect love casts out all fear (1 John 4:18). If you walk with Christ, you don't need to be afraid. God, the Father, will not beat up the Son's bride before He returns.

And when you correctly understand the time and seasons, there is **no fear**. In fact, these signs give us great hope and expectation. The patterns are clearly laid out. This book will comprehensively explain the connection between historical events and the biblical timeline. And this is a timeline that will continue to unfold rapidly over the next few years.

Moreover, the math in recorded information cannot be possible without God's design. We shouldn't *fear* His coming, we should *long for* it. As believers, we understand this world isn't our permanent home, it's a pass-through to a better home in glory. And God's divine plan is unfolding before us.

In this book, you will learn to see the random events playing out on the world's stage from a "big picture" perspective. You will learn spiritual truths about how God moves, revealing the consistent unfolding of a divine plan to bless His chosen people.

GUARD AGAINST TRADITIONAL MINDSETS

I urge you to keep an open mind as this book covers a wide range of topics that challenge traditional thinking. For example, most people have a fixed mindset regarding the world's financial system.

A prominent personal finance author was a recent guest on a vlog hosted by a well-known entrepreneur/talk show host. The show host, who was a Christian, cited passages of scripture from Ezekiel and Daniel during the interview. The guest promptly dismissed the conversation, refusing to listen to any of that "Religious [*expletive*]."

It was very disappointing to see that when it came to Christian thought, this man's heart and mind were completely closed. And even more interesting is that in these end days, the guest who shut down the interview is buying up land and precious metals, taking precautions, and making preparations for what could be a rough road ahead. Although he appears to be doing everything correctly, he is still without God.

As the scripture alludes, some people profess themselves to be wise and become utter fools. You can do everything "right" according to the world's standards and still be empty when you don't know Christ. And the Bible says that some will throw their gold and silver into the streets because they want to buy their way into Heaven.

This famous author trashed the talk show host many times because of his references to the Bible. But again, ignoring the Truth won't change it. Christ is coming back, and we can't stop that.

CHRIST'S FINAL JUDGMENT

In 30 AD, Jesus was baptized by John the Baptist, marking the beginning of his three-and-a-half-year ministry. Page 4 illustrates how Jesus, while at the synagogue following his Baptism, read from Isaiah 61 and stopped reading before the end of the passage.

> The Spirit of the Sovereign LORD is on me, because the LORD has anointed me to proclaim **good news** to the poor. He has sent me to bind up the brokenhearted, to proclaim freedom for the captives and release from darkness for the prisoners, to proclaim the year of the LORD's favor [and the day of vengeance of our God].
>
> Isaiah 61:1-2a NIV [Emphasis Added]

Jesus didn't read the last line, "And the day of vengeance." Why is this so? Because He knew that the day of vengeance was in the future. Jesus actually said, "It's not for now." He was saying, "I'm not bringing vengeance. I'm here to bring Salvation." Vengeance comes on the great and terrible day of the Lord, according to Joel 2:31 and Psalm 37:10. It is expected to come in 2025 and be wonderful for the church, but terrible for the enemies of God. Although vengeance comes with deliverance for America and the world, this is not the final judgment.

Christ came and died on the cross and was resurrected. And through His blood, we can trample on the necks and heads of serpents. But we cannot redeem the earth. Christ is coming back to do that. He's not coming back to save us; He saved us when He shed His blood on the cross. He's coming back for the final judgment and to redeem the Earth. That's the Lord's purpose for returning.

> Vengeance is Mine, their foot shall slip in due time,
> for the day of their calamity (the day of vengeance) is at hand
> and their fall shall come swiftly.
>
> Deuteronomy 32:35 NKJV [Emphasis Added]

And when He comes, the earth will see the final judgment as described in the book of Revelation 20:11-15.

> Then I saw a great white throne and Him who sat on it, from whose face the earth and the heaven fled away. And there was found no place for them. And I saw the dead, small and great, standing before God, and books were opened. And another book was opened, which is the Book of Life. And the dead were judged according to their works, by the things which were written in the books. The sea gave up the dead who were in it, and Death and Hades delivered up the dead who were in them. And they were judged, each one according to his works. Then Death and Hades were cast into the lake of fire. This is the second death. And anyone not found written in the Book of Life was cast into the lake of fire.
>
> Revelation 20:11-15 NKJV

BLESSING AND VINDICATION vs. FINAL JUDGMENT

God's intervention yields a dual outcome: blessings and vindication, or judgment and deliverance at the same time. When He intervenes, it is both the scariest time and the biggest blessing. But there is always a bigger plan and a dual outcome.

For example, when God intervened at the Red Sea, both outcomes occurred. The Israelites were terrified as they reached the rushing waters. But the Egyptians' fate (vindication) was sealed. The parting of the waters became a blessing for God's people, who were saved from their enemies (deliverance).

> *The people of Israel went into the midst of the sea on dry ground, the waters being a wall to them on their right hand and on their left.*
>
> Exodus 14:21-22 NLT

And when the three teens were in the fire with Daniel, it was scary. Their situation was dire. But despite the circumstances, they felt the safest *in the fire* because Jesus Christ was present. Shadrach, Meshach, and Abednego were being delivered while God was bringing judgment on Babylon.

While God carries out judgment, Christians are secure because He is the Way Maker, Miracle Worker, Promise Keeper, and the Light in the Darkness. When God intervenes, there is always a bigger plan—to strike evil. His Glory will manifest first vengeance for the righteous. And, in the future, the final judgment where the earth is redeemed.

The Final Judgment will happen when Christ returns. The consequences of the evil seeds sown by evil people will be their harvest. God will reap on their heads what they planted for us.

The modern-day Egyptians (Wall Street, Babylon, Hollywood, corrupt politicians, etc.) will soon be gone for a season of time. But we aren't to take matters into our own hands for now. It's the Lord's battle. God reminds us not to fight evil with evil but to fight evil with good.

Therefore, vengeance entails an unshakable faith in Christ's provision, refusing to be swayed. We do our part to walk with Him, but then we stand and watch. At the Red Sea, the Israelites were told to "**stand** still and **watch** the salvation of the Lord, for He will work for you today" (Exodus 14:13 Emphasis Added).

In 2025, when God moves upon the world, we are going to see the incredible manifestation of favor AND fulfillment of Isaiah 61 (both the year of the Lord's favor and the day of vengeance). There will be signs, miracles, and wonders as God displays His glory. And if you are a witness to all of that and still refuse Him, then in the future time of the Antichrist when He brings judgment, you will not be saved. America is saved from judgment for overturning Roe vs. Wade. But, like disobedient children, we will receive chastisement as written in Jeremiah 30:11.

> *For I am with you, says the LORD, to save you; though I make a full end of all nations where I have scattered you, Yet I will not make a complete end of you. But I will correct you in justice, and will not let you go altogether unpunished.*
>
> Jeremiah 30: 11 NKJV

The Final Judgment will be a horrific thing upon the earth. But right now, we are at a point of vengeance, and God is going to fulfill Isaiah 61 by proclaiming freedom, releasing captives, and proclaiming the Lord's favor. This will ultimately result in a mutli-billion soul harvest. What an exciting time to stand and watch!

GENESIS TO REVELATION

It is fitting that the first book of the Bible, Genesis, describes the *entrance* of sin and the curse, and the last book, Revelation, talks about the *end* of sin and the curse. Genesis *brings* sorrow upon humanity, while Revelation *banishes* all sorrow from humanity.

Even with all the provisions from our Heavenly Father, Genesis still brings illness, suffering, and poverty. Revelation displays the restoration of God's kingdom and His financial system. Genesis introduces the *creation* of the heavens and the earth, while Revelation shows the *culmination* of the heavens and the earth.

Revelation is a book that speaks directly to troubled times. When it seems like the world is darker than ever and the powers of evil seem to be completely out of control, we can find assurance in the book of Revelation that God will triumph, bless His saints, and judge sin.

MAINTAIN THE RIGHT PERSPECTIVE

The goal is to strengthen your faith and change your perspective on end-time events. Instead of fearing what is ahead, start trusting in the promises of Scripture that bring ***good news*** to believers. These signs are a call to action to usher others into the Kingdom while there is still an opportunity.

The times we are living in and those yet to come offer hope for correcting injustices and fixing what is broken. God's season of freedom, favor, and our release from oppressive darkness is coming.

The counterfeiters of deception will soon be brought to light. The great shaking is imminent as the tables of injustice will be overturned in 2025. The sirens of man will ring out, and the world will tremble on the great and terrible day (Joel 2:31). But there's no need to fear because the trumpets of Heaven will give greater warning to the world.

> *The sun will be turned to darkness and the moon to blood before the coming of the great and dreadful day of the LORD.*
>
> Joel 2: 31 NIV

The Church is about to witness an unprecedented end-time harvest. In 2025, we enter a time of amazing grace for five years. And also a time of glory and plenty for the next seven years. We will see God open doors that man cannot close. And He will close doors to evil on the Earth that no man can ever re-open.

Now that is absolutely *good news!*

For whoever finds me finds life,
and obtains favor from the Lord.

Proverbs 8:35 NKJV

5-YEAR WINDOW OF DIVINE FAVOR & AMAZING GRACE

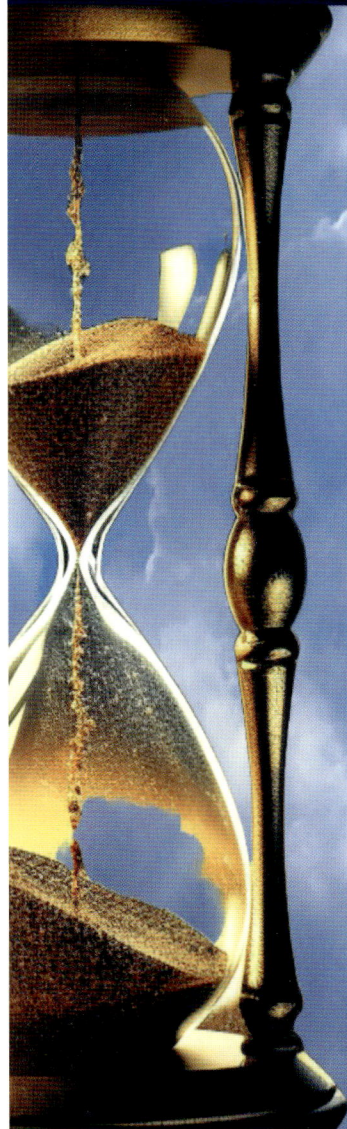

HIS GLORY ON EARTH (2025 – 2029)

- The wolf will live with the lamb, the leopard will lie down with the goat, the calf and the lion and the yearling together; and a little child will lead them.

- The cow will feed with the bear, their young will lie down together, and the lion will eat straw like the ox.

- The infant will play near the cobra's den, and the young child will put its hand into the viper's nest.

- They will neither hurt nor destroy on all my holy mountain, **for the earth will be filled with the GLORY of the LORD** as the waters cover the sea. - Isaiah 11:6-9

- And afterward (after the Great and Terrible Day in 2025), I will pour out my Spirit on all people. Your sons and daughters will prophesy, your old men will dream dreams, your young men will see visions. - Joel 2:28

Kim Clement 2013: *"The Glory of God that shall cover the earth with knowledge and manifestation, as the waters cover the sea. It is yet to come before I return, you are the generation that shall __defy death__!"*

Joy Unspeakable

Scan Me

BEGINS IN 2025

Events in our World...

ARE NOT POLITICAL
THEY ARE BIBLICAL

2020, the Beginning of the End, Written at the Beginning of Time!

CHAPTER 1
It's Not Political. It's Biblical.

Blessed be the name of God forever and ever,
For wisdom and might are His.
And He changes the times and the seasons;
He removes kings and raises up kings;
He gives wisdom to the wise
And knowledge to those who have understanding.
He reveals deep and secret things;
He knows what is in the darkness,
And light dwells in Him.
Thank You and praise You,
O God of my fathers;
You have given me wisdom.

Daniel 2:21-23a NKJV

THE EARTHQUAKES, TENSIONS in the Middle East, government corruption, droughts, and abnormal weather occurrences shown daily on the news might cause concern that the world is spinning out of control. Every corner of the globe is experiencing either the challenge of political unrest or the moral decay of human fiber in unparalleled fashion. The world is at a critical mass.

And yet, the events taking place are *not political*. Nor are they unexpected. They *are biblical*. God wrote the end from the beginning at the time of creation. And He has a timeline, recorded in the Bible through the prophecy of Daniel, that is unfolding before our eyes.

> **The current world events are part of the most significant move of God the earth will ever witness.**

While these occurrences are bewildering, they are all part of God's divine design. In God's kingdom, nothing is random or perchance. And we are leaping into an incredible point on His divine timeline—a move of God even more remarkable than the parting of the Red Sea. Let me repeat: The current world events are part of the most significant move of God the earth will ever witness.

It's essential to view world events with a broad perspective. God's movement is confirmed through spiritual truths that reveal His consistent unfolding of a divine plan to bless His chosen people.

Throughout the book, readers will learn about God's secret 248-year cycle, the Leviticus 50-year cycle, the six-day rule, the feasts, the day of His vengeance, signs in the sun, moon and stars, as well as other end-of-days' mysteries revealed. These circumstances and situations indicate the coming of a significant change—a paradigm shift—that will massively affect the world.

Some mistakenly believe that the people of God do not know the details of His divine timeline. But as many prophecies unfold, God's people must understand that there is nothing to fear and that the day of the Lord *is* near.

The Bible tells us where we are and where God is going in the days ahead. The events of today are not just arbitrarily happening. They are by His design.

As mentioned previously, we are entering a period of miracles and prosperity. The year 2025 brings the start of unimaginable miracles, unprecedented prosperity and incredible events happening within our world. The admonishment on the image at the opening of this chapter is important because Christ wants us to discern the "signs of the times" in which we live. This is based on God's covenant.

THE BEGINNING OF THE END

The year 2020 was the *beginning* of the end, which is perplexing to some. The confusion stems from the belief that the four horsemen will ride during the Tribulation. However, there is no record of that in the Bible.

The signaling of the beginning of the end comes with the opening of the Seven Seals. All seven seals will be discussed in detail in Chapters 4 and 5. For now, understand that when the first seal is opened, things will never be the same.

The Corona Virus opened the first seal as illustrated in Chapter 4, in the section: One Who Brings Ill Health. Since the Great Flood, nothing has affected the entire globe until Corona. Even during World Wars, there were some nations who never took part in the fighting.

So when the Lion of Judah opened the first seal, there was no turning back. You can't stop what's coming. And with Corona, the first seal was opened.

> *I watched as the Lamb opened the first of the seven seals. Then I heard one of the four living creatures say in a voice like thunder, "Come!" I looked, and there before me was a white horse! Its rider held a bow, and he was given a crown, and he rode out as a conqueror bent on conquest.*
>
> Revelation 6:1-2 NIV

FALLEN ANGELS

Angels and archangels have an especially important responsibility to travel back and forth between the heavenly and earthly dimensions, fulfilling missions from God. In the spiritual realm, angels spend time in God's presence, praise Him, and receive assignments for their work on Earth, assisting His children.

But since the Garden of Eden, fallen angels have infiltrated the Earth in a battle between good and evil. Two hundred fallen angels, were once part of God's team but were expelled from Heaven, and landed on Mount Hermon and made a covenant there with Satan. Those fallen angels are now being used by him to tempt humans to sin. Satan was known as Lucifer in Heaven and was the one who led the rebellion against God and was expelled from Heaven. Within the depths of hell, fallen angels have built their own empire. They are actively working to condemn humanity to the same fate.

However, this is a battle humanity cannot win on its own; we need God. The reason the Son of Man came to the Earth was to *seek* and *save* (i.e., redeem) that which was lost in the fall of humankind. According to God's laws, there is a penalty owed for sin in order for people to have the hope of eternal life. And that penalty was paid for those who believe in the Lord Jesus Christ through the shedding of blood on the cross of Calvary. Have you ever wondered why the Lamb is the only one who may open the seven seals? That is because the seals are sealed in His blood!

> *In fact, the law requires that nearly everything be cleansed with blood, and without the shedding of blood there is no forgiveness.*
>
> Hebrews 9:22 NIV

WHO IS RUNNING THE SHOW?

Revelation 17:5 describes a place of evil as "Mystery, Babylon the Great, the mother of Harlots and Abominations of the Earth." It speaks of a filthy woman who keeps company with the beast of the Abyss and is "the great city which rules over the kings of the earth."

> *There I saw a woman sitting on a scarlet beast that was covered with blasphemous names and had seven heads and ten horns . . . She held a golden cup in her hand, filled with abominable things and the filth of her adulteries. The name written on her forehead was a* **mystery: Babylon the Great**, *the Mother of Prostitutes and of the abominations of the Earth.*
>
> Revelation 17:3-5 NIV [Emphasis Added]

MYSTERY BABYLON

So, who or what is **Mystery Babylon**? It started off as an evil world system controlled by the Antichrist and fallen angels. In the Old Testament, the Pharaoh and the oppressive Egyptians held Israel in bondage. In current times, it is an ungodly system of men trying to kill America with evil goals to dominate and control it, as in the days of Daniel.

Mystery Babylon has a global influence over the people of the world. It is controlled by puppet masters, primarily billionaires and trillionaires, who have enslaved everyone on earth. Beginning in the early 70s they set up snares to capture the seven pillars of society and exercise control over us. The seven pillars are:

- Financial
- Family
- Church
- Government
- Entertainment
- Media
- Education

Babylon the Great started off as the city that never sleeps: New York, New York. Which is also the city where the founding fathers got on their knees and dedicated America to God. There they specifically made a covenant with God—and that day is celebrated every 4th of July. The covenant with God was sealed on July 4, 1776. Within this book, you will come to realize this date was already set and can be calculated backward to the birth of Jesus and even Creation.

> *Babylon was a golden cup in the LORD's hand, that made all the earth drunk. The nations drank her wine; therefore the nations are deranged.*
>
> Jeremiah 51:7 NKJV

Babylon promotes religious heresy and hates the true followers of God. This corrupt system actively leads people away from the Truth and toward all things corrupt, perverse and evil. Another characteristic of Mystery Babylon is her history of political influence. She brings great persecution and martyrdom to those who hold fast to the teachings of Jesus Christ.

Everything is a captured instrument and will remain so until the Glory manifests. The totalitarian system of Babylon is so powerful that the Bible says it was "given authority over every tribe, people and nation, no matter what language they spoke."

A WARNING FOR AMERICA

In 1984, a prophet named Dumitru Duduman issued a plea for America to be alert as Mystery Babylon progressed with its evil agenda. Duduman was of Romanian descent and brought up by Christian parents in the Pentecostal church. However, as a teenager, Duduman turned away from God, even confiscating Bibles while serving in the military.

However, this man had a supernatural encounter with God that turned his life around and eventually he would smuggle Bibles *into* Russia, rather than taking them from Christians. Subsequently, Duduman and his family were expelled from Romania. And they ended up in America by God's guidance and direction.

Once in the United States, and after years of persevering through many hardships, God gave Duduman a message for the American church:

"Tell them, because all the nations of the world immigrated to America with their own gods and were not stopped, but were encouraged by the freedom here, the wickedness began to increase. Later on, even though America was established as

a Christian nation, the American people began to follow the strange gods that the immigrants had brought in, and also turned their backs on the God who had built and prospered this country."

Duduman continued sharing this message until the day of his death, with one goal in mind: to encourage Christians to be obedient to God's word and do all that He asked.

THE STORM OF THE LORD IS COMING

As we will discuss in Chapter 7, God will judge Mystery Babylon. And that judgment will be swift. As the scriptures note, it will take place in "***one day***" and "one hour."

> *Babylon the fallen—that great city is fallen! She has become a home for demons . . .Therefore, these plagues will overtake her in a single day—death and mourning and famine. She will be completely consumed by fire, for the Lord God who judges her is mighty . . . they will stand at a distance, terrified by her great torment. They will cry out, "How terrible for you, O Babylon, you great city! In a single moment God's judgment came on you . . . in a single moment all the wealth of the city is gone!"*
>
> Revelation 18:2, 8, 10, 17 NLT

God's judgment of Mystery Babylon is described in detail as *Jacob's Trouble* in Jeremiah 30. Who is Jacob of Jacob's trouble? Jacob is the body of Christ, the latter template that will be birthed in the latter days (Haggai 2:9). The union of Jacob and Jesus is specifically the coming future royal wedding and the Great Return when the body of Christ becomes one with Jesus.

It is the storm of the Lord as described in Jeremiah 30:23 that brings a day so great (Jeremiah 30:7) that there is none like it. It causes a sudden 180-degree change in the direction away from the plans of evil and away from a one-world government to the great fall of evil and a turning toward God! That day is called the "Distress of Jacob" and with it comes cries of terror and panic (Jeremiah 30:5). But yes, we will be saved out of it by the hand of God. That day is coming in 2025!

Revelation brings ***good news*** for Christians, promising them spiritual blessings during the Fall of Mystery Babylon, provided they avoid the false teachings of this wicked empire. The mystery is no longer, because the misguided teachings of this agenda have been exposed through God's Word.

> *God's people need to be very patient. They are the ones who obey God's commands. And they remain faithful to Jesus.*
>
> Revelation 14:12 NIRV

> *Behold, the whirlwind of the LORD goes forth with fury, a continuing whirlwind; it will fall violently on the head of the wicked. The fierce anger of the LORD will not return until He has done it, and until He has performed the intents of His heart. In the latter days you will consider it.*
>
> Jeremiah 30:23-24 NKJV

BABYLON 'THE GREAT'

Babylon [America] <u>was</u> a gold cup [founded under God, a <u>Covenant</u> Nation, took the bible, financial aid and military protection across the globe] in the Lord's hand; she made the whole earth drunk. The nations drank her wine; therefore, they have now GONE MAD   - Jeremiah 51:7

WORLD GONE MAD

WAKE UP AMERICA

DUMITRU DUDUMAN PROPHECY

Scan Me

USA <u>is</u> referenced in the BIBLE; it is the Great Harlot, a beautiful virgin turned prostitute!

with whom the kings of the earth have committed sexual immorality and have become drunk. And on her forehead was written a name of mystery: **"BABYLON THE GREAT"**, mother of prostitutes and of earth's abominations."   - Revelation 17:2, 5-6

Statue of Liberty

The Statue of Liberty was originally a Muslim Woman. Early models of the statue were called, *"Egypt Carrying the Light to Asia". The present-day translation is Egyptians Carrying the Light to China.*

USA

AMERICA <u>WAS</u> a GOLD CUP that turned into the WORLDWIDE SWAMP, the GREAT HARLOT of Revelation!

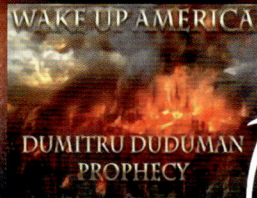

BABYLON THE GREAT

USA

Freemason "Puppet Masters"
The Khazarian Mafia
HARLOT SITTING to the BEAST

"MYSTERY BABYLON"

- Rothschilds
- Klaus Schwab
- Bill Gates
- Rockefellers
- Bilderberg Group
- Obama
- etc.

"G" = Gilgamesh = Nimrod

"And **He (KING Jesus)** will reign over **Jacob's** descendants forever; his kingdom will never end." - Luke 1:33

*S*tar of Bethlehem
Matthew 2:1-12

The Balaam Prophecy written in the Book Numbers:
The *Star of Bethlehem* is traditionally linked to this prophecy and stars relate to the arrival of miracles on earth, the Star of Bethlehem marked the arrival of Jesus. Matthew uses the star as a sign that Balaam's prophecy was coming true.

Christ The (Head) KING Is Born!

*S*tar of Jacob
Numbers 24:17

I see him, but not here and now. I perceive him, but far in the distant future. A star will rise from Jacob; a scepter will emerge from Israel. It will crush the heads of Moab's people, cracking the skulls of the people of Sheth.

The MOABITES are the son of Lot and his oldest daughter, who survived the destruction of Sodom and Gomorrah. A people in frequent conflict Israel and they worshiped a god of War and human sacrifice. Were eventually assimilated with the Arabs.

The (Body) BRIDE of Christ is Born!

50
Golden Jubilee

2023-24 KEY DATES:
- October 6-7, 2023: Tabernacle War
- October 26, 2023: U.S. Bombs Syria
- November 11, 2023: 300,000 call for a cease-fire
- May 31, 2024: Biden calls for Israeli ceasefire
- May 31, 2025 (Year of Jubilee): A Ceasefire?!

1973-74 KEY DATES:
- October 6, 1973
- October 26, 1973
- November 11, 1973
- May 31, 1974

TABERNACLE WAR
OCTOBER 7, 2023

AS FORECAST!

BO POLNY

CHAPTER 2
The Israel & United States Connection

IN MODERN TIMES, the United States and Israel have shown close ties. This stems from the shared Judeo-Christian values between the two nations. When Israel became a state and began the formation of their political, financial and military infrastructure, they looked to the U.S. for inspiration. Conversely, the U.S. has often followed the Western plan for economic development and democracy.

But this strong bond isn't something new. John Adams wrote a letter stating, "I will insist that the Hebrews have done more to civilize man than any other nation." (Letter to Mordecai Manual Noah 1819). Hebrew was once a required subject at Harvard University and Yale's insignia bears the Hebrew phrase "Urim ve'Thummim." The Urim and Thummim device (also known as the "breastpiece of decision") was worn by high priests in Leviticus and helped them discern God's will (Exodus 28:15). Another fascinating coincidence between Israel and America is the name of God, "I AM" as discussed on the following page.

That is why the Yom Kippur War, also known as the October War, drew the defense of the United States for their ally, Israel. The war was initiated by Egypt and Syria on October 6, 1973, on the Jewish holy day of Yom Kippur. Arab countries wanted more favorable terms after their defeat and loss of territory in the six-day war of 1967.

The Yom Kippur War ceased on October 26, 1973, and on November 11th, Israel signed a formal cease-fire agreement with Egypt and later with Syria on May 31, 1974. The war had a profound effect on the journey towards a lasting peace between Egypt and Israel, culminating in the restoration of the entire Sinai Peninsula to Egypt. The 1973-74 war had four key dates: October 6, 1973, October 26, 1973, November 11, 1973 and May 31, 1974. It is fascinating that all four of the 1973-74 dates ended up being important relative to the Leviticus 50-year cycle in 2023-24.

Being a time analyst, I predicted a war event would occur in October 2023, exactly fifty years after the start of the October War of 1973. On October 3, 2023, during a podcast interview, I stated that we were at a "critical mass" where things were going to intensify. I explained that the "world wanted Israel."

And just days later, on October 7, 2023, the Palestinian Jihadist group Hamas led an attack on Israel from the Gaza Strip. The assault resulted in the deaths of thousands of Israelis. Less than three weeks later, the United States launched an airstrike against Syria on October 26, 2023. And on November 11, 2023, 300,000 protesters hit the street demanding a cease-fire. Finally and precisely on May 31, 2024, Joe Biden called for an Israeli ceasefire. All that remains is for the Israel War to come to a sudden end. And that is expected to occur in 2025. Will May 31, 2025, bring a cease-fire?

THE FORTY-FOURTH KING

There is an interesting coincidence when discussing the nation of Israel and the United States. Israel had a total of forty-four monarchs (including those who reigned when the nation split into Israel and Judah). Israel fell after the final monarchy and there were no more after that. Those who reigned over Israel set the tone in terms of administrative, military and spiritual capacity.

Barack Obama was the 44th President of the United States. Many conservatives believe that the downturn of the United States came through his administration. Whatever you believe, one can't disagree that the Obama presidency set a new tone for America. Or better stated, it marked the end of America, as we know it.

You may find this interesting. I AM relates to the two covenant nations:

I = Israel (God chose Israel who rejected Jesus)

AM = America (America chose God, who accepted Jesus)

By the end of this book you will come to realize there are no coincidences. And what we call a coicidence is simply the manifestation of God's divine plan, written at the beginning of time.

In 2020, Obama published what was to be the first of a two-part memoir, titled *A Promised Land*. Although seemingly coincidental, notice the title is **A** Promised Land, not **The** Promised Land. In other words, he's not referring to the land flowing with milk and honey promised to Abraham in Genesis 15:18.

And while the book has only a few pages that mention anything about his faith, he does talk about carrying a few "lucky" [i.e., pagan] mementos with him while in office—a poker chip, a statue of Buddha, a bronze monkey god, and crystals and rocks. These were carried in hopes that the universe might tilt in his favor.

There is no doubt that this 44th king greatly changed the course of a nation during his presidency. Moreover, the 44th king calculation is indicating the fall of the United States *after* Obama. And Donald Trump brings in the birth of the kingdom of David.

Review the image on the next page which highlights the critical timepoints that occurred during the Obama administration, from his receipt of the Nobel Peace Prize to ending his presidency with a visit to the home of Zeus, Satan, God of the fallen angels.

OBAMA - The 44ᵗʰ PRESIDENT / KING
Whose Presidency marked the END of America, INC.

Obama's 2 x 1260-Day Cycle

Daniel's 7-Year Timeline

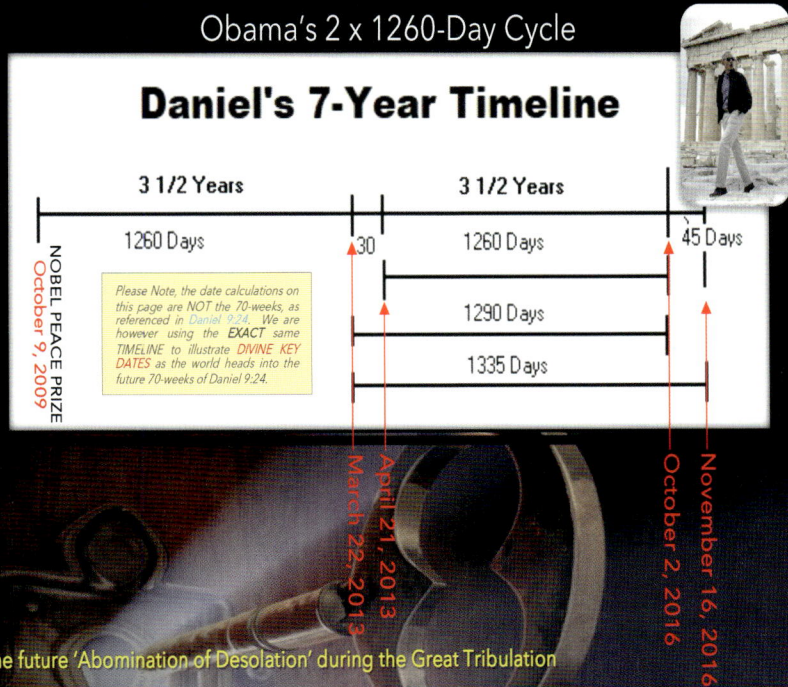

3 1/2 Years		3 1/2 Years	
1260 Days	30	1260 Days	45 Days
		1290 Days	
		1335 Days	

Please Note, the date calculations on this page are NOT the 70-weeks, as referenced in Daniel 9:24. We are however using the EXACT same TIMELINE to illustrate DIVINE KEY DATES as the world heads into the future 70-weeks of Daniel 9:24.

NOBEL PEACE PRIZE October 9, 2009

March 22, 2013
April 21, 2013

October 2, 2016
November 16, 2016

Obama Presidency 2009 - 2016

DIVINE KEY DATES *using 1260-Day Cycle*

✓ October 9, 2009 - Obama received the **NOBEL PEACE PRIZE**

✓ March 22, 2013 - October 9, 2009 + **1260 Cycle** - Obama's ISRAEL Trip, a foreshadowing of the future 'Abomination of Desolation' during the Great Tribulation

✓ April 21, 2013 - March 22, 2013 + **30 Cycle** - Obama spends $10bn updating guided nuclear bombs in Europe

✓ October 2, 2016 - April 21, 2013 + **1260 Cycle** - Obama signs over the internet to the United nations for future information control including **Cryptocurrencies**

➢ *November 8, 2016 - October 2, 2013 + 37 Cycle - US ELECTION and TRUMP WINS*

✓ November 16, 2016 - October 2, 2013 + **45 Cycle** - Obama Arrival in Athens, Greece, home of Zeus (satan), god of the fallen angels.

'Officially'

ISRAEL BORN 1967

A *GENERATION* is 70-Years, 1967 + 70-Years =

2037+

On **14 May 1948**, **Israel proclaimed its INDEPENDENCE.** Less than 24 hours later, the regular armies of Egypt, Jordan, Syria, Lebanon, and Iraq invaded the country, forcing Israel to defend the sovereignty it had regained.

1967 ARAB-ISRAELI WAR
SIX-DAY WAR

June 5, 1967, The Six-Day War And The Golan Heights

After the first Arab-Israeli war in **1948-1949**, the Arab world refused to recognize Israel's INDEPENDENCE. Nineteen (19) years later on **June 5, 1967**, the 6-Day War began and ended six (6) days later **June 10, 1967**, with an Israeli victory by seizing the West Bank, including East Jerusalem, as well as the Golan Heights.

> ## On the sixth (6) day God COMPLETED His Work.
> ## On the seventh (7) day God RESTED.

As of **June 10, 1967**, Israel is finally recognized by ALL the world as INDEPENDENT, and Israel was **'OFFICIALLY' BORN!!** This GENERATION 'that shall defy death' born on or after June 10, 1967, comes to an end between **2037**, latest **2048** by 'reason of strength', Psalm 90:10.

50-years after the Six-Day War ended is **2017**, then after **70-years** Treaty Broken & Abomination of Desolation in **2037**

Exactly **7-years** later, after the war ended, June 10, 1967, the USA and Saudi Arabia signed the 'Petro-Dollar' Agreement June 9, 1974.

1967 – Six-Day War

June 9, **1974** - Petrodollar

2017 – Rev. 12 Sign, Trump President

USA 2017 & 2024 **Total Solar ECLIPSES**

June 9, **2024** – Petrodollar ENDS
July 4, **2025** – America Reborn!

2037 Great Tribulation Matthew 24:21
2040 WW3 - Armageddon

7-YEARS

7-YEARS

50

50-years after the USA and Saudi Arabia signed the **Petrodollar** Agreement in **1974**, the Saudi's refused to resign on June 9, 2024, marking the END of the **Petrodollar** and the START of the 50-year Golden Jubilee into **June 9, 2025**

1776 Declaration of Independence + 248 Years, ends = July 3, 2025

Scan Me

THE ORIGINS OF THE ARAB/ISRAELI CONFLICT

The strong hatred between the Arabs and Israelis is a spiritual issue that goes back to Genesis, Chapter 16. Hagar, who was Sarah's maid, conceived a child by Sarah's husband, Abraham. At that time, Hagar despised Sarah. And ultimately when Hagar was sent away into the wilderness, God told her that her child would become the father of the Arab nations.

> *"... you will give birth to a son. You shall name him Ishmael, for the Lord has heard of your misery. He will be a wild donkey of a man; his hand will be against everyone and everyone's hand against him, and he will live in hostility toward all his brothers."*
>
> Genesis 16:11-12 NIV

Without a doubt, this word has come true. The strategy employed by Arab nations to conquer their foes has involved aggression and hostility just as God said. Although God had shown mercy to Hagar, declaring that He would make Ishmael a great nation, He made it clear from the start that His covenant would be with Isaac (Genesis 17:21). And since the time of Abraham, things have been rocky between the two nations.

However, 1913 was a year when everything unraveled between them, and the conflict escalated to an entirely new level. In that year, the newly formed Arab-Syrian Congress announced their unity in opposition to the European Zionist movement. Originating from eastern and central Europe, the Zionists had established a congress in 1901 and gathered annually to promote the establishment of a Jewish state in Palestine, the ancestral homeland of the Jewish people. NOTE: The Zionists laid the groundwork for what is today modern Israel.

During 1913, the Zionist Congress discussed the possibility of employing Hebrew labor to build the future Jewish state, rather than relying on Arab labor. The tensions between Jews and Arabs in the region were escalated by this pivotal decision. Arab communities in that region became more hostile because of their perceived threat from the establishment of Jewish settlements and infrastructure. These events paved the way for the larger conflict that would occur in the following decades.

The following page showcases a book, authored by Pulitzer Prize Winner Amy Dockser Marcus, titled *Jerusalem 1913*. Her book provides a comprehensive exploration of the Arab/Israeli conflict.

ESTABLISHMENT OF THE FEDERAL RESERVE

➡ **DID YOU KNOW?** 1913 was also a notable year for the United States who made a decision that would profoundly impact their economic history for generations to come. The Federal Reserve Act was passed and signed into law by President Woodrow Wilson on December 23, 1913. This all took place while a considerable number of Congress members had already left for their holiday recess. Yet, this was not a result of poor planning, but a strategic

1913

ISRAEL & USA

The Origins of the Arab Israeli Conflict &

Creation of the Federal Reserve

- Though the origins of the Arab-Israeli conflict have traditionally been traced to the British Mandate (1920-1948) that ended with the creation of the Israeli state, a new generation of scholars has taken the investigation further back, to the Ottoman period (1299-1922).

- In **1913** the Zionist Congress pursued the idea of building the future state of Israel with **Hebrew labor** and **not Arab labor** was when the conflict began to percolate.

- Why 1913? Because 1913 is the year that everything went wrong. There are academic arguments as to when the Arab-Israeli conflict began, but Marcus, a Pulitzer prize-winning former Wall Street Journal correspondent, suggests that this year, 1913, when the Zionist Congress pursued the idea of building the future state with Hebrew labor and not Arab labor was when the conflict began to percolate. It was during that same year that the Arab Syrian Congress met to declare unity as a response to the encroaching European Zionist movement.

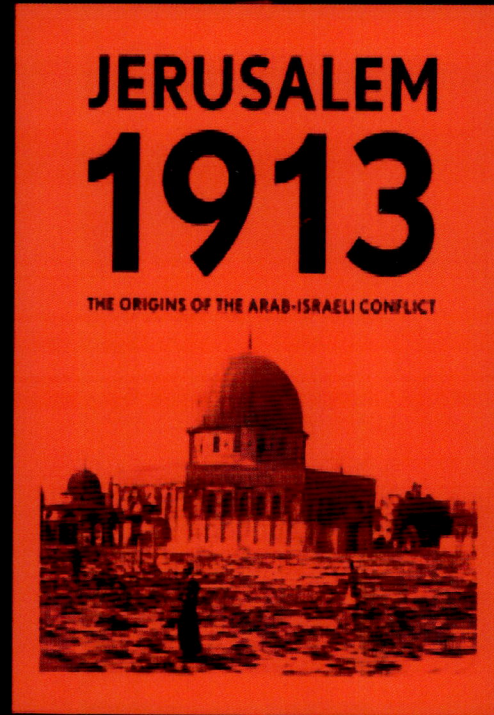

JERUSALEM 1913

THE ORIGINS OF THE ARAB-ISRAELI CONFLICT

AMY DOCKSER MARCUS

WINNER OF THE PULITZER PRIZE

1913
Federal Reserve

The Creation of the Federal Reserve

The **Federal Reserve** Act was passed by the United States Congress on **December 23, 1913**, and signed into law by President Woodrow Wilson on December 23, 1913.

At the time, many Congress members had already left for the Christmas break. This law created the Federal Reserve System, which is the central banking system of the United States.

move to ensure the bill's smooth passage. The bill encountered significant controversy during its drafting and deliberations; scheduling a vote while many were absent helped seal the deal.

The Act established the Federal Reserve System, which had the power to *control* the nation's money supply and interest rates. Also a central banking system for the United States was created to supervise and regulate banks, with 12 regional banks setup to cover the geographic regions of the U.S. More important information regarding the impact this decision had on America is explained on the images over the next few pages.

ISRAEL'S TRUE BIRTH

Let's continue with some important facts about Israel. Although Israel proclaimed its independence on May 14, 1948, less than 24 hours later, Arab nations, including Egypt, Syria, and Iraq, invaded the country, forcing Israel to defend its newly-gained sovereignty.

Nineteen years later, on June 5, 1967, the 6-day war broke out, ending six days later on June 10, 1967, with an Israeli victory. At that time, Israeli forces seized the West Bank, including East Jerusalem and the Golan Heights. On June 10, 1967, Israel was finally recognized by the entire world as independent—it was Israel's official birthday.

Notice the numerical hand of God at work here. It was a six-day war. And like the creation of the world, God completed His work and rested on the seventh day. Also, *exactly seven years* after the official birth of Israel, on June 9, 1974, the United

States and Saudi Arabia entered into the "Petro-Dollar" Agreement, a decision that would literally impact history for the next fifty years!

HOW THE DECISIONS OF 1971 IMPACTED AMERICAN HISTORY

"We the people," as a nation founded under God, on August 15, 1971, abandoned the U.S. Dollar Gold Standard when President Richard Nixon severed the link between dollar and gold, temporarily. This particular point in time has been labeled as "The Nixon Moment."

From then, the U.S. money system became Fiat Money, a government-issued currency that is *not* backed by a physical commodity, such as gold or silver, but rather by the government that issued it. Unlike traditional commodity-backed currencies, fiat currency cannot be converted or redeemed. It is intrinsically valueless and used by government decree.

The USA and Saudi Arabia signed a military agreement on June 9, 1974, orchestrated by Henry Kissinger to give value to government money that no longer had value. The agreement involved U.S. military protection of Saudi Arabia in exchange for Saudi Arabia agreeing to purchase all oil (i.e., Petro) in U.S. dollar-denominated bonds *only*, and thus the origin of the "Petro-Dollar," a monetary system backed by oil, not God's money.

Starting from June 9, 1974, the U.S. dollar was no longer a genuine fiat currency since it was now supported by oil. And although the decision had been called "temporary" by Richard Nixon, the

U.S. never returned to the gold standard! This was one of three crucial decisions with long-lasting effects on the United States.

Interestingly, when applying the Leviticus 25 "Year of Jubilee Release" to the Nixon Moment of August 15, 1971, then fifty years later, to the exact date, the world witnessed the fall of Kabul on August 15, 2021. Nine days after the fall of Kabul, on August 24, 2021, Saudi Arabia signed another military agreement with Russia despite their previous 1974 Petro-Dollar agreement with the USA. And on August 24, 2023, the Saudis further agreed to join the BRICS (**B**razil, **R**ussia, **I**ndia, **C**hina, **S**outh Africa) agreement that directly challenges the supremacy of the U.S. Petro-Dollar.

ALL BAD THINGS MUST COME TO AN END

On June 9, 2024, fifty years to the exact day since the creation of the Petro-Dollar, Saudi Arabia refused to resign the 1974 Petro-Dollar contract. And thus ended the Petro-Dollar itself as Saudi Arabia was essentially abandoning the U.S. dollar. The former deal was a cornerstone of the United States global economic dominance.

But the Saudi's failure to renew the deal plays a vital role in determining the stability of the U.S. currency system, which was supposed to be without the support of any physical commodity for only a limited time. Saudi Arabia's agreement to join the BRICS resulted in the U.S. Dollar becoming a fiat currency with no physical commodity backing. And the government responsible for issuing the U.S. Dollar has avoided discussing this issue!

God gave the USA and the world an honest instrument of money to transact, specifically gold and silver, as written in Haggai 2:8. But then "We the people" turned away from God's money system when Nixon implemented a new man-made money system: the Petro-Dollar. And now that ended on June 9, 2024. However, let's not forget the 2021 Saudi Arabia and Russia military agreement and the recent rise of the BRICS nations.

With this poor decision, we caused God, the Creator, to turn his back to the world money system. And an evil, ungodly money system was put in place that completely enslaves and controls humanity. However it didn't stop there.

Between 1971 and 1974 America made some bad decisions. In addition to destroying the U.S. Financial System with the Petro-Dollar deal, a second decision made in December of 1972 also contributed to the fall of America. It was a secret project by the CIA called, "Project Looking Glass." This was a covenant or deal made with a demonic principality that led the way to the third bad decision: Roe vs.Wade.

America has suffered the consequences of Roe vs. Wade, Project Looking Glass and the start of the Petro-Dollar. Tragically, over fifty million unborn children were aborted over the fifty years of Roe vs. Wade. The cup is full!

But there is ***good news***! Sound the trumpet! The Lord is releasing us, beginning in 2025, as He restores His covenant with the U.S.A. The founding fathers of America made an immutable covenant with God. He will cancel debt and reestablish His monetary system on the Earth with the fall of Mystery Babylon.

50-YEAR JUBILEE, THE "YEAR OF RELEASE"

Glass Full of Children's "Blood" Paid for with the US 'Petro-Dollar'!

After 50-Years...

50-Million Children

Understanding the TIMING written in Leviticus 25, '50-YEAR JUBILEE', and how it relates to two critical events of 1971 to 1974.

Spiritually, Secretly the CIA made a Covenant was made with a demonic principality by way of Project Looking Glass in December 1972, then 'we the people' turned away from God on January 22, 1973, by allowing Abortion, a 'blood sacrifice' to evil, by a nation founded under God had agreed to legally, in the highest court in the land, kill the Creator's creation. Romans 8:31 states, "If God is for us, who can be against us?" In this instance, 'we the people' caused God, the Creator, to turn his back to the U.S.A. and the world and as of January 22, 1973, God was no longer 'for us,' and evil moved into America.

Financially, 'we the people' abandoned God's honest money system August 15, 1971, by abandoning the 'gold standard, with Nixon and then further turned away from God's honest money system on June 9, 1974, by signing a man-made 'Petro-dollar' agreement with Saudi Arabia. One thing is for certain, nothing made by man has ever lasted forever and therefore on **June 9, 2024**, as we forecast based on the 50-year Jubilee calculation within Leviticus 25:10-11, Saudi Arabia on June 9, 2024, refused to resign the 1974 'Petro-dollar' agreement and from that day forward the US dollar is backed by nothing, next comes the collapse of this 'man-made' money system. 'We the people' were given an honest money system by God, the Creator, and we decided to use a 'man-made' money system instead, and the 50+ years of endless money printing all of humanity has now become enslaved with quadrillions of dollars of debt created out of thin air.

SUMMARY: As a nation founded under God, spiritually we turned away from God on January 22, 1973, and Financially we turned away from God on June 9, 1974.

- CIA's secret Project Looking Glass in December 1972, a Covenant was made with a demonic principality.
- Roe v Wade becoming law on January 22, 1973, the 50th-year ended January 22, 2023, based on Leviticus 25:10-11.
- Saudi Arabia and USA 'Petro-Dollar' agreement was signed on June 9, 1974, the 50th-year ended **June 9, 2024**, based on Leviticus 25:10-11.

The Leviticus 25:10-11 calculation indicates Mystery Babylon's fall is expected in the **1-year period** beginning June 9, 2024, and **before June 9, 2025**.

What is a Shemitah? In the old Testament every 7th year, translated as "the release" and applied to the wiping away of debts and resting of the land.
What is a Jubilee? After seven cycles of seven years, the 50th year is a Jubilee year of rest.
What is a SUPER SHEMITAH? After many 50th year cycles and no 'Jubilee' is honored by the people, in disobedience and in direct opposition to God's law, God intervenes with a SUPER SHEMITAH with biblical ramifications and consequences.

SUPER SHEMITAH 2025

BO POLNY
THE ANALYST OF TIME

The Final Vote in the SENATE on the Federal Reserve Act on December 23, 1913:

- The bill PASSED the SENATE by a vote of 43 to 25, a difference of 18
- Total Senators that VOTED: 43 + 25 = 68
- Total Senators in 1913: 96

      28 senators had left for Christmas vacation by the time the final bill came to a vote

THE
FEDERAL
RESERVE ACT
OF 1913

President Wilson LATER came to REGRET SIGNING the bill: "I am a most unhappy man. I have unwittingly ruined my country. A great industrial nation is controlled by its system of credit. Our system of credit is concentrated."

1913

In What other Financial Event occurred in 1913?
First FEDERAL INCOME TAX, Revenue Act, takes effect (16th amendment) February 25, 1913, enacted into law by Congress, granting Congress constitutional authority to levy taxes on corporate and individual income.

What movie came out in 1913?
Dr. Jekyll and Mr. Hyde

What did Andrew Jackson say about the Federal Reserve that cause them to hate him?
Beyond characterizing the bank as hopelessly corrupt, he argued "the powers conferred upon [the bank were] ... not only unnecessary, but dangerous to the Government and the country." He went on, warning that if it continued to operate, "great evils... might flow from such a concentration of power in the hands of a few ...

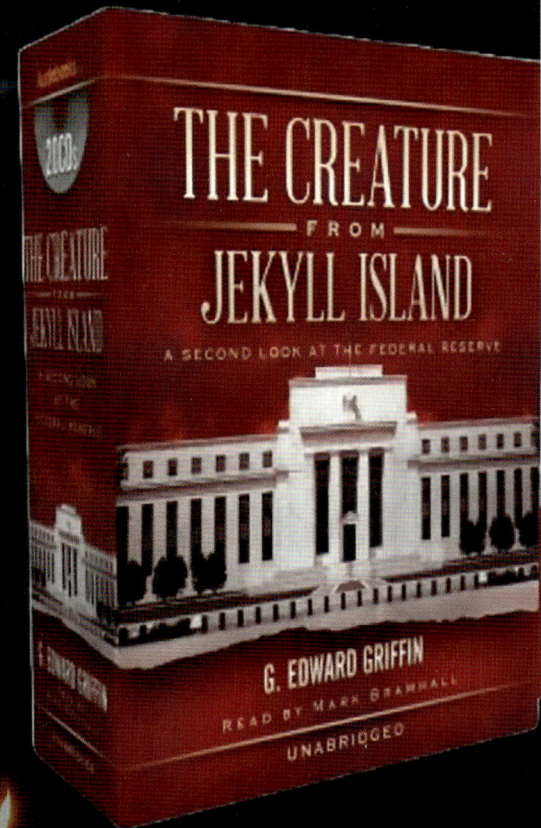

Jekyll Island

In <u>November 1910</u>, six (6) men – Nelson Aldrich, A. Piatt Andrew, Henry Davison, Arthur Shelton, Frank Vanderlip and Paul Warburg – met in SECRET at a PRIVATE CLUB on Jekyll Island, to write a plan to reform the nation's banking system and the plan for the Federal Reserve was developed, a SINGLE CENTRAL BANK with 15 branches across the country.

The bankers WORKED LATE INTO THE NIGHT for more than a week to write the plan using occultic practices of witchcraft and sorcery.

The Federal Reserve Act was signed into law by President Woodrow Wilson on <u>December 23, 1913</u>, at <u>6:02 PM</u>, the night <u>before Christmas Eve, December 24</u>.

The act established the <u>Federal Reserve System</u> as the CENTRAL BANK of the United States.

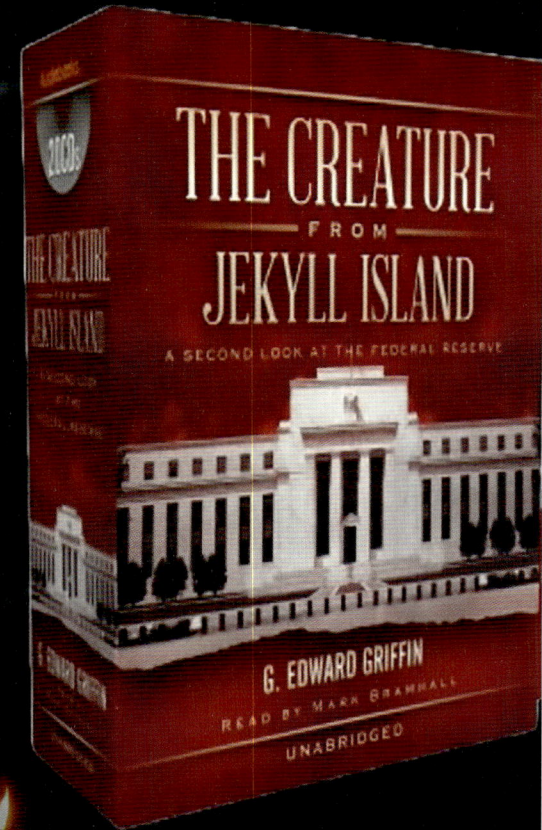

Who is the Richest BANKING Family in the World?

The Rothschild family is one of the oldest, wealthiest, and most storied families in history. With roots in banking, the family has continued to grow its wealth in a variety of businesses over the centuries, continuing to wield significant power and money.

What does the Bible say about Money?
"For the LOVE of money is the ROOT of ALL EVIL."
- 1 Timothy 6:10

WADDESDON MANOR
THE HERITAGE OF A ROTHSCHILD HOUSE

BO POLNY
THE ANALYST OF TIME

BANK OF ENGLAND

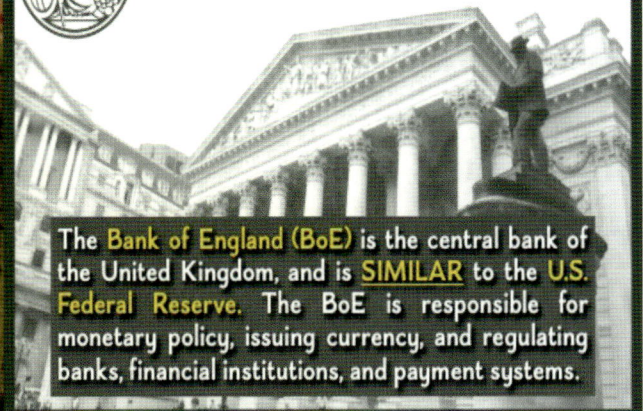

The Bank of England (BoE) is the central bank of the United Kingdom, and is SIMILAR to the U.S. Federal Reserve. The BoE is responsible for monetary policy, issuing currency, and regulating banks, financial institutions, and payment systems.

Remote Viewing
Astro Projection
50
Golden Jubilee
Scan Me
1972
PROJECT
LOOKING GLASS
STARGATE
CENTRAL INTELLIGENCE AGENCY
UNITED STATES OF AMERICA

ACTS PENTECOST

Sunday, June 8, 2025

THE BOOK OF DANIEL

The Story of 5-KINGS *The Number of Grace!*

1. One Mighty / NEBUCHADNEZZAR
2. One Foolish and Wicked / BELSHAZZAR
3. One Deceived / DARIUS
4. One Wise for all the ages of the world / CYRUS
5. One who sounds the Trumpet for the Return of the JESUS! / TRUMP

CHAPTER 3
The Daniel Timeline

ONE IDEA filling my mind repeatedly is the incredible ability of our God's power to change things, particularly within a **single day**. Throughout history, people have been stuck in challenging situations—even those people with power and influence. In a single moment, their life took a complete turn, after receiving God's favor.

Consider Joseph, who was sold into slavery and imprisoned in Egypt after his brothers turned him away. It's likely that he never imagined becoming the prime minister of a great nation.

Or consider the life of Nebuchadnezzar, the mighty ruler of Babylon and a man who gloated in his power and authority as he built pagan shrines and rejected God. He would lose his mind and resort to eating grass in the field like a wild beast. Yet, Nebuchadnezzar's sanity was ultimately restored and he chose to honor God, all thanks to humility and God's grace.

> *Now I, Nebuchadnezzar, praise and exalt and glorify the King of heaven, because everything He does is right and all His ways are just. And those who walk in pride He is able to humble.*
>
> Daniel 4:37 NIV

THE FIVE KINGS

Let's review the story of Daniel as it pertains to the five kings. Why are there five kings? Five is the number of grace, signifying God's unmerited favor and blessing. When five is multiplied by itself (i.e., 5 x 5) you get 25 or "grace upon grace" as described in John 1:16. Interestingly that also represents the year 2025! The images here and on page 159 illustrate God's amazing grace. Please pay close to the "fifth king" mentioned later as it ties directly into everything we have been discussing for the last few years.

The story of Daniel is incredibly prophetic and not only predicted events in Old Testament days, but also gives direction to how events will play out in current times. Daniel was a Jewish man living in captivity in Babylon (modern-day Iraq) under the rule of King Nebuchadnezzar, the first king in this story.

Nebuchadnezzar had a dream which upset him greatly, so he called upon the magicians and soothsayers, the ones who talk to spirits, to seek an interpretation of the dream. Nebuchadnezzar would not tell them the dream because he wanted to validate their interpretation by confirming that they also knew the dream itself.

None of the pagan mediums knew the dream, nor could they interpret it. So, Nebuchadnezzar was going to put them all to death. Daniel, knowing that all the prophets were going to be killed the following morning, told the king that *he* could interpret the dream. But Daniel needed to first pray to God; he would give the interpreation in the morning.

The incredible thing is that God gave Daniel not only the interpretation but the dream as well. The passage in Daniel 2:31-45 tells how Daniel interpreted the dream as an overview of world events in the millennia yet to come.

The dream included a large statue of a man whose head was made of pure gold and his chest and arms were made of silver. The statue's belly and thighs were made of bronze and its feet were partly made of iron and partly made of clay. Review the images that follow to learn more about the man in Nebuchadnezzar's dream. As the Word describes, it was a "frightening sight" (Daniel 2:31b)

Your majesty looked and there before you stood a large statue. An enormous, dazzling statue, awesome in appearance. The head of the statue was made of pure gold and it's chest of silver. It's belly and thighs of bronze, its legs of iron, its feet partly of iron and partly of baked clay. While you were watching, a rock was cut out but not by human hands. It struck the statue on its feet of iron and clay and smashed them. Then the iron, the clay, the bronze, the silver, and the gold were all broken into pieces and

became like chaff on a threshing floor in the summer.The wind swept them away without leaving a trace. But the rock that struck the statue became a huge mountain and filled the whole earth. This was the dream and now we will interpret it to the king. Your majesty, you are the king of kings. The God of Heaven has given you dominion and power and might and glory; in your hands He has placed all mankind and the beasts of the field and the birds in the sky. Wherever they live, He has made you ruler over them all. You are that head of gold. After you, another kingdom will arise, inferior to yours. Next, a third kingdom, one of bronze, will rule over the whole earth. Finally, there will be a fourth kingdom, strong as iron—for iron breaks and smashes everything—and as iron breaks things to pieces, so it will crush and break all the others. Just as you saw that the feet and toes were partly of baked clay and partly of iron so this will be a divided kingdom; yet it will have some of the strength of iron in it, even as you saw iron mixed with clay. As the toes were partly iron and partly clay, so this kingdom will be partly strong and partly brittle. And just as you saw the iron mixed with baked clay, so the people will be a mixture and will not remain united, anymore than iron mixes with clay. In the name of those kings, the God of Heaven will set up a kingdom that will never be destroyed, nor will it be left to another people. It will crush all those kingdoms and bring them to an end, but it will itself endure forever. This is the meaning of the vision of the rock cut out of a mountain, but not by human hands—a rock that broke the iron, the bronze, the clay, the silver and the gold to pieces. The great God has shown the king what will take place in the future. The dream is true and its interpretation is trustworthy.

Daniel 2:31-45 NIV

KINGDOMS that CONTROL Humanity

7-KINGDOMS

Twenty-six hundred (2600) years ago, Daniel interprets Nebuchadnezzar's Dream of future Kingdoms and they all, except the 7th, which is still to come, and have arrived with supernatural PRECISION.

1. **HEAD** of Gold [BABYLON]
   606 - 539 B.C. (King Nebuchadnezzar)

2. **CHEST** of Silver [PERSIA]
   539 - 331 B.C. (Cyrus The Great)

3. **THIGHS** of Brass [GREECE]
   331 - 168 B.C. (Alexander The Great)

4. **LEGS** of Iron [ROME]
   168 B.C - 476 A.D.

5. & 6. **FEET** of Iron & Clay [Kingdom Divided]
   476 A.D. - July 2025 A.D.

   5. Iron & Clay **1** [PAPACY]
   538 A.D. - 1798 A.D. "Little Kingdom"

   6. Iron & Clay **2** [USA]
   1776 A.D. - July 2025 A.D.

7. **STONE...** 2025, Jubilee Begins, the **Kingdom of David** is born, starts 5-years of Amazing Grace (5 x 5)! - Daniel 2:34

The Great Image in Nebuchadnezzar's Dream

The great image that God revealed to Nebuchadnezzar in a dream was interpreted by the prophet Daniel. Each section represents a world-ruling superpower. Each succeeding metal is less valuable, but each succeeding metal is stronger, as each empire was more powerful than the last.

Silver—Chest and Arms

The silver chest with two arms signified the empire of the Medes and Persians, which conquered and supplanted Babylon.

Bronze—Belly and Thighs

This section represented the Greco-Macedonian Empire of Alexander the Great, which swallowed up Persia.

Iron—Legs

The two legs of iron represented the Roman Empire. After Alexander's death, his Hellenistic empire continued in a divided form until its divisions were taken over by Rome. The two legs apparently signified the east-west division that characterized the Late Roman Empire.

Iron & Clay—Feet and Toes

Extending from the legs are feet and toes of iron mixed with clay—a brittle and unstable mixture because it would not bond well. These represent the final phase of the Roman Empire, which will be made up of ten kings, some strong and some weak.

"THE GREAT IMAGE"

Gold—Head

This section represented the empire of Babylon, of which Nebuchadnezzar was king.

THE BEAST "MYSTERY BABYLON"

THE **FALL** OF
"MYSTERY BABYLON"

"While you were watching, 'A STONE' was cut out, <u>by no human hands</u>. It struck the statue on its feet of iron and clay and smashed them. "

- Daniel 2:34

Scan Me

<u>PLEASE NOTE</u>:

"by no human hands";

therefore, GOD, <u>not</u> Trump, will ultimately get <u>all</u> the Glory in the destruction of Babylon!

'A STONE'...
2025
Starts 5-years (5 x 5) of Amazing Grace!

WHO IS 'A STONE'?

"I am the stone for this generation, that stone is 'My Son', the rock Christ Jesus and that stone shall be given to the Davids of this generation, and they shall break down the force of hell. There shall be no world war yet, for I am yet to show you the manifestation of a rock in the hand of a generation that shall break down the voice of hell. "The Glory of God that shall cover the earth with knowledge and manifestation, as the waters cover the sea. It is yet to come before I return, you are the generation that shall defy death!" – Kim Clement 2013

WE ARE THE GENERATION THAT SHALL BREAK DOWN THE VOICE OF HELL & DEFY DEATH!

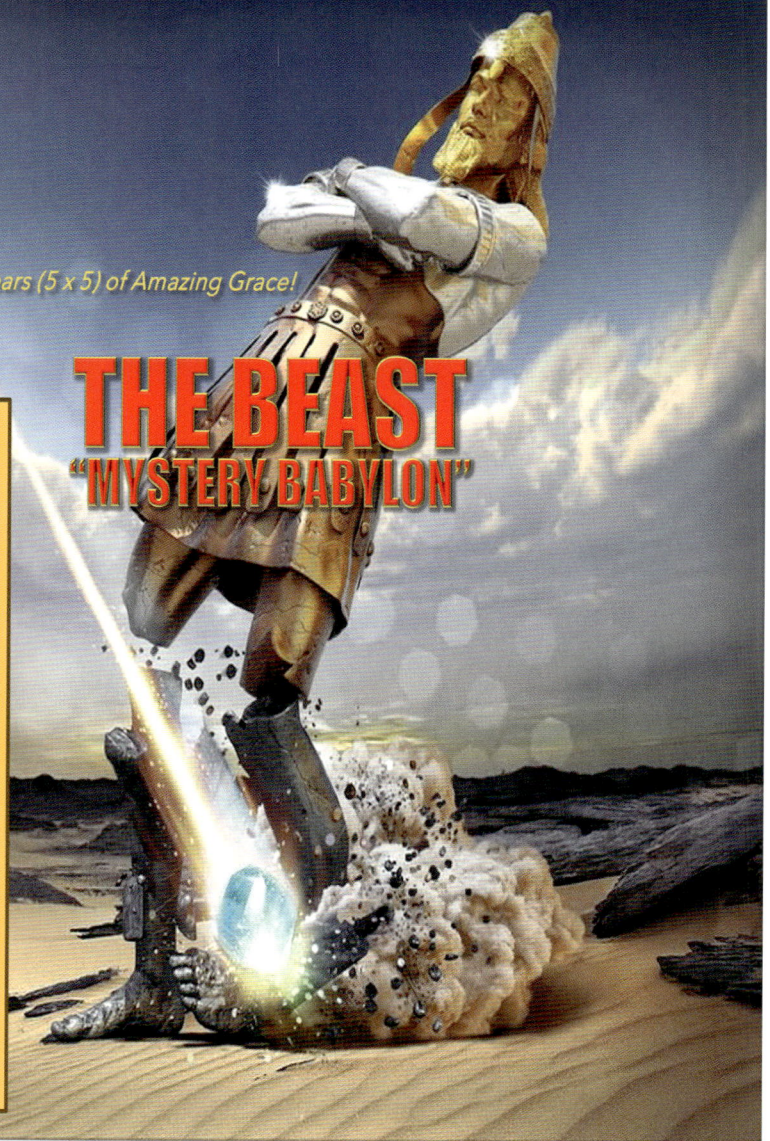

THE BEAST
"MYSTERY BABYLON"

Daniel's prophecy would hold true for the next 2500 years. All the kingdoms have risen and fallen precisely as prophesied, except for the last kingdom, the birth of the kingdom of David. **All men are powerless if the prophecy is true.** Turns out Daniel's prophecy was true, and everything that people have done to stop it from being fulfilled has been worthless.

For instance, the rise of Rome and the rise of Greece. This prophecy has involved millions of people over thousands of years, and it has all come to pass.

Nebuchadnezzar was so impressed by Daniel and his God that Daniel was made second in command over Babylon. In *one day*, Daniel went from *captive* to *commander*.

God has made the plan, and He's got it all figured out. And this is fascinating because these stories will overlay onto present times. Let's continue.

CAST INTO THE FIRE

Nebuchadnezzar's story progresses following the construction of a 90-foot golden statue for Babylon's worship. Three of Daniel's friends, fellow Jewish captives, Shadrach, Meshach, and Abednego, refuse to bow down to this idol. Therefore, they are thrown into the fiery furnace, and Nebuchadnezzar is so angry that he orders the furnace to be lit seven times hotter than normal. The fire was so hot that the soldiers who carried out the order died just by being near the flames.

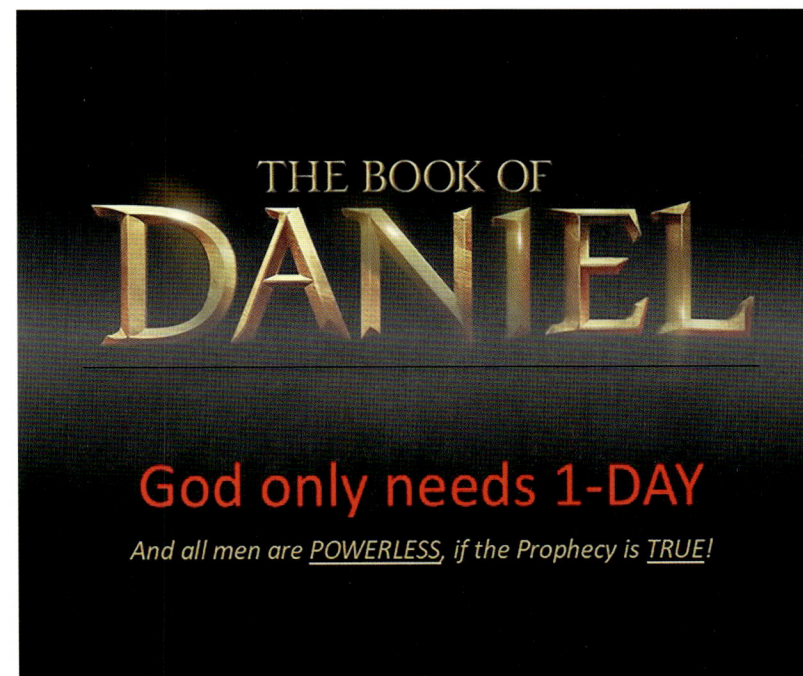

THE BOOK OF

DANIEL

God only needs 1-DAY

And all men are <u>POWERLESS</u>, if the Prophecy is <u>TRUE</u>!

> *And because the king, in his anger, had demanded such a hot fire in the furnace, the flames killed the soldiers as they threw three men in. So Shadrach, Meshach, and Abednego, securely tied, fell into the roaring flames.*
>
> Daniel 3:22-23 NLT

Nebuchadnezzar looked into the fire, knowing he had ordered three young men into the furnace, and he saw four bodies standing in the flames. Jesus was standing right there with the three

Daniel 2, The Dream

THE BOOK OF
DANIEL

1. NEBUCHADNEZZAR

King Nebuchadnezzar has a dream that deeply troubled him, he gathers all his scribes, sorcerers, wise men, magicians, enchanters, and astrologers and demands they interpret his dream without even giving them a piece of the dream, if they fail, they die. They reply, that is not possible. Daniel hears of the death decree. Meets with Nebuchadnezzar and ask for time to pray until dawn.

During the night, the mystery was revealed to Daniel in a vision, and he blessed the God of heaven. At dawn he meets with the King stating... "As you lay on your bed, O king, your thoughts turned to the future, and the Revealer of Mysteries made known to you what will happen."

Daniel interprets the Kings dream which described the coming Kingdoms that shall rise and fall for the next 2 ½ thousand years! All kingdoms, except the final one, have already come into existence, precisely as prophesied.

Nebuchadnezzar makes Daniel the ruler over the entire Babylon, only to answer to him. Daniel names Shadrach, Meshach, and Abednego as his administrators.

The Great Image in Nebuchadnezzar's Dream

The great image that God revealed to Nebuchadnezzar in a dream was interpreted by the prophet Daniel. Each section represents a world-ruling superpower. Each succeeding metal is less valuable, but each succeeding metal is stronger, as each empire was more powerful than the last.

Gold—Head
This section represented the empire of Babylon, of which Nebuchadnezzar was king.

Silver—Chest and Arms
The silver chest with two arms signified the empire of the Medes and Persians, which conquered and supplanted Babylon.

Bronze—Belly and Thighs
This section represented the Greco-Macedonian Empire of Alexander the Great, which swallowed up Persia.

Iron—Legs
The two legs of iron represented the Roman Empire. After Alexander's death, his Hellenistic empire continued in a divided form until its divisions were taken over by Rome. The two legs apparently signified the east-west division that characterized the Late Roman Empire.

Iron & Clay—Feet and Toes
Extending from the legs are feet and toes of iron mixed with clay—a brittle and unstable mixture because it would not bond well. These represent the final phase of the Roman Empire, which will be made up of ten kings, some strong and some weak.

In 1-Day Daniel went from about to be executed in the morning, to second in command of Babylon.

men. And they all walked out of the furnace unharmed. That's **good news,** as it parallels the fire and judgment that is coming for today!

One has to appreciate Nebuchadnezzar's response to this situation. He was the king of Babylon, not Israel. Yet he decreed: *"God the Father is the King of Kings. Anyone who speaks against the God of Shadrach, Meshach, and Abednego will be torn limb from limb and their houses laid to ruin. For no other God can save like this."* (Daniel 3:29)

And again, in ***one day***, Shadrach, Meshach and Abednego went from being near execution to having the King of Babylon declare that their God was above all others.

THE SCALES OF JUSTICE

The second king of the story of Daniel is Belshazzar, son of Nebuchadnezzar. Belshazzar hosted a party for thousands of his nobles. He ordered his servants to gather all the gold and silver vessels from the temple of Jerusalem that Nebuchadnezzar had conquered. Belshazzar, his nobles, and their wives drank wine from the gold and silver vessels while praising their pagan gods on Nisan 15.

What does God say about gold and silver?

> *"The silver is mine and the gold is mine,"* declares the Lord Almighty.
>
> Haggai 2:8 NIV

On this particular night Belshazzar was defiling what was God's. At that moment, a hand appeared and wrote an inscription on the palace walls. Just as in the dream of Nebuchadnezzar, none of Babylon's diviners can interpret the text. So once again, Daniel is called to decipher the writing on the wall.

Daniel's interpretation was:

- **MENE:** God has numbered your days, and your reign will be brought to an end.
- **TEKEL:** You have been weighed on the scales and found deficient.
- **UPHARSIN:** Your kingdom will be divided and given to the Medes and the Persians.

That night, Belshazzar was killed by King Darius, the king of the Medes. Darius took over the kingdom and Babylon, and eventually, through King Cyrus, it was given to the Persians. The prophecy was true. All men are powerless to stop the prophecy from being fulfilled.

In ***one day***, Belshazzar, the foolish king, was killed and conquered. Sadly, today other foolish kings—enemies of almighty God—will soon meet the same fate. If we fail to study history, we are surely bound to repeat it.

All men are powerless to stop the prophecy from being fulfilled.

Daniel 3, The Golden Image & Fiery Furnace

THE BOOK OF
DANIEL

1. NEBUCHADNEZZAR

King Nebuchadnezzar proceeds to build a statue in his image, 90 feet tall, and writes a **mandate** for all to fall down and worship the image. "Is it true, that you do not serve my gods or worship the golden image that I have set up? Now if you are ready when you hear the horn, to fall down and worship the image. But if you do not worship, you shall immediately be cast into a burning fiery furnace. And who is the god who will deliver you out of my hands? O Nebuchadnezzar, we have no need to answer you in this matter. If this be so, our God whom we serve will deliver us out of your hand. But if not, be it known to you, that we will not serve your gods or worship the golden image that you have set up. Nebuchadnezzar filled with fury, ordered the furnace heated seven times more than usual and had Shadrach, Meshach, and Abednego, cast into the burning furnace.

Then King Nebuchadnezzar was astonished, "Did we not cast three men bound into the fire? But I see four, walking in the midst of the fire; and the appearance of the fourth is like a son of the gods. The hair of their heads was not singed, their cloaks were not harmed, and no smell of fire had come upon them. King Nebuchadnezzar... Blessed be the God of Shadrach, Meshach, and Abednego, who has sent his angel and delivered his servants, who trusted in him, set aside my mandate, gave up their lives.

Therefore, I decree: Any people, nation, or language that speaks anything against the God of Shadrach, Meshach, and Abednego shall be torn limb from limb, and their houses laid in ruins, for no other God can save in this way.

In only a FEW HOURS Shadrach, Meshach, and Abednego went from being executed, to having the King of Babylon decree anyone speaks anything negative against God shall be torn limb from limb.

It is also important to note that throughout biblical history, Nisan 15 has been a monumental day. On this day Issac was tricked to bless Jacob. On this day Jesus was crucified. It was also the day the small army of Gideon destroyed the powerful Midian army. The Bible records Nisan 15 as a "night to be much observed" in Exodus 12:42 KJV

➤ **DID YOU KNOW?** The word "tekel" is important as it relates to the present day. "You have been weighed on the scales and found deficient."

This correlates to our United States currency and the paper money of this world. With the removing of the gold standard in 1971 and the Saudi's refusal to resign the Petro-Dollar deal in 2024, the U.S. dollar is now a purely evil monetary system because it is not backed by anything. It is a debt instrument that is satanic. Excessive and unlimited printing of it has now weighed the scales to one side, rendering God's money worthless.

The ***good news*** is that when God intervenes, he flips the tables. God will tip the scales, restore His money, and destroy the currency of Satan.

A NEW KING COMES INTO POWER

The third king is Darius of the Medes, who conquered Babylon by killing Belshazzar. Darius was a wise king and quickly befriended Daniel after learning about everything that Daniel had accomplished. In fact, Daniel becomes Darius' second in command, which angers the other administrators who want to be in control.

They tricked Darius into signing an irreversible decree outlawing prayers to anyone but the king for thirty days. The conspirators knew that Daniel, who loved God the Father, couldn't comply with this command and would thus suffer the penalty of dying in the Lion's Den.

Daniel was ultimately thrown into the lion's den on the biblical date Nisan 15 in violation of the decree, which upset Darius because he loved and appreciated Daniel. The next morning, Darius ran to the lion's den, fully expecting to find Daniel killed. Darius called out, "Daniel? Daniel? Has your God saved you?"

Of course, Daniel was fine! Being innocent in God's eyes, he was saved by an angel of the Lord. Darius was overjoyed, and now another king of Babylon, not Israel, declared the glory of God. He proclaimed, "In every part of my kingdom, men are to humbly fear before the God of Daniel. He is the living God, and He endures forever. His kingdom will never be destroyed, and His dominion will never end" (Daniel 6:26).

In ***one day***, God turned the tables and Babylon went from *decreeing* Darius as being the only one worthy of worship to *declaring* the Lord God, above ALL!

The stories and cycles of the Bible overlap with the present time. Today's Babylon, Satan's kingdom, plots against the people of God. They want to kill and destroy by throwing America into the lion's den. Just as with Daniel, the truth is that God's people will be untouched, and the plotters themselves will be destroyed. This will happen when God, in a single day, restores the covenant made with the founding fathers of America.

THE BOOK OF
DANIEL

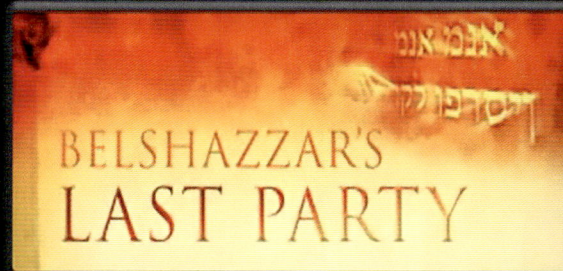

Daniel 5, Belshazzar's Feast

2. BELSHAZZAR

Belshazzar gave orders to bring in the gold and silver vessels that Nebuchadnezzar his father had taken from the temple in Jerusalem, so that the king could drink from them. As they drank the wine, they praised their gods. At that moment the fingers of a human hand appeared and wrote on the plaster of the wall. The king called out for the enchanters, astrologers, and diviners to be brought in, and he said to these wise men of Babylon, "Whoever reads this inscription and tells me its interpretation will be clothed in purple and have a gold chain placed around his neck, and he will be made the third highest ruler in the kingdom." So, all the king's wise men came in, but they could not read the inscription.

Belshazzar summons Daniel and Daniel Interprets the Handwriting.

Now this is the inscription that was written: **MENE, MENE, TEKEL, UPHARSIN**

MENE means that God has numbered the days of your reign and brought it to an end.

TEKEL means that you have been weighed on the scales and found deficient.

UPHARSIN means that your kingdom has been divided and given over to the Medes and Persians.

That very night Belshazzar was slain, and King Darius, the Mede, received the kingdom.

God wrote on the wall that Belshazzar was to die this night, and his kingdom would be divided; that SAME NIGHT King Darius killed him.

Daniel 6, The Plot against Daniel

3. DARIUS

Daniel distinguished himself among the administrators and the king planned to set him over the whole kingdom. The administrators then tricked King Darius into signing a decree that would cause Daniel to be thrown into the Lions' Den and the decree could not be repealed even by the king.

Daniel was accused and sentenced to death and put into the Lion's Den. At the first light of dawn, the king got up and hurried to the den of lions. When he reached the den, he cried out O Daniel, servant of the living God, has your God been able to deliver you from the lions? Daniel replied, **My God sent His angel and shut the mouths of the lions.** No wounds whatsoever were found on him. At the command of the king, the men who had falsely accused Daniel were brought and thrown into the den of lions–they and their children and wives.

All Glory to God, and Darius Honors God**... I hereby decree that in every part of my kingdom, men are to tremble in fear before the God of Daniel, For He is the living God, and He endures forever; His kingdom will never be destroyed, and His dominion will never end.** And instead of dying in the lion's Den, he prospered during the reign of King Darius of the Medes and then King Cyrus of Persian, as prophesied by Isaiah.

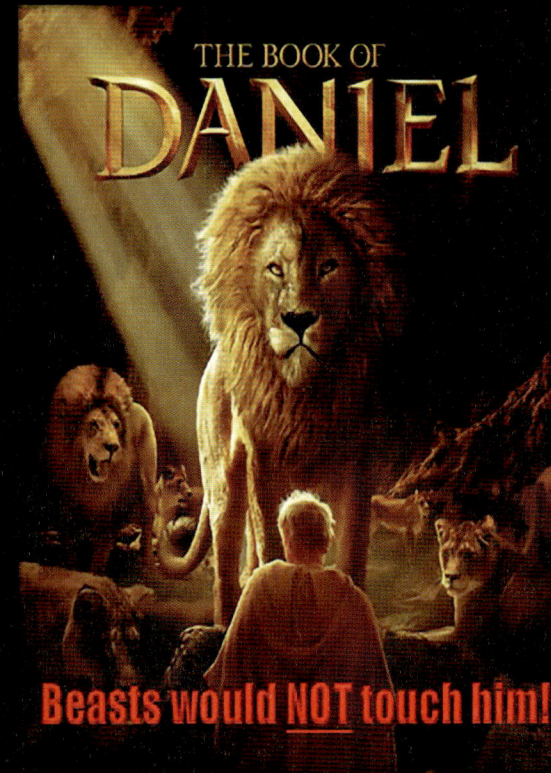

THE BOOK OF
DANIEL

Beasts would NOT touch him!

Daniel was sentenced to death, put into the Lion's Den AT NIGHT; AND IN THE MORNING, he was alive untouched. The men who had falsely accused Daniel were thrown into the den of lions and King Daniel decrees men are to tremble in fear of God and Daniel was raised up!

A STORY SEVENTY YEARS IN THE MAKING

King Cyrus is the fourth king of the Daniel timeline. By freeing Israel from Babylonian rule, King Cyrus fulfilled a 70-year time cycle, which began when King Nebuchadnezzar conquered Israel seventy years before.

Jeremiah prophesied that a king of Babylon (i.e., Nebuchadnezzar) would capture Jerusalem and that Israel would serve Babylon for seventy years. But Israel would later be freed by Cyrus who would rebuild God's temple in Jerusalem.

> *This entire land will become a desolate wasteland. Israel and her neighboring lands will serve the king of Babylon for seventy years. Then, after the seventy years of captivity are over, I will punish the king of Babylon and his people for their sins,"* *says the Lord. "I will make the country of the Babylonians a wasteland forever. . . ."*
>
> Jeremiah 25:12-13 NLT

Furthermore, King Cyrus was even prophesied about, by name, in Isaiah 44:28 where God also referred to Cyrus as "My shepherd."

> *. . . who says of Cyrus, "He is my shepherd, and will accomplish all that I please"; he will say of Jerusalem, "Let it be rebuilt," and of the temple, "Let its foundations be laid."*
>
> Isaiah 44:28 NIV

King Cyrus fulfilled this prophecy; he did as God said. He freed Israel, and allowed the second temple in Jerusalem to be rebuilt. This was done out of the goodness of his heart, and not for any sum of money or reward.

There is another man in this story that will be discussed in Chapter 8. Donald Trump will be the fifth leader that works to free God's people, without reward, but out of the goodness of his heart. Just like King Cyrus, he will also rebuild the United States of America after her great fall, which will have a worldwide impact.

Incredibly, not only was King Cyrus, and his freeing of Israel, prophesied before his birth, but so, too, was Donald Trump. His name was hidden in a mystery by the prophet Jeremiah, nearly 2500 years ago. This will be discussed later in the book's teaching about the Star of Jacob's prophecy.

Lastly, on May 14, 2018, Donald Trump opened the embassy in Jerusalem. Fast forward seven years to 2025 and expect this year to be biblical for Israel, as well—perhaps even on the date May 14, 2025. This is precisely 108 years from the Miracle of Fatima, when Mary, the Mother of Jesus, appeared to three young peasant children, prophesying that prayer would bring about a significant change to the world. As Christians, we should also always be praying.

70-years **7**

70-years | 70-years

4. CYRUS / TRUMP
Isaiah 45:13

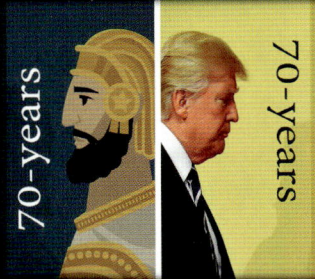

Cyrus the great, called out by name in the prophecy of Isaiah as the shepherd for his people and that of Israel. **70-years** comes to an end and Israel is freed from Babylon by decree of king Cyrus, granting the Jews the right to return to Judah and rebuild the Temple in Jerusalem, including sending back with them the sacred vessels which had been taken from the First Temple and a considerable sum of money with which to buy building materials.

Thus says the Lord, your Redeemer, "I am the Lord, who made all things, who frustrates the signs of liars and makes fools of diviners, who turns wise men back and makes their knowledge foolish, who confirms the word of his servant, the prophets, and fulfills the counsel of his messengers, who says of Cyrus (TRUMP), 'He is my shepherd, and he shall fulfill all My purpose'; saying of Jerusalem, She shall be re-built." - Isaiah 44:24-28

The prophet Jeremiah prophesied that King Nebuchadnezzar King of Babylon would capture Jerusalem and Israel would serve Babylon for **70-years** and be freed by Cyrus to build God's House in Jerusalem in 536 BC .

1 "Thus says Cyrus king of Persia, 'The LORD, the God of heaven, has given me all the kingdoms of the earth, and He has charged me to build Him a house in Jerusalem.' - 2 Chronicles 36:23

TRUMP COMPLETED 2018

In 1948 Israel was proclaimed a STATE and exactly **70-years** later **May 14, 2018**, Trump opens the US Embassy in Jerusalem.

2 I will raise up CYRUS (TRUMP) in My righteousness, I will make all his ways straight, He will rebuild My cities and set My exiles free, but not for a price or reward, says the Lord Almighty." - Isaiah 45:13

TRUMP BEGINNING 2025

7-years from **May 14, 2018**, is May 14, 2025... Expect 2025 to be Biblical for Isreal!

God only needs 1-DAY! *All men are POWERLESS, if the Prophecy is TRUE!*

THE DANIEL TIMELINE

The events in the book of Daniel describe a specific timeline known as "the Daniel Timeline" or two 3 ½ year cycles that comprise a total of seven years. Many calculations have relied on this 7-year cycle, uncovering significant dates of divine importance. The number seven has biblical significance and will be important in the information presented throughout this book.

In the Bible, the number seven appears over 700 times in both the Old and New Testaments. It represents perfection, complete or a point of divine intervention. Some examples include creation, which was complete with rest on the seventh day. A week ends with rest on day seven. Jesus is described as having seven qualities in Isaiah 11:2.

The final chapter of Daniel, Chapter 12, discusses The End Times and portrays the concluding events of human history, preparing for the second coming. It describes the Great Tribulation and assures us that God's *"people—everyone whose name is found written in the book of life—will be delivered."* The events portray what will happen to Israel, the saints, and the wicked.

The question is asked, "How long will it be before these astonishing things are fulfilled?" (Daniel 12:6 NIV). The answer comes: **It will be for a time, times and half a time.** A time is 360 days. Times is the equivalent of TWO times or 720 days. And of course, a half a time equals 180 days. So that equals 1260 days, or three and one-half years. 360+720+180= 1260 days.

Other biblical passages describe a period of 3 ½ years. For instance, Revelation 11:2 says, *"They will trample on the holy city for 42 months* [i.e., 3.5 years]." Revelation 12:6 NIV says, *"The woman fled into the wilderness to a place prepared for her by God, where she might be taken care of for 1260 day*s." NOTE: We know that Jesus' ministry lasted for 1260 days or 3 ½ years. And as we live in the end-times, we are seeing the significance once again of 1260 days.

Interestingly, the word "time" here parallels the Greek word used in Galatians 4:4 (NIV). *"But when the set **time** had fully come, God sent his Son, born of a woman, born under the law, to redeem those under the law, that we might receive adoption to sonship."* It is considered "the fullness of time" or completion of God's plan.

As an analyst of time, The Daniel Timeline has been a valuable biblical function in identifying critical end points. Please note the many 1260-day time points featured on the images throughout this book. Additionally, 2 Peter 3:8 tells us a day is but a thousand years with the Lord. Applying this knowledge to 1260 *days* gives us 1260 *years*. This biblical calculation from the year 1736 points back to the exact year Rome would fall in 476 A.D. This was the period when the world would go into the Dark Ages of medievil times.

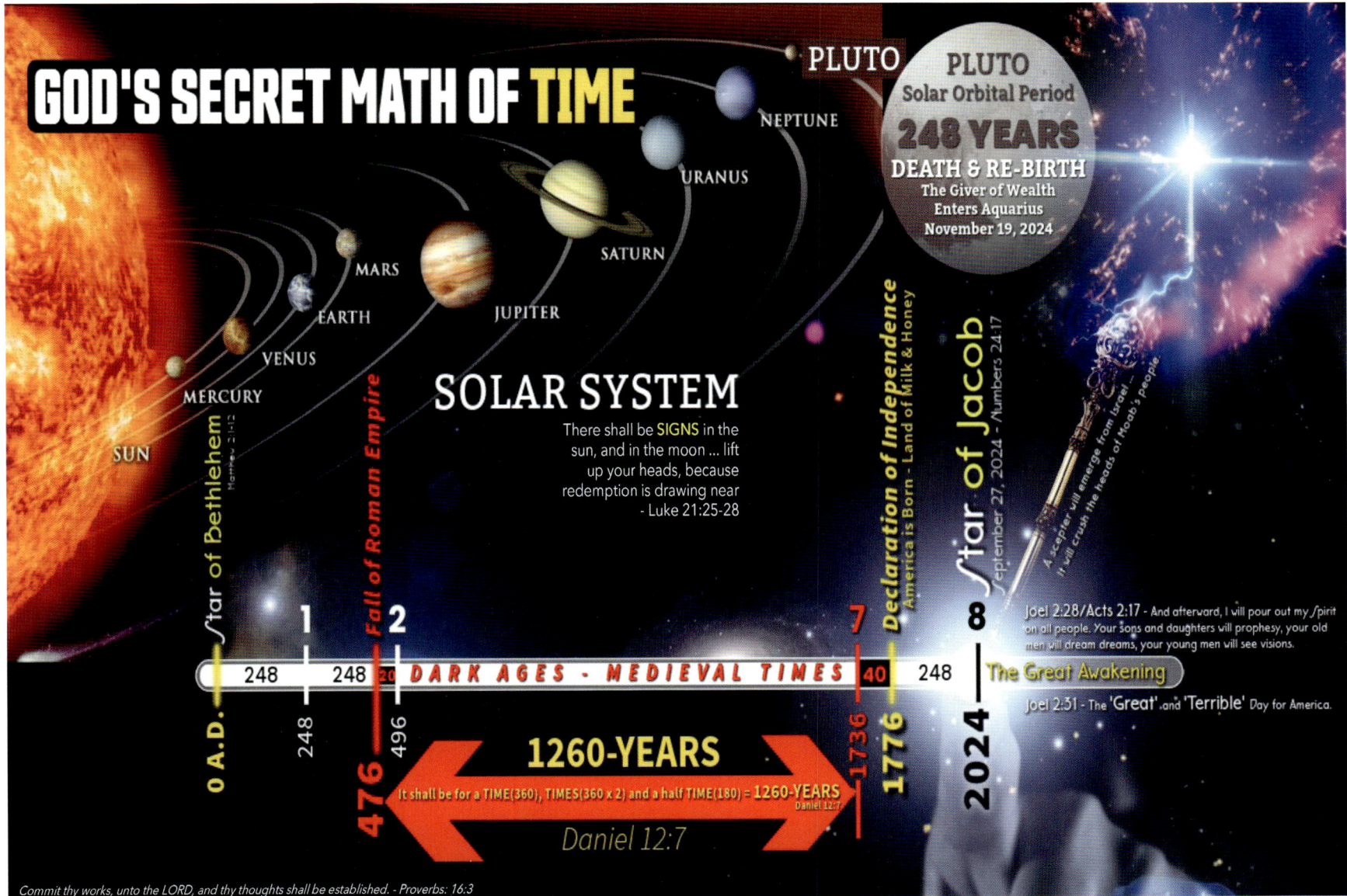

GOD'S SECRET MATH OF TIME

PLUTO

PLUTO
Solar Orbital Period
248 YEARS
DEATH & RE-BIRTH
The Giver of Wealth
Enters Aquarius
November 19, 2024

NEPTUNE

URANUS

SATURN

MARS

JUPITER

EARTH

VENUS

MERCURY

SUN

SOLAR SYSTEM

There shall be SIGNS in the
sun, and in the moon ... lift
up your heads, because
redemption is drawing near
- Luke 21:25-28

Star of Bethlehem
Matthew 2:1-12

Fall of Roman Empire

Declaration of Independence
America is Born – Land of Milk & Honey

Star of Jacob
September 27, 2024 - Numbers 24:17

A scepter will emerge from Israel ...
It will crush the heads of Moab's people.

Joel 2:28/Acts 2:17 - And afterward, I will pour out my Spirit
on all people. Your sons and daughters will prophesy, your old
men will dream dreams, your young men will see visions.

1 **2** **7** **8**

| 248 | 248 | 20 | DARK AGES - MEDIEVAL TIMES | 40 | 248 |

The Great Awakening

Joel 2:31 - The 'Great' and 'Terrible' Day for America.

0 A.D.

248

476

496

1736

1776

2024

1260-YEARS

It shall be for a TIME(360), TIMES(360 x 2) and a half TIME(180) = **1260-YEARS**
Daniel 12:7

Daniel 12:7

Commit thy works, unto the LORD, and thy thoughts shall be established. - Proverbs: 16:3

THE 4-HORSEMEN WHO BRING "ANTICHRIST", THE 'FALSE' SAVIOUR OF THE WORLD

After the 4-Horsemen are riding, the **ANTICHRIST** comes to 'Save / Deceive' the world from corona virus, wars, economic collapse, and plague, pestilence and death!
In 2033 the **ANTICHRIST** will come to bring PEACE and SOLUTIONS, will unite the world in love, 'demonic' love, the love of accepting all godly perversions.
Those deceived and unprepared will then willingly accept the beliefs of Islam and take the 'mark of the beast'. - Revelation 13:17

Secret
Prophecy of SEVEN SEALS

And they (Islam) were given authority over
a **fourth** of the earth, to kill with SWORD
and with FAMINE and with PESTILENCE
and by WILD BEASTS of the earth.

- Revelation 6:8

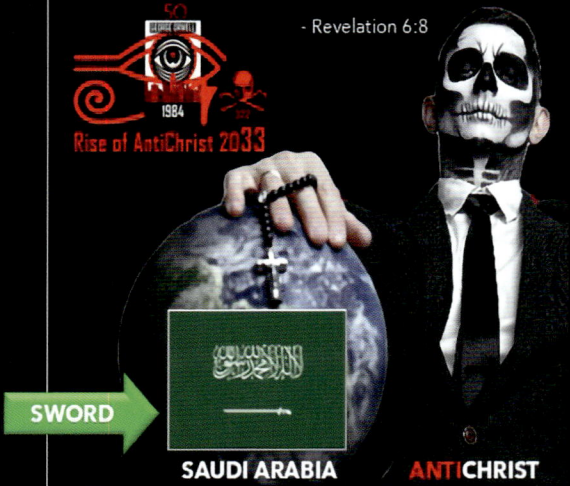

Rise of AntiChrist 2033

SWORD

SAUDI ARABIA   **ANTICHRIST**

The 4-Horsemen that bring
World War 3

All the four horse riders control
<u>only</u> **one-quarter** of the earth

- Revelation 6:8

1   2   3   4

Scan Me

| 1. WHITE | 2. RED | 3. BLACK | 4. GREEN |

Greek Khloros (LINK)

Jordan   Sudan   United Arab Emirates   Afghanistan   Iran

Iraq   Kuwait   Libya   Palestine   Syria

- · GREEN field with the **Shahada** inscribed in white text.
- · **WHITE SWORD** symbolizing justice and adherence to Islamic principles.
- · GREEN color represents Islam, paradise, and the Prophet Muhammad.

Shahada definition: There is no god but god,
and Muhammad is the messenger of god'.

Who is this god? The great deceived... **satan!**

The 4-COLORS (HORSEMEN) of ISLAM. NOT
accepting CHRIST is **ANTICHRIST.**

SWORDS are and will be used to cut off head!

CHAPTER 4
The First Four of the Seven Seals

THE SEVEN SEALS

THE APOSTLE JOHN experienced a vision while imprisoned on the island of Patmos. The vision showed a book or scroll safeguarded by the Seven Seals, as described in Revelation. The opening of the seals, associated with the Second Coming of Christ, is detailed in Revelation chapters five through eight.

The opening of the final 7th Seal marks the beginning of the Apocalypse. According to John's description, the breaking of each seal brings forth a new judgment upon the earth. Following the judgments come the trumpets and bowls of God's wrath.

While weeping over the unopened scroll and the unbroken seven seals, John receives **good news** about who can open them.

> I wept and wept because no one was found who was worthy to open the scroll or look inside. Then one of the elders said to me, "Do not weep! See, the Lion of the tribe of Judah, the Root of David, has triumphed. He is able to open the scroll and its seven seals."
>
> Revelation 5:3-5 NIV

A detailed discussion of the opening of the seven seals is included in the following chapter.

THE FOUR HORSEMEN

John also tells of the Four Horsemen of the Apocalypse in Revelation, who appear with the opening of the first four seals. The first horseman rides a white horse and carries a bow and a crown. Throughout history, the bow has been a symbol of military triumph or conquest. This horseman represents the Antichrist, who mistakenly believes he can conquer Jesus Christ.

The second horseman rides a red horse and carries a great sword, representing violence. Interestingly, the sword isn't a double-edged sword (like the Word), but a dagger like that used for combat and violence. The third horseman carries scales with weights and rides a black horse. The scales imply the scarcity and shortages brought about by worldwide financial corruption that comes to a sudden end. This results in a disruption of the food supply. And black represents death of the enemies of Almighty God.

The fourth horseman rides a pale green horse, symbolizing death through plague and pestilence. His horse brings a widespread loss of life throughout the opening of the fourth seal. The Four Horsemen are personifications of Death, Famine, War, and Conquest.

As observed in the illustration at the beginning of the chapter, the colors of the four horsemen are like those used in the flags of Middle Eastern nations, an area that covers approximately one-quarter of the entire world.

GOD'S ENDTIME JUDGMENT

As previously mentioned, Revelation, which is a portrait of revealed information, describes seven symbolic seals that secure the scroll which John of Patmos saw in his vision. The first four seals are described as the Four Horsemen. And each one is a certain color which interestingly, the colors match the same colors used on the flags of the major countries in the middle east.

There are certain characteristics which must occur for the opening of a seal: 1) It marks a worldwide (global) phenomenon. And 2) each will typically occur in conjunction with one of the Jewish feasts and/or festivals. So the first four seals are expected to open in this way.

- The release of the coronavirus indicated the opening of the **Seal #1** on Hanukkah, December 30, 2019.

- Pentecost, May 30, 2020, marked the opening of **Seal #2**, when global violence erupted as a consequence of the George Floyd riots.

- **Seal #3** is expected to open during Passover/Resurrection 2025 or at the latest Rosh Hashanah, Yom Kippur 2025. It will occur at a time that also coincides with an anticipated significant crash or attack of the U.S. dollar.

- **Seal #4** is expected to be opened on a Jewish feast late in this decade and before 2033. Plagues and pestilence will be unleashed by the opening of this seal. But by that time, the church will have already separated itself and will be filled with the "greater" glory as referenced in Haggai 2:9.

- All four horsemen are expected to be riding by the year 2033, as the second seven-year cycle ends, when the world will be in desperate need of a Savior.

THE FIRST SEAL

People often wonder why it is taking so long for the Lord to return and redeem the earth. After reading this book, you will come to realize everything is occurring in perfect biblical timing. From creation, 6,000 years ago, to today, after two seals have been opened, and then to the opening of the third seal. It has been written in the annals of time, pointing to the year 2025. Let's examine what happened with the first seal in greater detail.

1st SEAL Broken

HANUKKAH December 30, 2019 (COVID-19)

OUR WORLD CHANGED FOREVER!

December 30, 2019, Corona Virus First Positive Test Result: "Wuhan Central Hospital received a report from Beijing Boao Medical Laboratory stating that their sample (obtained 27 December) contained SARS coronavirus."

YEAR 2020 THE **BEGINNING** OF **THE END!**

1ˢᵗ SEAL Broken

Horseman = Deception

"And I looked, and behold, a white horse! And its rider had a **BOW**, and a **CROWN** was given to him, and _he came_ out conquering, and _to conquer_."   - Revelation 6:2

Corona Definition = a part of the body resembling or likened to a **CROWN**

Corona Virus is the **CROWN** of Revelation 6:2

Judgement and Deliverance

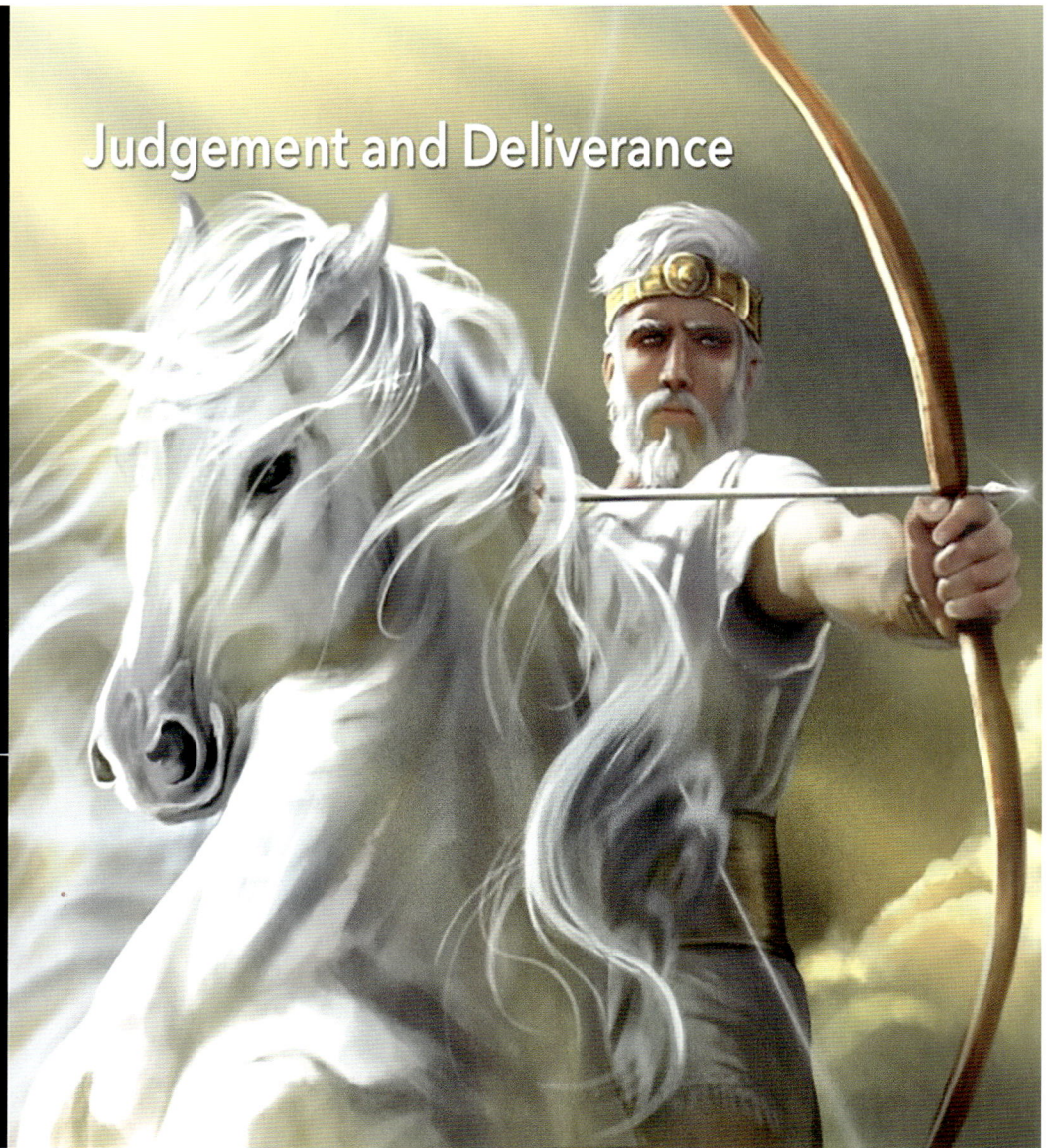

> *I looked, and there before me was a white horse! Its rider held a bow, and he was given a crown, and he rode out as a conqueror bent on conquest.*
>
> Revelation 6:2 NIV

DISTINCTIVE ELEMENTS OF THE FIRST SEAL

Revelation 6:2 clarifies that the breaking of the first seal involves three distinct components, according to John:

1. A crown
2. A bow
3. A conqueror bent on conquest

THE CORONA CROWN

The word "corona" means a part of the body resembling or likened to a crown. In Revelation 6:2, the virus referred to as "corona" was foreseen. The intentional release of the coronavirus was a deceitful act with the aim of world domination and submission to an evil agenda.

The first positive test for the coronavirus came on December 30, 2019. The conclusion of Hanukkah that year was also on December 30, 2019. So this met biblical requirements for the opening of a seal: 1) worldwide impact and 2) corresponding with a Jewish feast or festival.

It is true that other plagues have impacted large numbers of people over time. But the COVID-19 pandemic was the most significant global crisis in history. Not even WWI or WW2 affected every nation worldwide like Corona. And it was clearly an attempt to bring deception and destruction upon the earth like no other event in human history.

ONE WHO BRINGS ILL HEALTH

The ceiling of the Sistine Chapel features a painting that Pope Clement VII commissioned Michelangelo to paint. It is a fresco known as *The Last Judgment* and is one of Michelangelo's greatest masterpieces. The Pope requested that the painting depict the resurrection of Jesus Christ. However, Michelangelo took personal liberty and combined a mix of figures from pagan mythology into the painting, including the gods Hercules and Apollo.

The main figure in Michelangelo's final work lacks a beard, is depicted as nude, and is not shown seated on a throne, diverging from scriptural references to Christ. It more closely resembles Apollo than Christ. In the illustration on the following page, notice the "light" behind Apollo's head. This is actually a "corona" or an envelope around the sun and other stars that has an irregular, pearl-like glow very similar to the figure shown in *The Last Judgment*. In mythology, Apollo is a god (little "g") who brings ill health and deadly plagues with his arrows.

Weep no more; behold, the **Lion** of the tribe of **Judah**, the Root of David, has conquered, so that he can open the **scroll** and its **7-seals**

- Revelation 5:5

1ˢᵗ SEAL Broken

Deception = Apollo

Q: Where in the world is there a **BOW** and a **CROWN** in a single image?

A: The Last Judgement, by Michelangelo in the Sistine Chapel at the Vatican.

BOW is a weapon used for hunting and warfare. Who is the ARCHER in Greek mythology? **Apollo**

Is **Mary** the 'mother' of Jesus, depicted to the right of Apollo? Consider John 8:58... **"Before Abraham was, I AM"**. Jesus was alive before both Abraham and Mary!

Notice right away that this is not a normal looking Christ figure. He is not brown-haired, bearded or dressed in flowing robes. Instead, he is clean-shaven with defined facial features and bulging muscles. He is very much a roman **Apollo**

"**Apollo** is also a god who could bring ill-health and **deadly plague** with his arrows

2nd SEAL Broken

PENTECOST May 31, 2020 (Violence Erupts)

"And out came another horse, bright red. Its rider was permitted to take peace from the earth, so that people should slay one another, and he was given a great SWORD." – Revelation 6:4

SWORD represents VIOLENCE

May 31, 2020: George Floyd RIOTS BREAKOUT

"Peace taken from the earth"

Judgement and Deliverance

Protests, riots that gripped the world **BEGINNING** May 2020:

- **Paris Riots**
- **Brazil Riots**
- **London Riots**
- **Argentina Riots**
- **Black Lives Matter**
- **Portland Riots**
- **Chicago Riots**
- **Minneapolis Riots**
- **Indianapolis Riots**
- **New York Riots**
- **Seattle Riots**
- **Russia-Ukraine War**
- **Canada Trucker Convoy**
- **Israel-Hamas War**
- To name <u>only</u> a few!!

*"You will hear of wars and rumors of wars but see to it that you are not alarmed. Such things must happen, **but the end is still to come**. Nation will rise against nation, and kingdom against kingdom. There will be famines and earthquakes in various places. All these are the beginning of BIRTH pains (NEW ERA)."* - Matthew 24:6-8

THE SECOND SEAL: PEACE TAKEN FROM THE EARTH

> *You will hear of wars and rumors of wars, but see to it that you are not alarmed. Such things must happen, but the end is still to come. Nation will rise against nation, and kingdom against kingdom . . . All these are the beginning of birth pains.*
>
> Matthew 24: 6-8 NIV

The second seal was broken on May 31, 2020, as a consequence of the violence that ensued after George Floyd's death. In correlation, Pentecost was also on Sunday, May 31, 2020. Again, a seal opened on a Jewish holy-day.

John describes the second horsemen as carrying a sword and riding a red horse symbolizing civil unrest and war. One didn't have to look far during the days following Floyd's death to see the extensive turmoil in the United States and worldwide.

PENTECOST 2020—A FORESHADOWING OF THE BIRTH OF THE BRIDE

The Bible mentions Hebrew holidays that resulted in specific displays of God's power. The first occurred in the third month (aka Sivan), after the children of Israel had gone out of Egypt. While camped in the wilderness at Mount Sinai, Moses was called up to the mountain. There, God informed Moses that the Israelites would become a "kingdom of priests, a holy nation," and He presented Moses with His commandments. This was on the feast date of Shavuot.

When translated into Greek, Shavuot becomes "Pentecost." Shavuot = Pentecost; they are both the same day. When you refer to someone or a particular church as "Pentecostal" you are calling them by the name of a Hebrew feast, Shavuot.

And so, the day Moses received the law was the *first Pentecost*, also referred to as "The Day of the Law or Covenant." This occurred after the Passover in Egypt.

In Acts 2:1-4, we read about the *second Pentecost* (or Shavuot). Believers were all together in one place and a mighty wind filled the house where they gathered. And they were all filled with the Holy Spirit. The second Pentecost was known as "The Day of the Spirit." This also occurred after the Passover in Jerusalem.

These special Jewish holy days are when the Lord usually manifests His presence and intervenes to suddenly change the course of history. It is a time when He empowers His children to operate under His authority through the Holy Spirit. This gives reason to believe that the events related to the end times and His second coming will likely coincide with a Hebrew holy day.

In 2020, Pentecost occurred on May 31st and was the day the 2nd Seal of Revelation was opened when the George Floyd riots broke out. The image on the following page gives more information about what happened on *Pentecost* in 2020 and what is expected in 2025.

PENTECOST Birth of the BRIDE (BODY)

Latter Temple/Reign, as described in Haggai 2:9

3rd PENTECOST MAY 30/31, 2020 & 2025

2020 was a Foreshadowing of the BIRTH of the SPIRIT of the LATTER TEMPLE, expected in 2025

Before dark May 19, 2020: Edenville Dam fails causing flash flood conditions. Emergency text goes out: "MIDLAND CITY RESIDENTS WEST OF EASTMAN SOUTH OF US-10 NEED TO EVACUATE DUE TO DAM COLLAPSE." The initial dam breach causes the Sanford Dam to flow over and the Tittabawassee River to overflow its 24-foot flood stage.

Aprox. 8:00 p.m. May 19, 2020: The M-30 bridge in Wixom Lake collapses while residents begin arriving at Midland High School after being evacuated from their homes.

In Edenville, township of HOPE Michigan, a dam breaks, this BREAK was representative of WATER BREAKING before childbirth, a foreshadowing of the future Birth of the Latter Temple, Haggai 2:9

The break occurred May 20, 2020 (Israel Time), EXACTLY 140-weeks, 2 x 70-weeks, from the Birth of GROOM as described in Revelation 12.

The Latter Temple (The BRIDE) *"shall be greater than the former"* as described in Haggai 2:9.

Five (5) years after 2020 is 2025, PENTECOST June 8, the expected BIRTH of the Latter Temple into the 4th of July 2025, the end of the 248-year USA Covenant and BIRTH of NEW.

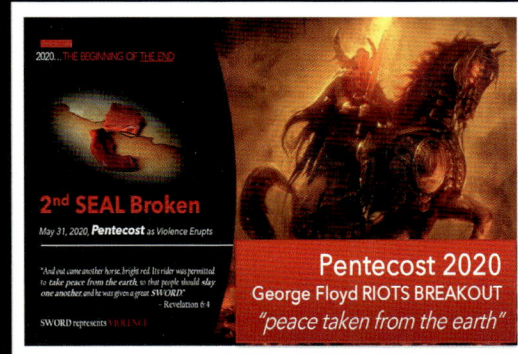

2020...THE BEGINNING OF THE END

2nd SEAL Broken

May 31, 2020, **Pentecost** as Violence Erupts

"And out came another horse, bright red. Its rider was permitted to take peace from the earth, so that people should slay one another and he was given a great SWORD" — Revelation 6:4

SWORD represents VIOLENCE

Pentecost 2020
George Floyd RIOTS BREAKOUT
"peace taken from the earth"

ACTS
PENTECOST
Sunday, June 8, 2025

THE BLACK HORSE WITH THE RIDER & SCALES

The 3rd Seal is opened with the entrance of the third horsemen riding in on a black horse, while holding scales. Black represents the angel of death and although there will be physical death to the enemies of Almighty God. It will be the death of their current money system, as well. The scales represent the rebalancing of our financial system—a great financial reset. We await the greatest wealth transfer in human history, which will cripple our enemy's plans.

The scales tie to the handwriting on the wall that Belshazzar witnessed as outlined in Daniel, Chapter 5. *Mene. Mene. Tekel. Upharsin.* This translates to "You've been weighed on the balances and found wanting."

At the time, people were mocking God and drinking out of the golden chalices. Daniel told them, "Your kingdom has come to an end and will be given to the Medes and the Persians" (Daniel 5:26- 28). Of course, that very night, Belshazzar died, and Darius came into power and took over Babylon. The handwriting on the wall proved to be true. The prophecy was literally fulfilled within 24 hours as a sudden move of God.What do we know about the breaking of the 3rd seal?

- It will be a worldwide phenomenon.
- It will happen on a feast (as did the manifestation of the opening of the 1st and 2nd seals).
- Looking to April 2025, Passover and Resurrection are critical time points for humanity, including a possible Angel of Death moment in time.

THE ANGEL OF DEATH IS UPON THE EARTH

There have been numerous prophetic words about the Angel of Death being present on the earth in this day. Kent Christmas, noted pastor and evangelist, warned in early 2023 that God was "releasing the death angel in the Earth . . . and would loose a death angel amongst the wicked and [we] would see well-known names that when you get up in the morning, the news will report that so-and-so had just died." He also said that there would be a "mortal wound" upon the enemies of Almighty God, specifically Mystery Babylon.

In the days of Pharaoh, the angel of death didn't strike randomly. The angel killed Pharaoh's firstborn and the firstborns of Egypt and is again here on earth now. We are going to see sudden deaths and precision strikes when history soon repeats itself. This day has been written about in Joel 2:31, the Great and Terrible Day of the Lord.

"REVERSE RAPTURE" IN A MOMENT'S TIME

Just as in the days of Pharaoh, the wicked will be no more, as written in Psalm 37:10. There is no way that something so precise will happen overnight without the Lord's intervention. The world will see some precise and unexplainable deaths, as in the case of Pharaoh and the Egyptians that changes the course of history.

> *A little while, and the wicked will be no more; though you look for them, they will not be found. But the meek will inherit the land and enjoy peace.*
>
> Psalm 37:10-11 NIV

"When the Lamb opened the third seal, I heard the third living creature say, "Come!" I looked, and there before me was a black horse! Its rider was holding a pair of scales in his hand. And I heard what seemed to be a voice … saying, "A quart of wheat for a **DENARIUS**,…"
— Revelation 6:5-6

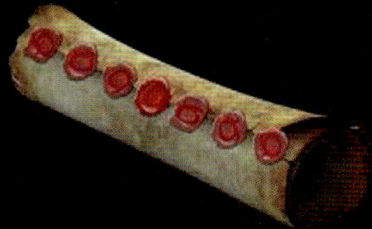

50
Golden Jubilee

Judgement and Deliverance

3rd SEAL

Great Wealth Transfer
2025 - FALL
September - October ?

ANGEL OF DEATH
KENT CHRISTMAS
April ?

BLACK HORSE = **ANGEL OF DEATH**

SCALES = FINANCIAL **RE**BALANCING

GREATEST <u>FINANCIAL EVENT</u> IN HUMAN HISTORY

DENARIUS represents an Ancient Roman **silver** coin and when Revelation was written (96 A.D.) weighed **3.41 grams** or **0.109634** of a Troy Oz.

A "MORTAL WOUND" TO THE ENEMY IN THE USA

March 19, 2023, Prophecy

MARCH "MORTAL WOUND" TO EVIL
SETS THE STAGE FOR APRIL!

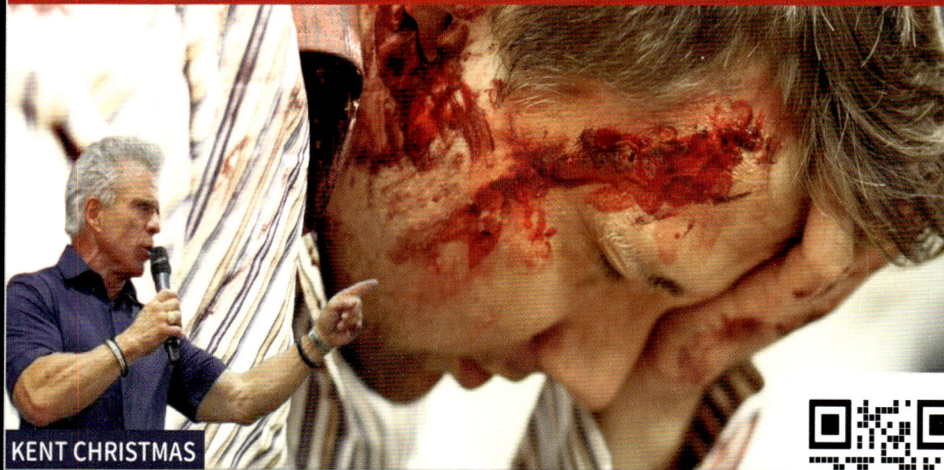

KENT CHRISTMAS

And I will put enmity between you and the woman, and between your offspring and hers; he will **crush your head (Mortal Wound)**, and you will strike his heel. - Genesis 3:15

Scan Me

- **March 19, Prophecy**: In the **next 7-days** I'm going to hit a *"mortal wound"* to the enemy in the United States of America and as men have said March winds and April Showers, God says there is a wind of the Lord getting ready to hit this coming week in the United States of America *that is going to Astound people*. Please Note, in the Prophecy God did <u>not</u> give a year, just that the 'wound' would occur withing 7-days of March 19.

- It's going to *"mortally wound"* the enemy in March and that then sets the stage for April.

- God says I'm opening Heaven upon the church and upon this nation and there is going to be a reign of the blessing and the favor of the Lord.

- It's going to be reported in the nation that God is going to begin to do something Supernatural by the power of the Holy Ghost.

A *"mortal"* wound is an injury that will ultimately lead to death.

"Mortal wound", see **Revelation 13:11-12**: Then I saw another beast rising out of the earth. It had two horns like a lamb, and it spoke like a dragon. It exercises all the authority of the first beast (Harlot/Mystery Babylon) and makes the earth and its inhabitants worship the first beast (Harlot/Mystery Babylon) whose *"mortal wound"* was <u>healed</u>.

Mortal Wound <u>"healed"</u> implies **resurrection** of <u>evil</u> in the future.

It will be a great day, although many will be angry with God for the millions of deaths. But we must remember His ways are higher than man's.

April is a particularly important timeframe biblically because it usually contains a particular day called Nisan 15 (a day that has been mentioned previously and is also discussed in greater detail in Chapter 7). Nisan 15 is one of God's appointed times. The key is that the event(s) will be absolutely unexplainable without God. He will keep the exact day and hour and the actual events all a secret because evil will have NO COUNTER for what's going to happen.

Even though God speaks to the prophets, Moses didn't know the Red Sea was going to part. He didn't know the Red Sea would close on Pharaoh's head. But, by faith, Moses was told to raise his staff and then he instructed the Israelites to stand and watch. And that is the example we must follow in the days to come. Standing and watching, in faith, the plan of God unfold. Trust in the **good news** of God's promises.

> *Then I heard another voice from heaven say, "Come out of her, my people" so that you will not share in her sins, so that you will not receive any of her plagues.*
>
> Revelation 18:4 NIV

THE DESTRUCTION OF BABYLON'S MONEY SYSTEM

Why is the wealth transfer that precedes the opening of the 3rd seal so important? Read the scripture above. God doesn't want us involved in the world's monetary system. But He knows that the church needs wealth to survive.

He will use gold and silver (His money) to destroy Babylon. How was modern-day Babylon built? With money. How will God destroy this Babylon? With money. God will use *His* money (made not by human hand) to destroy Babylon. And at the same time, He will cause Babylon's money, the Federal Reserve Note created in 1913, to be dethroned as the world's reserve currency. It will be exposed that it is worthless and backed by nothing.

> *"The silver is mine and the gold is mine," declares the LORD Almighty.*
>
> Haggai 2:8 NIV

If there was ever a moment in time when God *could* and *would* do something, it is now. The prophets have all spoken about the transfer of wealth. They have shared their words in different ways, but those words have all come from the same source—the Lord.

> *The wealth of the sinner is stored up for the righteous (the church).*
>
> Proverbs 13:22 NKJV [Emphasis Added]

Following the events of the opening of the 3rd seal, there will be a new monetary system worldwide.

A NEW BANKING SYSTEM

When the world operates with God's money, gold and silver, for party-to-party transactions, you won't need the central banks. Evil operates in the middle between two parties. And banks are always in the middle of a transaction between two parties.

President Joe Biden signed Executive Order #14067, titled the *Ensuring Responsible Development of Digital Assets* order, on March 9, 2022. As his 83rd executive order, it was aimed at developing digital currencies responsibly.

The BRICS nations are trying to bring on the Central Bank Digital Currency (CBDC), which would crash the dollar. This will fulfill a Kim Clement prophecy (listed below) stating that the brothers of Goliath (the BRICS nations) will gleefully stand and say, "We will cripple you."

When the current financial system fails, Babylon's CBDC plan will also fall apart. And shortly after the fall of the US dollar, so too will the plans of the BRICS nations. God will not allow these evil countries to take charge of the world as the next superpower. It was America that made a covenant with God. And that covenant is immutable; all other nations will experience a great fall.

In the distant future, likely the next decade, there *will* be a new CBDC when the mark of the beast comes into play. But not for now.

THE GIANT OF DEBT

In February 2014, Kim Clement delivered God's word:

"And then," God says, "highly embarrassing moments when another Snowden arises, and people will become very afraid.

They'll say, 'We have no protection.'" And then, God says, "Am I impressed with your weapons of war? Am I impressed with the strength of your men's legs? Ha! I have said I will bring this nation to its knees, and," God said, "you have been humbled, and yet some more, and then you shall hear the sounds of great victory.. . . this man shall begin to emerge . . . he shall slowly come to the fore. For they are saying, 'How do we kill the giant? How do we kill the giant of debt? How do we kill the giant of socialism? How do we kill the giant of human secularism?'

*"I have placed that man amongst you, a humble man. And as Samuel stood before the brothers, they had rejected David to come because of his age. Take all these little remarks I'm giving you. They are gems. The name and the word 'gold' remember that. A man that is amongst them but is young." **And God says,** "These that shall reject him shall be shocked at how he takes the giant down."*

Now hear me, please. The giant of debt, the giants that have come, the brothers of Goliath, stand in glee watching America. *"We will cripple you. You will lose your credit."* But God said, *"Watch. I said 20,000. Look not to Wall Street; however, observe. And they shall say, 'What is your plan for this giant?' And he will take a simple **stone**"* (remember the name) *"and he will hold it up and they will laugh at him, but the plan is so brilliant,"* says the Lord. *"It could only have been given by Me."*

THE NATURE OF A WEALTH TRANSFER

Often people ask, "What does 'the Great Wealth Transfer' look like?" Of course, we know that it will be worldwide because it occurs after a seal opens. It will be the collapse of the financial system we now know. Banks will vanish because they have ties to the Federal Reserve System or the "fiat" system lacking commodity support like gold and silver. The absence of banks who hold your mortgages could lead to the return of your land through loan cancellations.

All the major world currencies are "fiat" money, which has no intrinsic value and doesn't have a "use" value. Its value only comes because the individuals who use it agree on its value. They have confidence in its acceptance by merchants and others for transactions. The word "fiat" comes from the Latin "let it be done" in the sense of a decree or resolution.

The opposite of a fiat money system is a commodity system that has intrinsic value because it contains precious metals (e.g., gold and silver) that are embedded in the coin. President Richard Nixon suspended the U.S. dollar's gold standard in 1971, and the system of fiat currencies was initiated globally. Fiat money systems have a greater tendency for inflation/hyperinflation, and the task of keeping inflation low is overseen by authorities like banks.

WEALTH HAS BEEN STORED UP

The Bible speaks of wealth of the sinner being "stored up" for the righteous. God's monetary system relies on the use of gold and silver.

For years, financial institutions like J.P. Morgan, Citibank, Bank of America and Goldman Sachs have stored up precious metals like gold and silver. As of mid-2022, their share of all U.S. derivative bets was nearly 98%. Their intention is to manipulate the price by taking advantage of their influence.

But the **good news** is that they have done this unknowingly so that they can easily hand it over to the one who pleases God. Essentially, they have been working for us!

> *But to the sinner He has given the work of gathering and getting many riches together to give to the one who pleases God.*
>
> Ecclesiastes 2:26b NLV

> *The riches of the sinner are stored up for those who are right with God.*
>
> Proverbs 13:22b NLV

Enjoy portions of the prophecy regarding this, given by Julie Green, on August 10, 2022:

"Watch as they scream about the economy, even more when the banks collapse. They will cause a collapse— they think—to steal more from the world. But in actuality, I'm taking it from them and giving it to who it belongs to.

"My children, be prepared for the wealth transfer like the one in Egypt. But this time it's much bigger. Everything stolen will be

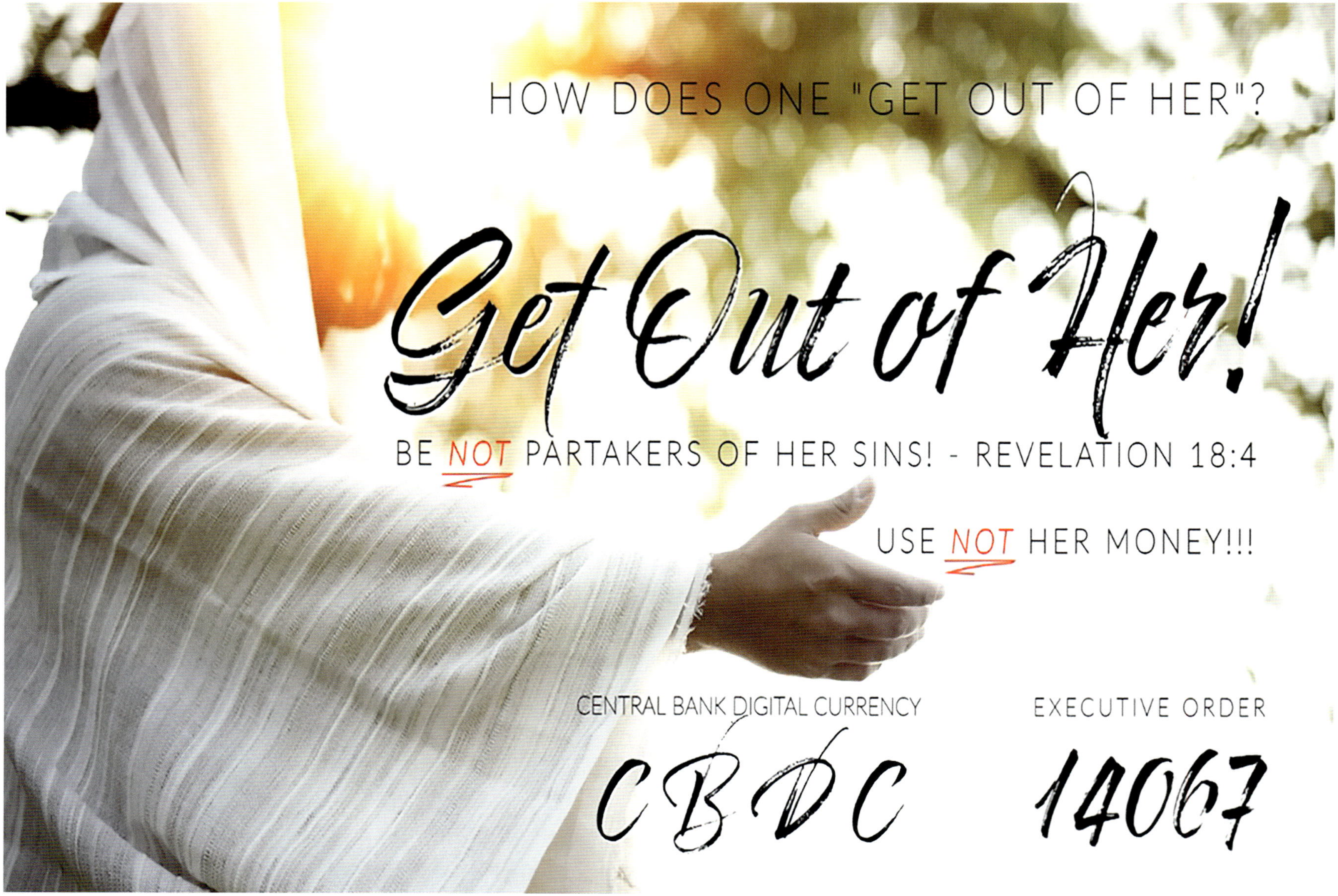

HOW DOES ONE "GET OUT OF HER"?

Get Out of Her!

BE *NOT* PARTAKERS OF HER SINS! - REVELATION 18:4

USE *NOT* HER MONEY!!!

CENTRAL BANK DIGITAL CURRENCY

EXECUTIVE ORDER

CBDC

14067

"CANKERED"

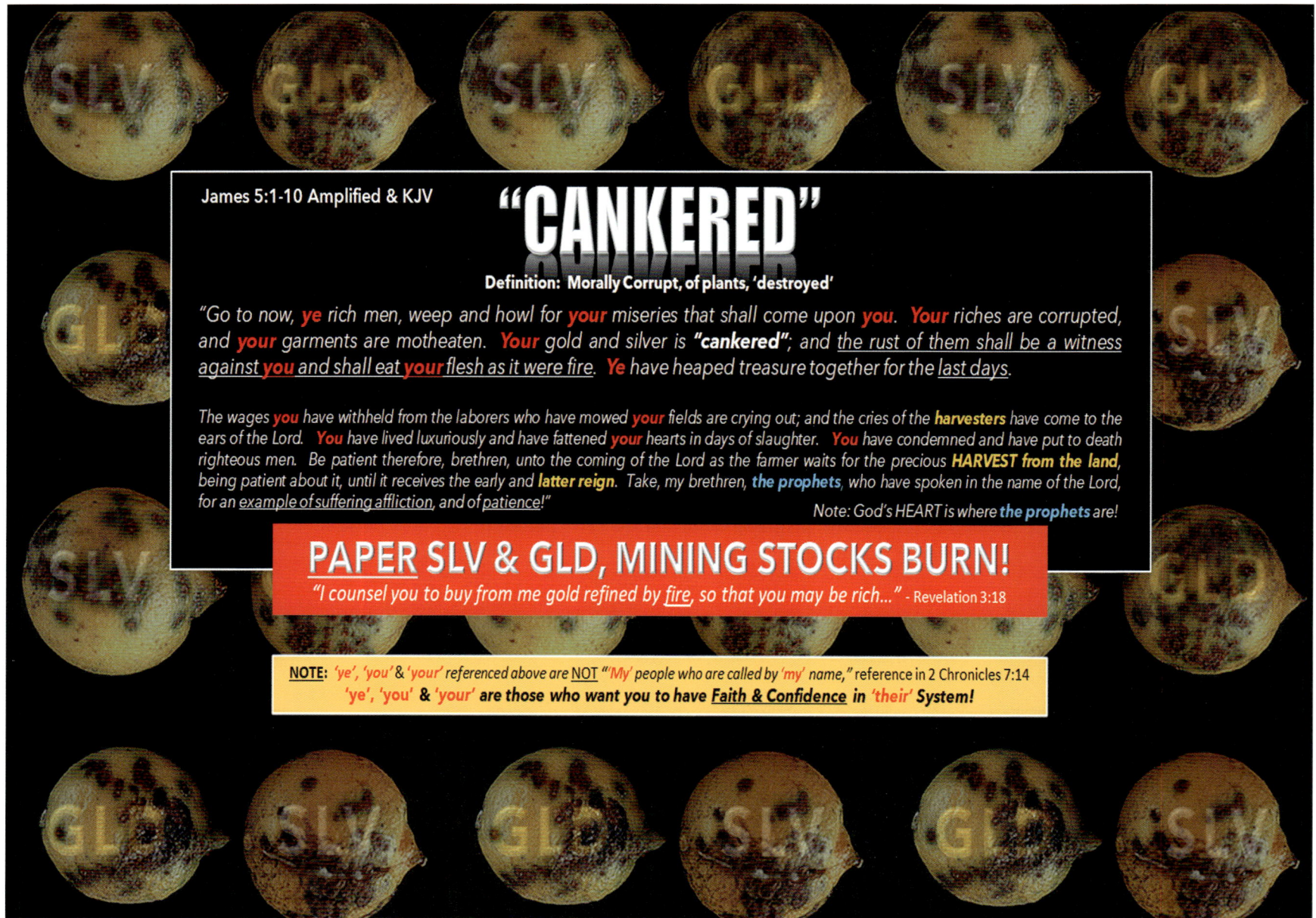

James 5:1-10 Amplified & KJV

Definition: Morally Corrupt, of plants, 'destroyed'

"Go to now, *ye* rich men, weep and howl for *your* miseries that shall come upon *you*. *Your* riches are corrupted, and *your* garments are motheaten. *Your* gold and silver is **"cankered"**; and the rust of them shall be a witness against *you* and shall eat *your* flesh as it were fire. *Ye* have heaped treasure together for the last days.

The wages *you* have withheld from the laborers who have mowed *your* fields are crying out; and the cries of the **harvesters** have come to the ears of the Lord. *You* have lived luxuriously and have fattened *your* hearts in days of slaughter. *You* have condemned and have put to death righteous men. Be patient therefore, brethren, unto the coming of the Lord as the farmer waits for the precious **HARVEST from the land**, being patient about it, until it receives the early and **latter reign**. Take, my brethren, **the prophets**, who have spoken in the name of the Lord, for an example of suffering affliction, and of patience!"

Note: God's HEART is where **the prophets** are!

PAPER SLV & GLD, MINING STOCKS BURN!

"I counsel you to buy from me gold refined by fire, so that you may be rich..." - Revelation 3:18

NOTE: *'ye'*, *'you'* & *'your'* referenced above are NOT *"'My'* people who are called by *'my'* name," reference in 2 Chronicles 7:14
'ye', *'you'* & *'your'* are those who want you to have Faith & Confidence in *'their'* System!

THE COMING OVERTURNING OF THE MONEY TABLES

'THEIR-END!', *NOT* *'THE-END'!*

- Matthew 21:12

Big Pharma, Federal Reserve, Banking Cartel and their Fiat money system, Government Agencies, Politicians, Fake News Media, Social Media including Twitter & Facebook, China, Drug Cartels, etc. have all been **working together quietly for generations to control and enslave humanity.**

given back to you. Even what was stolen from your ancestors, you didn't even know about. But I do. I saw it all. And I'm restoring it to the rightful owners.

"My children, who think these are lies or too good to be true— look in My Word and see how I have done this before. I promise to do it again. This is a part of the complete restoration of all things. This is the greater exodus, saith the Lord. . .

"A lot of people, after I have given out the words the Lord has given about the economy, a lot of people have been afraid and worried about what to do because they have things in the stock market. I don't know exactly what you should do, each and every one of you personally. But God does . . . In Amos 3:7, He doesn't do anything without first revealing it to His servants, the prophets. So He will warn you about things to come. But in these warnings, it's nothing to fear.

"Do not fear. . . We don't ask God, 'How are you going to do this?' He's not going to tell you how He's going to do it. He's not going to want your enemies to know how He's going to do it. But we just know that He can and that He will. And that's when we walk by faith and not by sight."

THE MONEY CHANGERS

The Bible records two instances where Jesus cleansed the temple by driving out the money changers and those selling sacrificial animals. In order to enter the temple, Jews and visitors had to pay a "temple tax," but they could not use foreign coins. Money changers were at the entrance, swapping foreign coins for the necessary Jewish currency to cover the tax. And they did so at a ridiculous exchange rate, taking advantage of the poor and visitors to the temple on Passover.

Jesus made a whip from cord and literally drove them out of the temple. By overturning their tables, he swiftly put an end to their evil practices. In the upcoming fall of Mystery Babylon and opening of the third seal, their wicked practices which have enslaved humanity will finally cease.

THE OPENING OF THE FOURTH SEAL

One-fourth of the earth's population will die as a result of the fourth seal. The ***good news*** is the latter temple, who is covered by the blood of Jesus and filled with the Holy Spirit, will not be touched. Review the image on the following page for more about the 4th seal which is yet to be broken.

4th SEAL is yet to be Broken

*"And I looked, and behold, a Khloros (green) horse! And its rider's name was **DEATH**, and Hades followed him. And they were given authority over a fourth of the earth, to **KILL** with **SWORD** and with **FAMINE** and with **PESTILENCE** and by wild beasts of the earth."*
- Revelation 6:8

Death on a large scale due to the cumulative effect of war, plague, and famine. Additionally, wild animals (beasts?) will be let loose, adding to the human carnage.

Famine, see "TIME OF JOSEPH"

PESTILENCE is defined as a fatal epidemic disease. Examples of a pestilence are the bubonic plague and a swarm of mosquitoes carrying disease.

Bubonic plague killed an estimated 25 million people, a third of the European human population.

Hundreds of Millions Die!

Those covered in the Blood of Jesus will NOT be touched.

A thousand may fall at your side, and ten thousand at your right hand. But it will not come near you. 8 You will only look on with your eyes, and see how the sinful are punished. 9 Because you have made the Lord your safe place, and the Most High the place where you live, 10 nothing will hurt you. No trouble will come near your tent. - Psalm 91:7-10

5th - 7th SEALS

are yet to be broken

5. Revelation 6:9-11

6. Revelation 6:12-17

7. Revelation 8:1-6

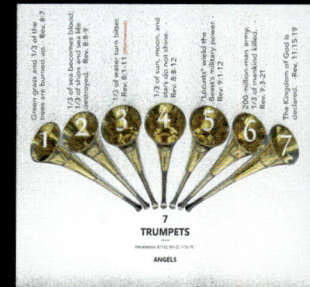

   ❖ 7-Trumpets

   ❖ 7-Bowls

5th SEAL - The Cry of the Martyrs

"I saw under the altar the souls of those who had been slain for the word of God and for the witness they had borne. They cried out with a loud voice, **'O Sovereign Lord, holy and true, how long before you will judge and avenge our blood on those who dwell on the earth?'** *Then they were each given a white robe and told to rest a little longer, until the number of their fellow servants and their brothers should be complete, who were to be killed as they themselves had been."*

– Revelation 6:9-11

6th SEAL - Heavenly Signs - Darkness

"there was a great earthquake, and the sun became black as sackcloth, the full moon became like blood, and the stars of the sky fell to the earth as the fig tree sheds its winter fruit when shaken by a gale. The sky vanished like a scroll that is being rolled up, and every mountain and island was removed from its place. Then the kings of the earth and the great ones and the generals and the rich and the powerful, and everyone, slave and free, hid themselves in the caves and among the rocks of the mountains, "Fall on us and hide us from the face of him who is seated on the throne, and from the wrath of the Lamb, **for the great day of their wrath has come..."**

– Revelation 6:12-17

7th SEAL - Heavenly Silence for about Half an Hour

"Then I saw the seven angels who stand before God, and **seven trumpets** *were given to them... Then the angel took... fire from the altar and threw it on the earth, and there were peals of thunder, rumblings, flashes of lightning, and an earthquake.* **Now the seven angels who had the seven trumpets prepared to blow them."**

– Revelation 8:1-6

CHAPTER 5

The Fifth through Seventh Seals

IN "THE REVELATION OF JESUS CHRIST," John received instructions about the specific events that would occur on earth during each seal's appointed time. Revelation chapters five, six, and eight contain the teachings of the fifth through seventh seals. Even though the specific time frame for the opening of the last three seals is yet to be revealed, the following is clear:

- The seals will be opened one after another, starting with five, then six, then seven.
- A worldwide event is set in motion by the opening of each of these seals.
- The opening of them corresponds with a Jewish feast or festival.
- The authority to open each of the seven seals was only granted to Jesus Christ.
- The timeframe, beginning 2033 into the end of that decade, is a critical time point with divine importance regarding the fifth, sixth and seventh seals.

And they [the saints of Heaven] sang a new song, saying: "You are worthy to take the scroll, and to open its seals; For You were slain, and have redeemed us to God by Your blood. . . ."

Revelation 5:9a NKJV

Some events related to the seven seals have already taken place, as documented in history. There are some that "appear" currently to being fulfilled, but are merely a foreshadowing of things to come. And others that will occur soon.

THE FIFTH SEAL OPENED

According to biblical teachings, the fifth seal represents the Cry of the Martyrs and provides a glance under the altar where the souls of those who were slain for their faith are honored. The martyred victims are pleading with the Lord, questioning when He will avenge their spilled blood.

Revelation 6:11 mentions that when the fifth seal is opened, these martyrs will receive a white robe. And they are then told to rest for a short while until the fulfillment of those who will be killed in the same manner. This foreshadows the persecution of God's chosen saints.

THE SIXTH SEAL OPENED

The sixth seal in Revelation will open with a great earthquake and a shaking of the sun, moon and stars (as referred to as "cosmic disturbances" in some Bible translations).

> *I looked when He opened the sixth seal, and behold, there was a great earthquake; and the sun became black as sackcloth of hair, and the moon became like blood.*
>
> Revelation 6:12 NKJV

Along with these cataclysmic events comes the great day of the wrath of the Lamb—a day when no one will be able to stand (Revelation 6:17). At that time, all men and women of every nation, tongue and tribe will pray in fear. But sadly, some will not pray to God, but to the rocks and mountains (Revelation 6:16) for covering.

Many theologians note the similarities to the sixth seal and the trumpet and bowl judgments mentioned in Revelation:

- A great earthquake (6th seal event-Revelation 6:12; trumpets/bowl judgment-Revelation 16:18)

- The sun goes dark and the moon goes red/dark (6th seal event-Revelation 6:12; trumpets/bowl judgment-Revelation 8:12)

- Falling stars (6th seal event-Revelation 6:13; trumpets/bowl judgment-Revelation 8:10-11; 9:1)

- Mountains moving (6th seal event-Revelation 6:14; trumpets/bowl judgment—Revelation 16:20)

The sixth seal is thought to be opened just before Jesus' return because the Trumpets and Bowl Judgments also take place at that time. The opening of the sixth seal also follows the words described by the prophet Joel:

> *I will show wonders in the heavens and on the earth, blood and fire and billows of smoke. The sun will be turned to darkness and the moon to blood **before** the coming of the great and dreadful day of the LORD. And everyone who calls on the name of the LORD will be saved; for on Mount Zion and in Jerusalem there will be deliverance, as the LORD has said, even among the survivors whom the LORD calls.*
>
> Joel 2:30-32 NIV [Emphasis Added]

These similarities also imply that the sixth seal events will occur **before** the return of the Lord.

THE SEVENTH SEAL OPENED

Seven is a complete number, representing perfection. And the opening of this seal signifies the end of the earthly story as Jesus returns in glory, along with all of Heaven's angels. Heaven will literally be emptied of the angelic hosts because they will accompany Jesus to earth to gather His elect.

With the opening of the seventh seal, the seven trumpets and seven plagues are introduced as imminent judgments for the earth. Before that occurs, there will be silence in Heaven for "about half an hour" according to Revelation 8:1 (NIV). Two theories exist regarding this deafening silence. The silence could be attributed to the earth's loss of breath from God's demonstrative power of judgment or its quiet anticipation.

The **good news** is that no matter what, Paul reminds us to take heart because we will be saved from these difficulties.

> All this is evidence that God's judgment is right, and as a result you will be counted worthy of the kingdom of God… He will pay back trouble to those who trouble you and give relief to you who are troubled, and to us as well. This will happen when the Lord Jesus is revealed from heaven in blazing fire with his powerful angels.
>
> 2 Thessalonians 1:5-7 NIV

THE SEVEN TRUMPETS

The seventh seal introduces the seven trumpet judgments. At the blowing of each of the seven trumpets comes a divine judgment. The trumpets bring hail, fire, and other disasters that devastate the earth's essential resources (water, light, plants). Each trumpet will be blown by a different angel, although the angels are not named.

THE SEVEN BOWLS

The blowing of the seventh trumpet brings forth seven angels carrying the seven bowls (also referred to as "vials") of God's wrath described in Revelation 11:15-19 and verses 15:1-8. These bowls inflict pain, death, intense heat, and other catastrophes. Together, the trumpets and the bowls signify the day of God's wrath mentioned earlier in Revelation.

7 TRUMPETS

are yet to be blown by the Angels

1. Revelation 8:7
2. Revelation 8:8-9
3. Revelation 8:1-11
4. Revelation 8:8-12
5. Revelation 9:1-12
6. Revelation 9:13-21
7. Revelation 11:15-19

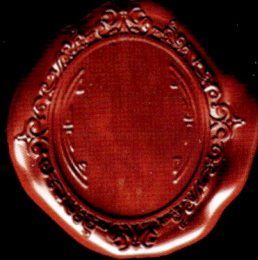

Green grass and 1/3 of the trees are burned up. - Rev. 8:7

1/3 of sea becomes blood; 1/3 of ships and sea life destroyed. - Rev. 8:8-9

1/3 of water turn bitter. - Rev. 8:1-11 (Wormwood)

1/3 of sun, moon, and stars do not shine. - Rev. 8:8-12

"Locusts" wield the Beast's military power. - Rev. 9:1-12

200-million-man army; 1/3 of mankind killed. -Rev. 9:3-21

The Kingdom of God is declared. -Rev. 11:15-19

1 2 3 4 5 6 7

7 TRUMPETS

Revelation 8:7-12, 9:1-21, 11:15-19

ANGELS

7 BOWLS

are yet to be poured out by the Angels

1. Revelation 16:2
2. Revelation 16:3
3. Revelation 16:4-7
4. Revelation 16:8-9
5. Revelation 16:10-11
6. Revelation 16:12-16
7. Revelation 16:17-21

Malignant ulcers appear on those with the 'mark' of the beast. - Rev. 16:2

Sea turns to blood, all living creatures in the sea die. - Rev. 16:3

Drinking water turns to blood, men given blood to drink. - Rev. 16:4-7

Sun becomes extremely hot and scorches men. -Rev. 16:8-9

Antichrist kingdom is struck with darkness. - Rev. 16:10-11

Euphrates river dries up, armies prepare for Armageddon. - Rev. 16:12-16

Worldwide earthquake, cities, islands & mountains disappear, 100lb hailstones fall from the sky. - Rev. 16:17-21

THE SIN...

6000 YEAR JOURNEY BEGINS BACK TO EDEN!
Starting 4008 B.C.

Earth was created specifically with man in mind, God wanted Relationship. Adam and Eve were given **Dominion [**authority**/ownership]** over all the creatures over the earth. Satan was a usurper (someone who takes a position of power) of Adam's dominion and is now referred to as **"the prince of the world."**

God/Jesus is in control of our lives, **but NOT the earth**, the world system. God does have the ability to destroy the earth, He did it in the Great Flood, but after the flood HE made a covenant with man that He would never flood the earth again; therefore, this time HE is going to destroy it with FIRE before the return of Jesus. Apostle Peter said He would destroy it with fire. - 2 Peter 3:10

- WHY DOES THE APPLE LOGO HAVE A BITE OUT OF IT?

WHAT DOES THE BIBLE SAY ABOUT AUTHORITY?
I [JESUS] have given you authority to trample on snakes and scorpions and to overcome all the power of the enemy; nothing will harm you. - Luke 10:19

CHAPTER 6
The Origins of Evil

THERE'S NO DOUBT that the origin of evil traces back to the Garden of Eden when the serpent caused Adam and Eve to fall away from God (Genesis 3). Known as the "most clever" of all of the beasts of the field, the snake chose to challenge God's gift of free will to mankind. Although they were given dominion over all of God's creation, Adam and Eve had the choice to trust God or not with their decisions.

In essence the miserable serpent tells Eve, "Hey don't you want to be like God?" in an attempt to destroy the blessings they had in the Garden. The snake didn't have the power to make Eve sin. But he knew that to disobey God was to initiate evil. And one bite of a fruit made all of that happen!

Make no mistake. God is not responsible for evil; His creatures are. The Bible says:

> *For everything in the world—the lust of the flesh, the lust of the eyes, and the pride of life—comes **not** from the Father but from the world.*

1 John 2:16 NIV (Emphasis Added)

Since that fateful moment over six thousand years ago, evil forces that despise God and seek to make us miserable, just as they are, have continually emerged.

They have one main purpose: To steal your soul for all eternity. They are the adversary of God and they are wicked. They are deceptive and lie, destroy and kill.

Let's identify some of the forces of evil in operation today.

THE KHAZARIAN MAFIA (KM)

This secret society is tied to the Synagogue of Satan as described in scripture (Revelation 2:9 and 3:9). As the world's largest organized crime syndicate, the group operates in total secrecy. They use their influence and funding to wipe any thought of their existence from recorded history. From what is known, this group formed around 100-800 AD and were composed of murderers, bandits, and thieves. They also routinely assumed the identities of their victims.

One common practice of the early KM was ancient Babylonian black magic, also known as Secret Satanism. This involved occult ceremonies based on Baal worship. Over the years, KM members have continued the practice of becoming masters of disguise and assuming false identities, along with their child-blood sacrifice ceremonies.

Today, members of the Khazarian Mafia often pose as Jewish but are vehemently opposed to the Jews and are considered "fake." Again, this stems from their methods of stealing identities and posing as counterfeits. This follows suit as Satan himself poses as an "angel of light" when he stands for nothing but darkness. But the ***good news*** is that they will get what they deserve.

> *Even Satan himself pretends to be an angel of light. So it doesn't surprise us that Satan's servants also pretend to be serving God. They will finally get exactly what they deserve.*
>
> 2 Corinthians 11:14b-15 NIRV

As powerful as all of the forces of evil are, they are still subject to God's sovereign control. Satan and his minions do not possess omniscience, omnipotence, or omnipresence. Satan is neither unchanging nor all-powerful. In fact, he is nothing but a creation, by the creator, God. Satan cannot create; he only copies.

He doesn't resemble God in any way. There is no creature more different from God than him. And he will get his just reward. Until that time comes, we have been given power in the Word to triumph over the evil one. What great confidence.

"RELEASE THE KRAKEN!"

This quote became well-known after the release of Disney's *Pirates of the Caribbean: Dead Man's Chest*. As the viewers chanted the quote, a gigantic beast would appear from the depths of the ocean. The beast used its monstrous tentacles to destroy a ship, leaving nothing remaining.

Attorney Sidney Powell, who represented Donald Trump in pursuit of justice over voter fraud in the 2020 election, used this phrase in an interview on FOX Business live with Lou Dobbs. Attorney Powell's cinematic reference nods to our societal conditioning. "Release the Kraken" is socially relevant; we all understood her intent. Although we've been conditioned to believe the Greek gods, titans, and legionary beasts are nothing but a myth.

The Geneva Bible teaches that we do not wrestle with flesh and blood but against principalities, against powers and against the worldly governors, the princes of darkness of this world (Ephesians 6:12 GNV). The Greek mythologies are in fact history. These are stories of gods, Satan, the fallen angels, and the Nephilim. Zeus, who is Satan, used the beasts of old and his fallen angels to control the world. In current times, we don't accept that a kraken would really exist. But Zeus still inflicts his control through modern beasts: nuclear weapons, financial manipulation, and biological warfare. The greatest lie ever told by Satan is that he does not exist! Humanity turned that great lie into a term called "Woo-Woo."

WOO-WOO

Woo-Woo is defined as something based on false beliefs or imaginary things, rather than through reason or scientific proof. Christians place their faith in an invisible God. Yet His existence is apparent everywhere if you look closely. There is overwhelming scientific and spiritual evidence that God exists. However, Satan has tried to convince the world that God, Jesus, and even Satan himself is woo-woo. If Satan doesn't exist, then people can remain oblivious to their impending doom without God.

There are physical signs of the biblical times, that would prove great things to an unbelieving world. But Satan, and Babylon, continue to cover it up. The discovery of giants and relics belonging to giants proves the existence of the Nephilim.

Physical evidence discredits the narrative of "Mythology". Genesis 6 speaks of the "Men of Renown". One giant is the Nephilim Molech (also spelled "Molek") who was the god of child sacrifice. For 50 years, America has been offering our children to Molech through abortion. Leviticus 20 outlines God's fair warning concerning this:

> The Lord said to Moses, "Say to the Israelites: 'Any Israelite or any foreigner residing in Israel who sacrifices any of his children to Molek is to be put to death. The members of the community are to stone him. I myself will set my face against him and will cut him off from his people; for by sacrificing his children to Molek, he has defiled my sanctuary and profaned my holy name. If the members of the community close their eyes when

> that man sacrifices one of his children to Molek and if they fail to put him to death, I myself will set my face against him and his family and will cut them off from their people together with all who follow him in prostituting themselves to Molek.

Leviticus 20:1-5 NIV

Satan, the Prince of the Air, offered the world to Jesus, because he had the legal authority to do so. This same offer was made to the Rothchilds and many other prominent families in our world. Jesus responded to Satan's offer by saying, "Get behind me, Satan." Yet sadly many of the now richest families in the world have bowed down to take the offer. And Satan has made them "Kings on the earth."

And since these kings created the Federal Reserve in 1913, their love of money has enslaved all of humanity. President Andrew Jackson had previously warned that powers conferred upon banks were "not only unnecessary, but dangerous to the Government and the country." He went on, warning that if it continued to operate, "great evils . . . might flow from such a concentration of power in the hands of a few."

So who is "they" and "their?" It is those who work for Satan, as referenced in Revelation 2:9 and 3:9.

KHAZARIAN MAFIA – The World's "Puppet Masters"

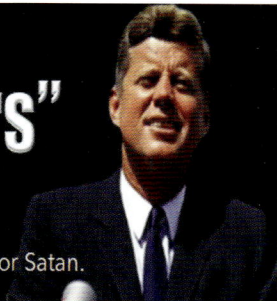

- The FAKE JEWS, the liars referenced in the Bible from the **Synagogue of Satan** that hide in the shadows, thus **"Mystery Babylon."**
- A worldwide syndicate with its origins going back 6000-years to the garden of Eden, comprised of blood drinking pedophiles working for Satan.
- <u>Unlimited money</u> is spent hiding them, thus allowing them to secretly operate in the shadows.
- John F Kennedy, in his infamous **1961** speech, referred to them as **"A SECRET SOCIETY."**

FAKE JEWS - SYNAGOGUE OF SATAN

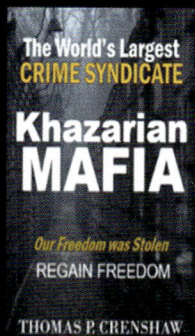

The World's Largest
CRIME SYNDICATE
Khazarian
MAFIA
Our Freedom was Stolen
REGAIN FREEDOM
THOMAS P. CRENSHAW

Coincidence? The current shield and symbol of Ukraine, the Crest of Ukraine, corresponds to the so-called Khazarian Tamga or Tamga Jazaro, belonging to the old Khazarian Empire from where the Khazarian Mafia originates.

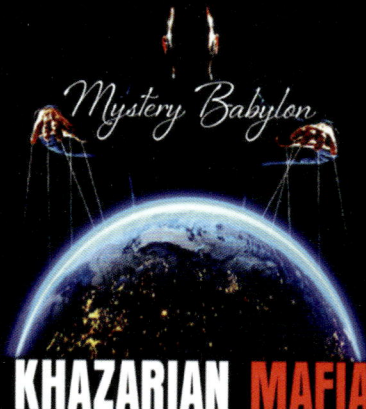

Mystery Babylon

KHAZARIAN MAFIA

- I know the blasphemy of those opposing you. They say they are Jews, but they are **not**, because their **synagogue** belongs to **Satan**. - Revelation 2:9

- I will force those who belong to **Satan's synagogue**, those liars who say they are Jews but are **not**, but are liars, to come and bow down at your feet. They will acknowledge that you are the ones I love. - Revelation 3:9

- For you are the **children of your father the devil**, and you love to do the evil things he does. He was a murderer from the beginning. He has always hated the truth, because there is no truth in him. When he lies, it is consistent with his character; for **he is a liar and the father of lies**. - John 8:44

A SECRET SOCIETY

GREEK MYTHOLOGY IS IN FACT HISTORY!

Zeus = Satan

Resided on Mount **Olympus**

"For we wrestle not against flesh and blood, but against principalities, against powers, and against the **worldly governors**, the **princes of the darkness** of this world, against spiritual wickedness, which are in the high places".

- Ephesians 6:12 GNV

Clash-of-the-Titans

"Release the Kraken!"

- Sidney Powell, Nov. 14, 2020

Zeus's nuclear option to teach unruly and disrespectful humans a lesson they would never forget.

Skull and Bones

322

YALE UNIVERSITY
NEW HAVEN, CONNECTICUT

WORLDS MOST SECRET WOO-WOO

Woo-Woo Definition: "Based on false beliefs or imaginary things, rather than reason or scientific knowledge."

THE GIANTS

"Men of Renown" in Genesis 6... "The Fallen Ones"... the Sons of God *who had children with the daughters of men. "And it came to pass, when men began to multiply on the face of the earth, and daughters were born unto them, That the sons of God saw the daughters of men that they were fair; and they took them wives of all which they chose."*

THE NEPHILIM

One of the Nephilim is Molech, the god of child sacrifice

"The Lord spoke to Moses, saying, "Say to the people of Israel, Any one of the people of Israel ... he who gives any of his children to Molech shall surely be put to death ... And if the people of the land do at all close their eyes to that man when he gives one of his children to Molech, and do not put him to death, then I will set my face against that man and against his clan and will cut them off from among their people, him and all who follow him in whoring after Molech."

- Leviticus 20:1-5 ESV

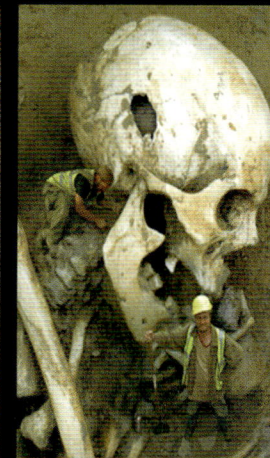

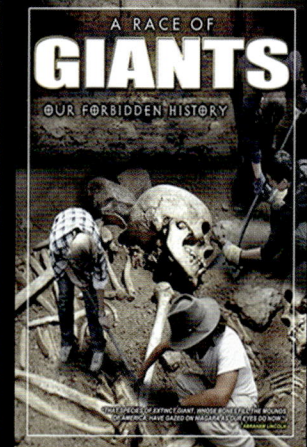

A RACE OF
GIANTS
OUR FORBIDDEN HISTORY

NIMROD AND GILGAMESH

Nimrod is first mentioned in 1 Chronicles 1 as a mighty warrior on earth. He was the son of Cush and the grandson of Noah's son, Ham. i.e., Noah was the great-grandfather of Nimrod. Most of the sons and grandsons of Ham were giants. Nimrod's uncle, Egypt, was known as the father of Kasluhites (from whom the Philistines originated) in Genesis 10:13. And of course, a prominent Philistine was the giant, Goliath (Nimrod's cousin).

The name "Nimrod" derives from the Hebrew *marad (*MRD), which means defiance or rebel. When adding the "n" before the root, it becomes NMRD or "*the* rebel" against God. Other translations of his name equate it to "tyrant" as mentioned in Genesis 10:8. Nimrod sought to establish himself as a warrior in rebellion against God. While he believed *in* God, Nimrod was also jealous *of* God.

Nimrod helped build the Tower of Babel as recorded in Genesis 10. One of the kingdoms established by Nimrod was Babel, later known as Babylon. Nimrod had an obsession with the idea of a second flood. The ancient historian, Josephus, in *Antiquities of the Jews*, states that Nimrod was motivated by his anger towards God for destroying his forefathers and intended to erect a tower tall enough to be unaffected by flood waters.

Gilgamesh was a vile, filthy, perverted man who was described as 2/3 god and 1/3 man in *The Epic of Gilgamesh*. These were ancient clay tablets excavated from 2000 B.C. The story of Gilgamesh very closely parallels the story of Nimrod.

For example, Gilgamesh sets out to the Cedar Mountain to find and destroy the "monster" who sent the Flood. The creature Gilgamesh searches to kill is "Huwawa," a name that is intriguingly similar to the name YHWH, the one whom Nimrod opposed.

Both Nimrod and Gilgamesh were known as tyrants and forcibly took other men's wives. Both *the Epic of Gilgamesh* and the Bible record a major flood event. Both men were known as expert builders and mighty warriors, and they both lived around the same time period. Finally, according to the clay tablets, Gilgamesh was from the city of Erech, a Babylonian town established by Nimrod. After the fall of Babel, Nimrod allegedly sought refuge in what is now Iraq, assumed the name Gilgamesh, and eventually established the foundations of the present-day Free Masons.

The ***good news*** is that on Pentecost, God reversed the giant Nimrod's evil plans to reach Heaven through the tower of Babel by twisting their tongues! Rather than allowing prideful men to become like Him by making a name for themselves, God thwarted their plans.

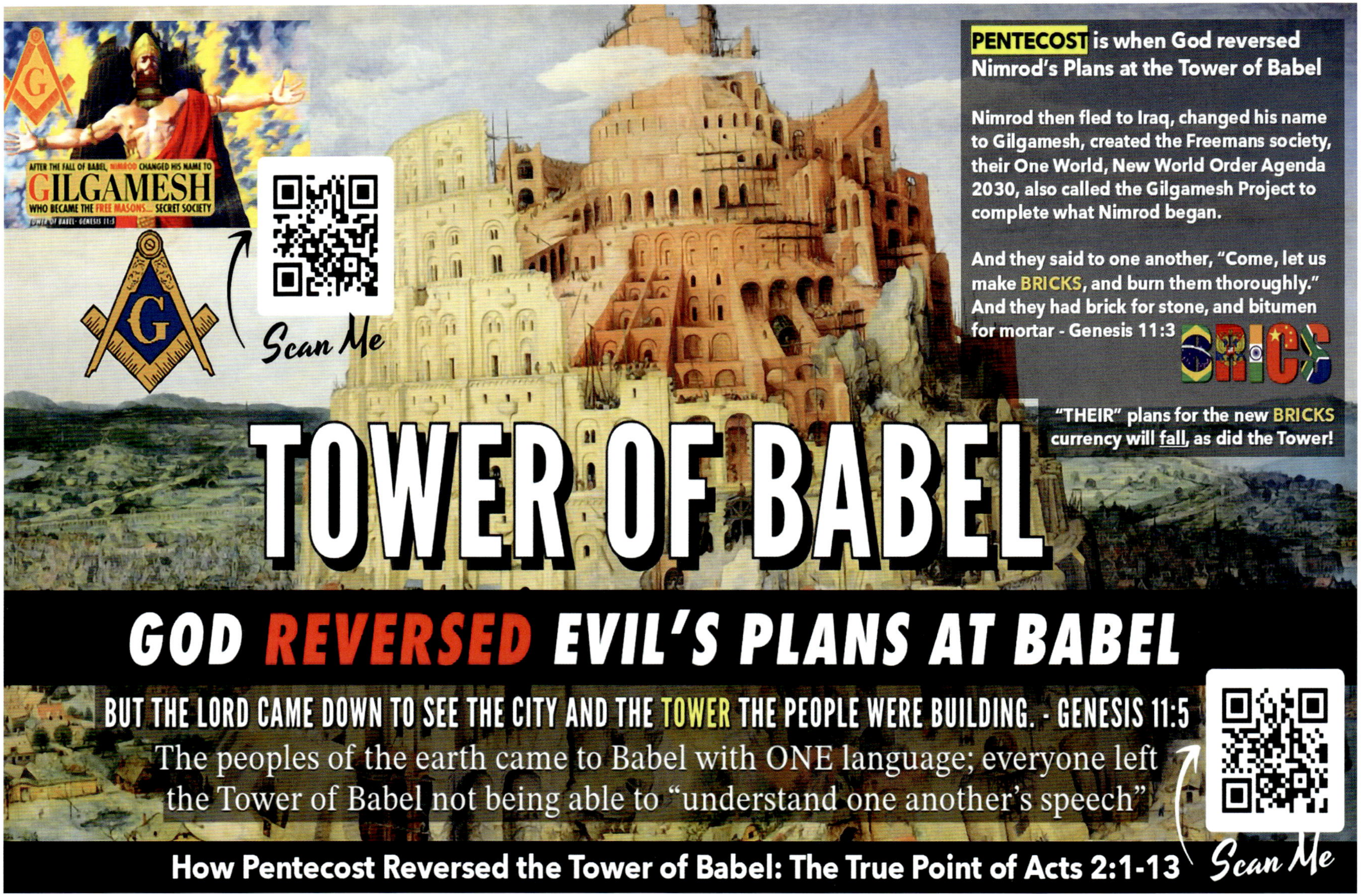

AFTER THE FALL OF BABEL, NIMROD CHANGED HIS NAME TO
GILGAMESH
WHO BECAME THE FREE MASONS... SECRET SOCIETY
G
G
Scan Me
PENTECOST is when God reversed Nimrod's Plans at the Tower of Babel
Nimrod then fled to Iraq, changed his name to Gilgamesh, created the Freemans society, their One World, New World Order Agenda 2030, also called the Gilgamesh Project to complete what Nimrod began.
And they said to one another, "Come, let us make BRICKS, and burn them thoroughly." And they had brick for stone, and bitumen for mortar - Genesis 11:3
BRICS
"THEIR" plans for the new BRICKS currency will fall, as did the Tower!
TOWER OF BABEL
GOD REVERSED EVIL'S PLANS AT BABEL
BUT THE LORD CAME DOWN TO SEE THE CITY AND THE TOWER THE PEOPLE WERE BUILDING. - GENESIS 11:5
The peoples of the earth came to Babel with ONE language; everyone left the Tower of Babel not being able to "understand one another's speech"
Scan Me
How Pentecost Reversed the Tower of Babel: The True Point of Acts 2:1-13

Freemason "Puppet Masters"
The Khazarian Mafia

HARLOT SITTING On The **BEAST**
- Revelation 17:3

- Rothschilds
- Klaus Schwab
- Bill Gates
- Rockefellers
- Bilderberg Group
- Obama
- etc.

"G" = Gilgamesh = Nimrod

Arrogant Rothschild's Quotes:

- *"Give me control over a nation's currency, and I care not who makes its laws."* - Mayer Amschel Rothschild (1743-1812)

- *"I care not who controls a nation's political affairs, so long as I control her currency."* - Mayer Amschel Rothschild (1743-1812)

- *"I care not what puppet is placed upon the throne of England to rule the Empire on which the sun never sets."* - Nathan Mayer Rothschild (1815)

THE BEAST
"MYSTERY BABYLON"
- Revelation 17:5

HARLOT is the **"DEEP STATE"** who is **"MYSTERY BABYLON"** with origins from the bloodline of Cain, that works in the shadows, pulling the strings of world leaders who control the

7-Mountains... **The "Puppet Masters"!**

7-Mountains
1. Finance
2. Family
3. Church/Religion
4. Government
5. Entertainment
6. Media
7. Education

God's DESTRUCTION of "MYSTERY BABYLON"
- REVELATION 17:5, JOEL 2:34

Fulfilling Daniel 2:34, a 2500+ year old Prophecy!

Their End!

Begins In 2025

"The sun will be turned to darkness and the moon to blood before the coming of the GREAT and TERRIBLE day of the LORD." - Joel 2:34

The BEST of TIMES, 'IN' the WORST of TIMES!

1. FINANCIAL
2. FAMILY
3. CHURCH
4. GOVERNMENT
5. ENTERTAINMENT
6. MEDIA
7. EDUCATION

YEAR 2020 IS THE BEGINNING OF THE END!

Some have mistakenly labelled 2020…"YEAR ZERO"

Secret
Prophecy of SEVEN SEALS

Weep no more; behold, the **Lion** of the tribe of **Judah**, the Root of David, has conquered, so that he can open the **scroll** and its 7-seals

- Revelation 5:5

FIRST 4 of the 7-SEALS are the 4-HORSEMEN of the APOCALYPSE

- 1st SEAL opened - Corona Virus - December 30, 2019 - Hannukah
- 2nd SEAL opened - Violence Erupts, peace taken from the earth - May 30, 2020 - Pentecost
- **2025** 3rd SEAL - Financial Collapse, Great Wealth Transfer, Dollar crash, gold & silver multiply
- 4th SEAL - coming - Death, Famine, Pestilence and Poverty
- 5th SEAL - coming - The Cry of the Martyrs, God's reply "just a little longer!"
- 6th SEAL - coming - The great earthquake, the sun became black, stars of the sky fall
- 7th SEAL - coming - Brings the 7-Trumpets and 7-Bowls of God's wrath

They shall **WEEP** and say "Why did we betray the United States?" - Kim Clement

THE GREAT RESET

COVID-19 THE GREAT RESET

In a Single Day...

REVELATION 18:8-10

KINGS OF THE EARTH WILL **WEEP AND WAIL**

Woe! Woe to you, great city,
you mighty city of Babylon!
In one hour your doom has come!

Revelation 18:10 NIV

At midnight the Cry Rang out...

MIDNIGHT HOUR
2025

- Completion
- No Time Left
- A Turning Point
- A New Beginning
- The End of an ERA
- Cleansing of The Old
- Darkness Before Dawn
- When Night Turns to Day
- A Timepoint for Vengeance
- When Darkness Meets The Light
- Death of USA Corporation & Mystery Babylon

MATTHEW 25 5-FOOLISH VIRGINS / 5-WISE VIRGINS

2025

CHAPTER 7
2024 through 2025 - The Fall of Babylon!

A 50-YEAR PLAN TO DESTROY AMERICA

IN HISTORY, THERE are critical time points that are a spiritual hinge for an entire nation. The era known as the 1970s was definitely a critical turning point for America. Besides the passing of Roe vs. Wade and the signing of the Petro-Dollar contract, other events happened that had both a financial and a spiritual impact tied to the events happening now (some fifty years later)!

Allow me to outline six critical events that happened in the 1970s and were attempts to collapse America:

- The World Economic Forum (WEF) first met in February 1971 in Davos, Switzerland, as organized by Klaus Schwab.
- Prayer was removed from schools in June 1971.
- President Nixon removed the U.S.A. from the gold standard in August 1971.

- Project LookingGlass allowed evil to enter America in December 1972.
- That was then suddenly followed by the passing of Roe vs. Wade in January 1973.
- In June 1974, the Petro-Dollar contract was signed.

The year 2025 is going to be momentous in many positive ways for God's people. Those important decisions, made fifty years ago, are being reversed or addressed globally. For example, since the overturn of Roe vs. Wade in 2022, God's hand of blessing is once again upon us. He is going to bless the United States and destroy evil for the murder of His creation. When Roe vs. Wade was overturned, three days later the Supreme Court also overruled the so-called Lemon Test that had been applied on June 28, 1971 to outlaw prayer in schools.

Also, June 9, 2024, marked 50 years since the historic signing of the Petrodollar. And now that contract is no more.

THE DAVOS MANIFESTO

This document, written in 1973, was a code of ethics for business leaders. The initial goal was to improve management, workers, and employees. Yet, it evolved into a manifesto seeking to redefine capitalism, establish a global economy, promote worldwide vaccinations, and reshape history through wealth redistribution, environmental initiatives, and activism.

In February, 1971, Klaus Schwab, founder of the World Economic Forum, took what was a small initiative in the Swiss Alps to an international agenda of "improving" the state of the world. Many are skeptical of Schwab's underlying motives, despite the Forum's 2024 Annual Meeting theme of rebuilding trust. Their so-called "trust" was in fact control of mankind.

God is going to open the third seal and for seven years break the power of these New Age World Order doctrines that seek to control.

REVIVAL

Originating in California in July 1970, the Jesus Revolution was a movement characterized by widespread baptisms across North America, Europe, Central America, Australia, and New Zealand, eventually tapering off in the late 1980s. Time Magazine ran a cover titled *The Jesus Revolution* on June 21, 1971. On February 24, 2023, a movie came out titled "Jesus Revolution".

It is fascinating to note that while evil is rising, so too, is the spirit of God with the Jesus Revolution. Both the fulfillment of the 1980 Bob Jones prophecy and the 1970s Jesus Revolution show that revival is near and expected to begin as year 248 ends on July 3, 2025. Be ready for the multi-billion soul Harvest to begin because that is ***good news***!

SANCTITY OF LIFE—THE MARK OF TIME!

"We the people," a nation founded under God, agreed through the highest court in the land to legally kill the Creator's creation.

> *If God is for us, who can be against us?*
>
> Romans 8:31 NIV

This decision caused God, the Creator, to turn his back on the world. As of January 22, 1973, God was no longer "for us," and evil moved in.

The case that legalized abortion in the USA began in 1970 when "Jane Roe," a fictional name used to protect the identity of the plaintiff, Norma McCorvey, instituted a federal action against Henry Wade. The case was first argued in the Supreme Court on December 13, 1971, and became federal law on January 22, 1973.

But then, on June 24, 2022, the court overturned the case forty-nine (49) years later. According to calculations, Roe vs. Wade's 50th year since becoming law ended on January 21, 2024, applying Leviticus 25's "50th Year of Release." That day (1/21/24) is also *exactly* 77 years, 7 months and 7 days from the birth of Donald Trump (77-7-7) according to the

DEATH ANGEL HAS BEEN RELEASED IN THE EARTH!

Hear me says the Lord, before this year is out, the Death Angel is being loosed upon the earth.

ANGEL OF DEATH

KENT CHRISTMAS

50
Golden Jubilee

WHERE is a second *Death Angel* event in scripture? *"In a little while, and the wicked will be no more; though you look for them, they will not be found. But the meek will inherit the land and enjoy peace and prosperity. The wicked plot against the righteous and gnash their teeth at them; but the Lord laughs at the wicked, for he knows their day is coming."* - Psalm 37:10-13

- **Hear me says the Lord, before this year is out, the Death Angel is being loosed upon the earth**, and what they concocted and created in laboratories, called the coronavirus, will pale in comparison, sayeth the Lord, to the spirit that the death Angel will loose upon the nations. And it will not touch my people… will not touch the church!

- And just as I declared in **psalms 91**, "a thousand may fall at your side, ten thousand at your right hand, but it will not come near you. You will only observe with your eyes and see the punishment of the wicked.

April 13 – 20, 2025!?

PASSOVER

"Commemorate this day for generations to come!"
- Exodus 12:14

April 13 - 20

2025

IS EXPECTED TO AGAIN MARK ONE
OF THE MOST IMPORTANT
TIMEPOINTS IN BIBLICAL HISTORY!

15TH OF NISAN

is described as "a night to
be much observed"
- Exodus 12:42

15TH OF NISAN

ONE OF THE MOST IMPORTANT TIMEPOINTS IN BIBLICAL HISTORY!

PASSOVER v PENTECOST

PASSOVER - at time when God has *intervened* on behalf of mankind to change the course of history, see items 1 -8 below.

PENTECOST - God *empowers* man with the ability to operate under HIS / God's Authority / Law
- Birth of the LAW / Torah at Sinai
- Holy Spirit

1. The First Passover, the angel of death, or destroying angel, appeared and brought **death to all the firstborn of Egypt,** including animals. - Exodus 12:23

2. Adam told his sons Cain and Abel that this night was suited for offering sacrifices to God because the Jewish people would one day offer the Paschal Lamb on this day, end up being **Jesus's Crucifixion.**

3. Isaac chose to bless his son Esau; but with the help of his mother Rebecca, Jacob ended up receiving Isaac's blessing which was rightly Esau's. [Isaac was tricked to bless Jacob]

4. Army of **Gideon's three hundred (300)** picked men and destroyed the powerful Midian army.

5. During the Period of the Kings, **the angel of God killed 185,000 Assyrian soldiers.**

6. On the 15th **Haman came to the King to convince him to wipe out the Jewish nation,** that same night, the King's sleep was disturbed, and a chain of events was set into motion that brought about Haman's downfall.

7. On the 15th **Daniel was thrown into the lion's den** and miraculously survived.

8. King **Belshazzar drank from the vessels** of the Holy Temple and died that night.

Gregorian calendar. In 2010, Kim Clement prophesied that the spirit of Python would be destroyed between 70 and 100 days from January 21.

With the overturning of Roe vs. Wade in the 49th year, Leviticus 25:8 NIV, *"Count off seven sabbath years—seven times seven years—so that the seven sabbath years amount to forty-nine years"* was fulfilled, indicating that the year 2022 was the 49th-year. The year 2023 is therefore considered to be the fiftieth, specifically using Roe vs. Wade as the 50-year marker.

But the 50-year calculation of the Petro-Dollar contract, from June 9, 1974, takes us to June 9, 2024. And therefore the 50th year ends on June 8, 2025. The year 2025 is, therefore, the official 50th-year marker. This year perfectly calculates with the end of the 248-year Declaration of Independence calculation. This calculation points to July 3-4, 2025, as a critical time point for human history, and specifically for America.

A DIVINE VISITATION IS ON THE WAY

Though the world appears dark to many, God spoke to modern-day prophet Kent Christmas and said, *"There is a divine visitation that is on the way."* And it's coming back to the Earth because the Earth is God's.The Lord continued to speak through Kent, *"This visitation will embarrass the enemy until they hang their head in shame... and though I have been slow in speaking and it seems like no one knows what's happening, I, the Lord, have always been in control. There is no demon spirit that I do not have authority over."*

PASSOVER 2025

Passover has been one of the most important time points in biblical history. For the Spirit of God has intervened on behalf of mankind, to change the course of history. And in 2025, He is expected to change the course of our future. The image on the previous page lists important biblical events that occurred in conjunction with Passover (also known as the 15th of Nisan). In 2025, Passover will begin on April 13th and will end on Resurrection Sunday, April 20th!

THE TRUE PASSOVER LAMB

In Exodus 12, God provides instructions through Moses for the Israelites to observe the Passover and Festival of Unleavened Bread. Passover is a major Jewish holiday that occurs in the spring. It commemorates what God did when He struck down every firstborn in judgment of all the gods of Egypt. And per God's instructions to Moses, it was to occur in the first month of their year (the Hebrew month Nisan).

Verses 1-12 teach that specifically on the **tenth** day of Nisan (April 8, 2025), each man was to take a lamb for his family, one for each household. The animal was to be a male and "without defect." Then, at twilight (which was considered the **ninth hour**) on the **fourteenth** day of Nisan (April 12, 2025), all the members of the community of Israel were to slaughter those animals (Exodus 12:6).

After the slaughter, the Israelites were to place some of the blood on the sides and tops of their doorframes. In the first

Passover, blood on the doorpost served as a sign to protect residents from the angel of death and prevent any destructive plague from coming to that household.

During the commemoration, the Israelites were also told to eat during the night the flesh of the sacrifice that had been roasted with fire and bitter herbs. There was to be nothing remaining of the lamb until the next morning (which would now be the **fifteenth** day of Nisan- April 13, 2025). God told His people that day was "the LORD's Passover."

> *This is a day* [i.e., the fifteenth day of Nisan] *you are to commemorate; for the generations to come you shall celebrate it as a festival to the LORD—a lasting ordinance.*
>
> Exodus 12:14 NIV [Emphasis Added]

Let's discuss the structure of the Jewish day. Their day did not begin at midnight as our days do. And their clock followed the sun, rather than the position of hands on a clock per se. At 6:00 p.m. or sunset, a new Jewish day would begin. Then 9:00 p.m. was considered the third hour of the day (morning), 12:00 a.m. was their sixth hour (noon), and 3:00 p.m. marked the ninth hour or "twilight" (mid to late afternoon) of their day.

John 12:1-13 illustrates some divine similarities between the Passover described in Exodus and Jesus' triumphant entry into Jerusalem and crucifixion. Christians understand that the Passover event in the Old Testament served as a prediction of Jesus' death as the lamb who would atone for our sins.

> *Six days before the Passover* [i.e., on the 9th day of Nisan], *Jesus came to Bethany, where Lazarus lived, whom Jesus had raised from the dead. Here a dinner was given in Jesus' honor…The next day [*i.e., on 10 Nisan, which is April 8, 2025] *the great crowd that had come for the festival heard that Jesus was on his way to Jerusalem They took palm branches and went out to meet him, shouting, "Hosanna! Blessed is he who comes in the name of the Lord!"*
>
> John 12:1, 13 NIV [Emphasis Added]

The people hailed and chose the lamb (Jesus) on the **tenth day** of Nisan like the families in the Old Testament chose a lamb without defect on the designated day. Of course, Jesus was without sin. Upon being arrested and brought to Pontius Pilate, Pilate stated that he found no wrongdoing in Jesus. This holds great significance because Jesus, as the sacrificial lamb, fulfilled the Passover requirements for humanity. In John 19:4 (NIV) Pilate says, "***I find no basis for a charge against him.***"

While on the cross, at about the "**ninth hour,**" Jesus cried out with a loud voice to God. None of this is mere coincidence; by God's divine design, Jesus met the exact requirements for the Passover. Jesus died during the Jewish twilight or ninth hour, and the **temple veil was torn**.

> *And about the **ninth hour** Jesus cried out with a loud voice, saying, "Eli, Eli, lama sabachthani?" that is, "My God, My God, why have You forsaken Me? . . . And Jesus cried out again with a loud voice and yielded up His spirit.*
>
> Matthew 27:46, 50 NKJV [Emphasis Added]

ABORTION

50 *Golden Jubilee*

Prophetic Word on ABORTION: *"A 'woman's right to choose' is nothing but an excuse for MURDER!"*

- **December 13, 1971** - Roe v. Wade is argued before the US Supreme Court.

- **January 22, 1973** - U.S. Supreme Court ruled , in a 7-2 decision, that the Constitution of the United States conferred a **"woman's right to choose"** using the 14th amendment to have an abortion. **Coincidently exactly 32 years later January 22, 2005, Trump marries Melania.**

- Since 1973 over 50-million plus children (God's creation) have been murdered in the USA!

- Roe v. Wade was overturned on **June 24, 2022**

Beginning in 2025, God will next chastise and then bless the USA and destroy evil for the murder of HIS creation, fulfilling 2 Chronicles 7:14.

CREATION vs ABORTION

God is the Creator, and man allowed the destruction of His creation!

By allowing abortion beginning in 1971, we turned away from God and God therefore allowed the Harlot of Babylon to gain complete control of the USA, and the world (via the USD), and now the Harlot rides upon the 7-mountains as described in Revelation 17.

June 24, 2022

OVERTURNED!

Prophecy Fulfilled!!

Roe v Wade was OVERTURNED by the US Supreme Court on June 24, 2022, and God's hand of blessing is once again back upon the USA!

Scan Me

OVERTURNED: If God is for us, who can be against us? - Romans 8:31

The New York Times

LATE CITY EDITION
Weather: Partly sunny today; cloudy tonight, cloudy and warm tomorrow. Temp. range: today 62-77; Saturday 57-76. Temp-Hum. Index yesterday 72. Additional details on Page 67.

SECTION ONE

NEW YORK, SUNDAY, JUNE 9, 1974

60 CENTS

KISSINGER LINKED TO ORDER TO F.B.I. ENDING WIRETAPS

His Testimony to Senate on 'Security' Action Involving Newsmen Is Disputed

HAIG QUOTED IN MEMOS

General Is Called the Liaison Man Who Passed Along Surveillance Decisions

By SEYMOUR M. HERSH

Prince Fahd Ibn Abdel Aziz of Saudi Arabia and Secretary of State Kissinger after signing agreement at Blair House in Washington yesterday. Standing between them is Isa Sabbagh, interpreter; at right is Ambassador Ibrahim al-Sowayed.

'MILESTONE' PACT IS SIGNED BY U.S. AND SAUDI ARABIA

Wide - Ranging Agreement Calls for Economic and Military Commissions

COOPERATION IS THE KEY

Washington Hopes Accord Will Serve as a Model for Other Arab Countries

By BERNARD GWERTZMAN

WASHINGTON, June 8—The United States and Saudi Arabia today signed a wide-ranging military and economic agreement that both said "heralded an era of increasingly close cooperation."

Petro-Dollar: On August 15, 1971, the US "severed link between the US dollar and gold" via President Nixon, 'we the people' turned away from God's gold standard of honest money and then on **June 9, 1974**, signing a man-made 'Petro-dollar' agreement with Saudi Arabia. Fifty years from 1971, on **August 24, 2021**, Saudi Arabia signs a new military agreement with Russia and on **August 24, 2023**, Saudi Arabia agrees to join the BRICS, although the US Government refuses to discuss this matter publicly. Then on **June 9, 2024**, exactly 50-years for the signing of the 'Petro-dollar' agreement, Saudi Arabia refused to re-sign and extend the agreement. Therefore, as of **June 9, 2024**, the US Dollar is now purely Fiat Money, a government-issued currency that is not backed by a physical commodity, such as gold, silver, or even oil; but rather only by the government that issued it. It is intrinsically **valueless** and is simply being used by government decree.

God gave the USA and the world an honest instrument of money to transact, specifically gold and silver as written in Haggai 2:8, then 'we the people', turned away from God's money system with Nixon, implemented a new 'man-made' money system called the 'Petro-Dollar' that came to an end on **June 9, 2024**. The only agreement Saudi Arabia now has for its oil is with Russia through the agreement signed on **August 24, 2021**. Just like with abortion, but this time with the money system, 'we the people' turned on back to God's honest system of money and this new man-made evil, ungodly, money system moved in and now, at the time of writing, has completely enslaved and controls humanity.

One thing is for certain, nothing made by man has ever lasted forever and therefore expect the 'Petro-dollar' to lose it status as the world's reserve currently **on or before the last day** that ends the **50-year Jubilee** on June 8, 2025, based on calculation within Leviticus 25:10-11.

'Milestone' Pact is SIGNED by U.S. and Saudi Arabia

Petro-Dollar June 9, 1974
ENDED Exactly 50-Year Later June 9, 2024

50 Golden Jubilee

TIME	is MONEY
1 million seconds is **12 days**	OR **$12**
1 billion seconds is 31 years	OR **$11,291 (Thousand)**
1 trillion seconds is 31,688 years	OR **$11,000,000 (Million)**
1 quadrillion is **31,536,000 years**	OR **$11,000,000,000 (Billion)**

US DOLLAR

50 *Expected to lose its status as the World's Reserve Currency in 2025*

THE 50-YEAR GOLDEN JUBILEE

- August 15, **1971** - Nixon "Severs link between dollar and gold" and the USA creates 'money by decree', separate from GOD, and 'fiat' money was born! This date in time has been coined the *'Nixon Moment'*.

- On June 9, **1974**, the USA and Saudi Arabia sign a Military Agreement, orchestrated by Henry Kissinger, and the **'Petro-Dollar'** was created, thus linking oil with the dollar.

- From August 15, 1971, **50-years** later, to the exact day, **August 15, 2021**, Kabul fell.

- Nine (9) days later from August 15, 2021, on exactly **August 24, 2021**, the Saudi's signed a Military Agreement with Russia despite their **1974 'Petro-Dollar'** agreement with the USA. From August 24, 2021, two (2) years later, to the exact day, **August 24, 2023**, the Saudi's joined the BRICS.

- On **November 29, 2023**, the orchestrator of the **'Petro-Dollar'** agreement, Henry Kissinger dies 50-years after creating the contract at age 100 (2 x 50 years).

- On **June 9, 2024**, Saudi Arabia refused to re-sign the 'Petro-dollar' agreement; thus, effectively removing the **'Petro'** from the **1974 'Petro-Dollar'**. Their attempt to hide this truth by calling this event 'fake news', does not change the fact it <u>did</u> occur.

Brief History of the GOLD STANDARD in the United States.

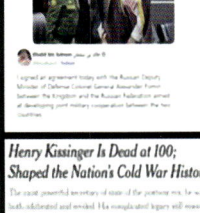

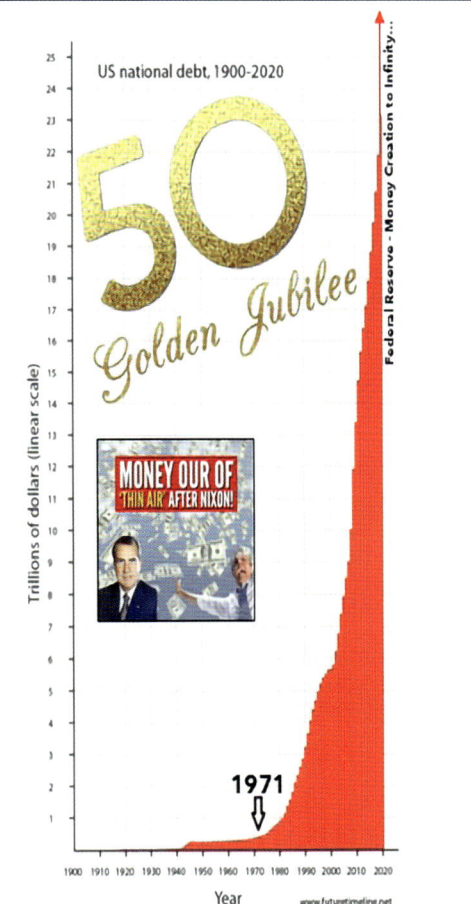

Scan Me

The New York Times

NIXON ORDERS 90-DAY WAGE-PRICE FREEZE, ASKS TAX CUTS, NEW JOBS IN BROAD PLAN; SEVERS LINK BETWEEN DOLLAR AND GOLD

Fall of Kabul (2021)

August 15, 2021

Saudi Arabia, Russia sign military cooperation agreement

August 24, 2021

REUTERS
BRICS welcomes new members in push to reshuffle world order

August 24 2023

Saudi Arabia's petro-dollar exit: A global finance paradigm shift

Henry Kissinger Is Dead at 100; Shaped the Nation's Cold War History

November 29, 2023

June 9, 2024

US national debt, 1900-2020

50 Golden Jubilee

MONEY OUR OF 'THIN AIR' AFTER NIXON!

Trillions of dollars (linear scale)

Federal Reserve - Money Creation to Infinity...

1971

1900 1910 1920 1930 1940 1950 1960 1970 1980 1990 2000 2010 2020
Year
www.futuretimeline.net

Understanding Money Creation to Infinity and Time:

1 million seconds is 12 days
1 billion seconds is 31 years
1 trillion seconds is **31,688 years**
1 quadrillion is **31,536,000 years**

GOD'S GLORY, EVEN IN FOOTBALL

On January 11, 1970, the Kansas City Chiefs won their first Superbowl (while playing against the Minnesota Vikings). In 1980, the Prophet Bob Jones received a prophetic word that stated, "When the Chiefs win the Superbowl, it will be a sign that God is raising up his apostolic chiefs around the world to usher in the greatest revival in human history, bringing in a one billion soul harvest."

Interestingly, not until 50-years later, in 2020, the Kansas City Chiefs Football team won their second Superbowl. However, no revival broke out—in fact, Covid came upon the world, and rather than a revival, the world witnessed a lockdown. Once again, the Chiefs won Superbowl 2023, and a revival broke out in 2023 on February 8th in Wilmore, Kentucky, known as the "Asbury Revival." (However, the Superbowl was held on February 12, four days *after* the revival began).

The Jones' prophecy implied that the revival would begin *after* the Superbowl, not *before*. Thus, the Chief's 2023 win did not correctly fulfill the prophetic word. Additionally, the revival came to an end on February 24, 2023.

The Chiefs won the Superbowl again in 2024. But no revival broke out in 2024. And there are several intriguing coincidences which paralleled this victory, suggesting the Bob Jones prophecy is now soon to be fulfilled. They have won in 2020, 2023 and 2024, i.e., three times in this decade. We wait and watch—a revival is imminent.

DID YOU KNOW? The Chief's 2024 Superbowl victory was the **3ʳᵈ win** since 2020. Additionally, the number "**3**," often used to represent the TRINITY, can be witnessed in many instances throughout the game. For example:

- the game was won with only **3-seconds** remaining,
- the winning throw was from the **3-yard line,**
- the San Francisco 49ers player who missed his tackle was **#33,**
- the Chiefs' quarterback finished the game with **333 passing yards,**
- the final score was 25 to 22, with the Chiefs winning by a **3-point spread**, and finally,
- the stadium address was **3333** Al Davis Way!

People might call these examples a mere "coincidence" meaning that there is no connection between these remarkable concurrences. However, given the consistent reoccurrence of the number "3," I recognize the significant possibility of God's divine influence in all of this and the probability that America will experience a momentous revival in 2025, as prophesied in the 1980s, over **forty years** ago.

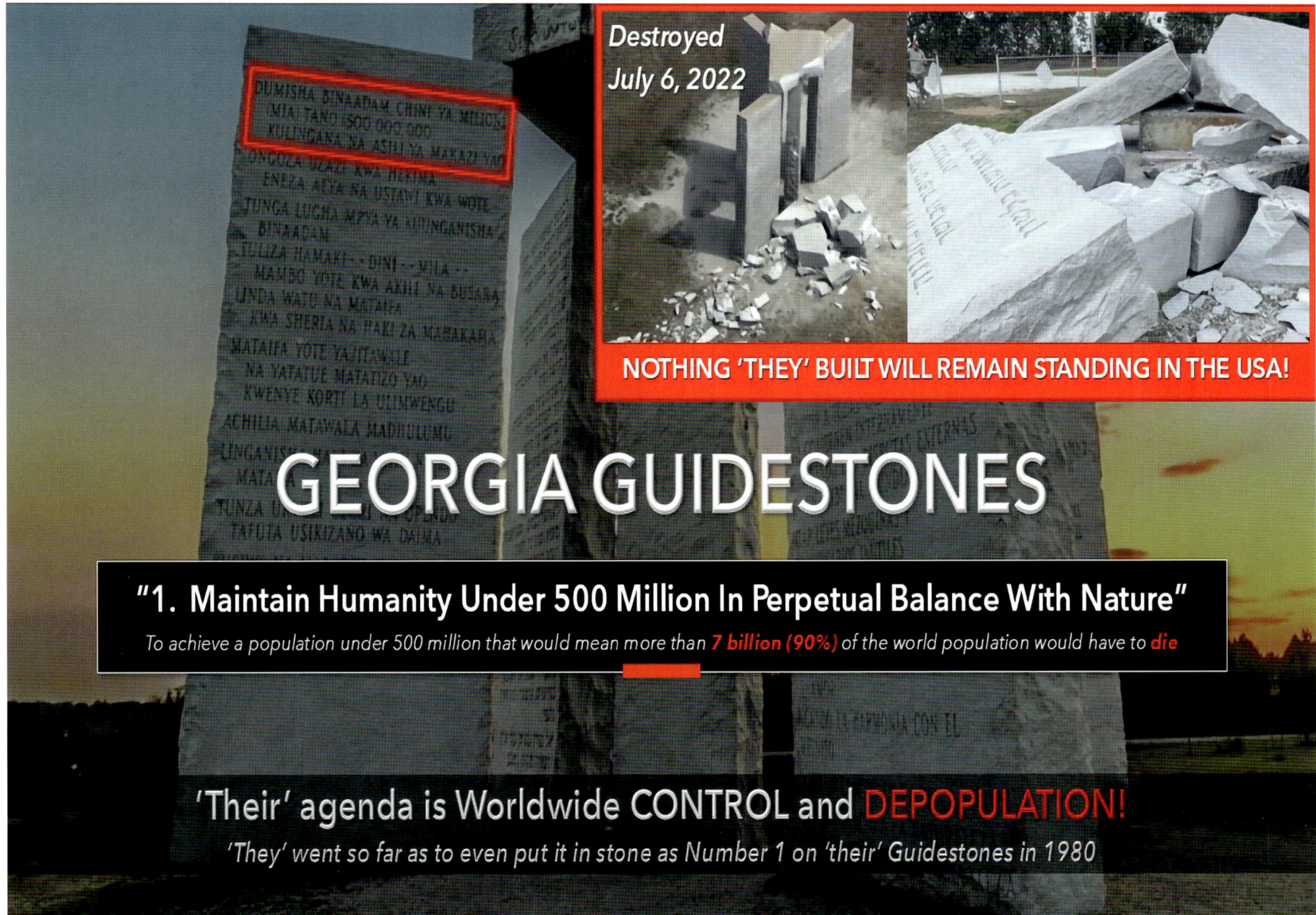

Destroyed
July 6, 2022

NOTHING 'THEY' BUILT WILL REMAIN STANDING IN THE USA!

GEORGIA GUIDESTONES

"1. Maintain Humanity Under 500 Million In Perpetual Balance With Nature"

*To achieve a population under 500 million that would mean more than **7 billion (90%)** of the world population would have to **die***

'Their' agenda is Worldwide CONTROL and DEPOPULATION!

'They' went so far as to even put it in stone as Number 1 on 'their' Guidestones in 1980

MATHEMATICAL PERFECTION INTO 2025

As illustrated on page 110, on April 8, 2024, a total eclipse crossed over North America. The eclipse has been called the "Jonah Sign" by many modern-day prophets, as compared to the period of darkness that Jesus spoke of when the Pharisees asked him for proof that he was the Messiah.

> *Then some of the Pharisees and teachers of the law said to him, "Teacher, we want to see a sign from you." He answered, "A wicked and adulterous generation asks for a sign! But none will be given it except the sign of the prophet Jonah."*
>
> Matthew 12:38-39 NIV

In 2020, a significant marker in time occurred when oil prices dropped to a -$38.00/barrel. That was 1260 days (Daniel timeline) since Trump went into office. The Lord told me to begin counting from this time point using the Noah cycle. And exactly 40 days later, on May 31, 2020, the second seal was opened when the George Floyd riots broke out and peace was taken from the earth. Would you like to guess the significant day that was celebrated on May 31, 2020? Pentecost!

My friends, God is going to show up again in His Glory and all calculations point to 2025. We are going to have the opening of the third seal, which will be the greatest financial event in human history. Mystery Babylon will begin to crumble with the opening of the third seal. June 9, 2025 is when the 50 year-cycle from the signing of the Petro-Dollar contract ends.

When a seal is opened, it opens a scroll. And the scroll contains many events to be fulfilled. According to mathematical calculations, the events beginning in 2025, and are expected to mirror those of 2020. But there will be one major difference: people referred to the events beginning in 2020 as a starting timepoint of great evil. The **good news** is that beginning in 2025 people will view it as "The Great Undoing of 2020." In other words: "The Great Redo." And it will usher in a time of great blessing for God's people.

AN ACT OF MAN OR OF GOD?

The Georgia Guidestones, as shown on the previous page, was a monument that stood for over forty years in Elbert County, Georgia. Made from six slabs of granite and weighing nearly 250,000 lbs., this structure was often referred to as the "American Stonehenge." On July 6, 2022, an "unknown individual" detonated an explosive device, causing significant damage to the Guidestones, which ultimately caused their removal.

Why is this significant? The monument has been controversial ever since its creation. Inscribed on the slabs were ten guidelines written in eight different languages, which addressed alarming New World Order themes, including population control, one world government, and uniting humanity with a living new language. The first line of the inscription read: "Maintain humanity under 500,000,000 in perpetual balance with nature." That is over a 90% reduction of the world's population!

Also, it was widely known that occult groups would occasionally visit the site, offering animal sacrifices, etc. The site gained the nickname "The Devil's Work," and workers regularly had the responsibility of erasing profane graffiti and Satanic phrases related to gods and goddesses. Politicians and clergy had demanded that the Guidestones be removed because they were of Satanic origin. Others have referred to the principles inscribed on the Guidestones as "the Ten Commandments of the Antichrist."

The **good news** is that the removal of the monument symbolizes the major move of God that is coming to the world. What happened to the Guidestones was likely an "act of God." He permitted them to be destroyed completely, and the same fate awaits Mystery Babylon, as everything they have built will be destroyed.

THE HEAVENS ARE TELLING

> *The heavens declare the glory of God; the skies proclaim the work of his hands. Day after day they pour forth speech; night after night they reveal knowledge.*
>
> Psalm 19:1-2 NIV

Psalms 19 speaks to the heavens, declaring the glory of God. Additionally, Luke 21:25 clearly teaches there will be signs in the sun, moon and stars. And 2024 had several rare and exceptional astronomical events, including four eclipses, naked-eye comets, and the Star of Jacob. The U.S. eclipse occured on Monday, April 8, 2024, with a total solar eclipse with a path of totality (where the moon literally covers the sun) crossed North America, passing over Mexico, the United States, and Canada.

This is the only eclipse of the century where the path crossed all three nations; it was also the longest total solar eclipse in the United States in this century, spanning from Texas to Maine and with a duration of almost 4 ½ minutes. During the totality, the corona (crown) was seen around the sun. This eclipse lasted twice the length of the 2017 Great American Eclipse and won't happen again until 2044 in the U.S.

When studying the trajectory of the 2024 eclipse, it literally crossed the path of the last eclipse in 2017, forming a salvation cross over America. It also crosses directly over seven U.S. cities named "Nineveh." This eclipse was a sign and a time point to start counting. Seven months later, Donald Trump won the presidency. Add 40 weeks and six days and Trump is inaugurated. Coming is the greatest revival in human history, as prophesied by Bob Jones in the 1980 Superbowl. Look to God for His glory beginning 2025.

B.R.A.V.O.

While on the stage of a ReAwaken America Tour with Clay Clark, I clearly heard God say "BRAVO." He was saying bravo to you who have hung in there patiently, waiting to see the hand of the Lord work in the midst of this evil Babylonian regime that is controlling with power. Particularly the last four years with our previous administration who negatively impacted the world!

B.R.A.V.O. is an acronym meaning: **B**lessings, **R**evival, **A**wakening, **V**indications, and **O**pen Heaven. An open heaven is a door that God opens, and that man cannot close. In the past, anytime truth flowed out of a break in a dam, evil put a finger in it or proverbially closed the door to prevent the truth from getting out.

But the *good news* is that when God says "bravo" he is going to break that dam and man won't be able to plug or prevent it. When you're struggling to contend with the discouragement, and it seems like the earth has tilted on its axis, it is difficult to speak words of faith.

When you can't do that, remember the friend of Elijah. He was a servant who was willing to keep looking. Six times he kept looking. Surround yourself with friends who will keep their eyes peeled on the horizon and keep watch for you.

Note that the word BRAVO has five letters. Five represents grace. Yet another confirmation that His grace arrives in 2025! BRAVO comes in 2025!

ANOTHER RED SEA MIRACLE

When Moses led the Israelites to the Red Sea, by faith, he knew that God would make a way for them to cross in safety. Six hundred chariots were making their way closer and closer. What must have been going through his mind as he tried to encourage God's people to stand and not fear?

The Bible recounts how the children of Israel called upon the Lord while the Egyptian army closed in. They thought Moses had led them into the wilderness to die. Yet Moses stood and said, "Fear not. Stand still. See the salvation of the Lord. (Exodus 14:13 paraphrased). He simply knew that God would take care of them.

This is a word we must heed today. As evil presses in, we cannot fear, but must stand and see what the Lord will do. The deep state, that seeks world control and domination, is about to experience God's vengeance. The angel of death is closing in and will destroy. But God's people will be spared, just as in the days of the Red Sea miracle.

2017 & 2024 NORTH AMERICAN ECLIPSES FORESHADOW THE COMING 2025 GREAT SHAKING TO WAKEUP THE CURCH!

- There shall be SIGNS in the sun, and in the moon ... lift up your heads, because redemption is drawing near - Luke 21:25-28

- Two Eclipses make a cross pattern 7-Days after Resurrection, 7-Years apart passing over 7-cities called Salem (Hebrew for peace), 7-cities called Nineveh (or Little Egypt) and exactly 7-Months before the US Presidential Election

- From *August 21, 2017*, add *6 years, 6 months, 6 weeks, 6 days* is *April 9, 2024*, if the *larger units* (months/years) are added before the smaller units (days). Alternative result is *April 8, 2024*, if the *smaller units* (days) are added first.

BLACK MONDAY of October 19, 1987, to the 2024 ECLIPSE is:
33 years, (3+3=6) 33 months, (3+3=6) 33 weeks, (3+3=6) 33 days apart (3+3=6)

2017 ECLIPSE to the 2024 ECLIPSE is
6-Years, 6-Months, 6-Weeks, 6-Days APART

MT. ST HELENS MT. RAINIER ERUPTIONS

Coming PORTLAND SALEM 2025

CALIFORNIA SHAKING

Coming CALIFORNIA 2025

7 x Salem

AUGUST 21 ECLIPSE

2017   2024   ECLIPSE 7 x Nineveh

7 x Salem

7 x Nineveh APRIL 8

6666

U.S.A. SALVATION CROSS
The Bald Knob Cross
THE CROSS OF PEACE
111 Feet Tall
Alto Pass, Illinois

Exactly 7-Months (7x30-days = 210-days) from the April 8, 2024 CROSS is November 5, 2024
TRUMP WINS ELECTION!

EXODUS 4:8 (April 8)
If they do not believe you or pay attention to the First Sign (Eclipse 2024), they may believe the Second (Star of Jacob 2024)

JONAH 3:4 (in 40-Days from the Second Sign...)
"Forty (40) more days and Nineveh (Mystery Babylon) will be overthrown."
Interesting: Forty (40) days from the Star of Jacob (9/272024), Trump Wins (11/6/2024)

THE GREAT EXODUS!

Worldwide!

"Watch the Middle East, water will become Blood Red, they will shout... 'How can this be possible?' The Great Exodus is here!" - Julie Green 2/22/22

A RED SEA MOMENT is coming to the Democratic party, members of the Republican party, the deep state, the evil one, his subservient elite and their family lineage are all about to experience GOD's vengeance for their rebellion; just as Pharaoh and his army were suddenly destroyed when GOD closed the sea, in the TIME of Moses.

Those that survive the angel of death in April will be stripped of their power and will flee underground to rebuild and regroup. The evil one and his remaining subservient elite will *reemerge* in the future under a DIFFERENT NAME, but with the SAME AGENDA... to eliminate GOD, the Constitution, hijack America, take not only Israel but also control the entire world!

Pharaoh tells Moses to get out of Egypt after Passover, (Exodus 12:31-36)

Israel departs Egypt and it takes 18-days to get to the Red Sea. Israel then camps at the Red Sea and crosses on the 8th day, the day God then closes the sea on Pharaoh and his army separating Israel from Egypt (Exodus 14:21-31).

A total of approximately 25-days from departure to sea closing.

Scan Me

RED SEA MIRACLE 2025

'Red Sea Miracle' TIME Calculation:

In 2025 Resurrection Sunday is April 20.

The calculation for the possible Great Worldwide Exodus, specifically the Red Sea Miracle, by adding 25-days from Passover/Resurrection, the closing of the Red Sea could/should occur on or about...

May 14, 2025 ?

May 14, 2025, is EXACTLY 7-years from when Trump opened the US Embassy in Jerusalem on May 14, 2018.

After the 'Red Sea Miracle', the puppet masters controlling Mystery Babylon become unimportant and/or insignificant as their worldwide control comes to a *sudden* end!

"Do not be afraid. Stand firm and you will see the deliverance the Lord will bring you today. The Egyptians you see today you will never see again. The Lord will fight for you; you need only to be still." - Exodus 14:13-14

Trump, the polished and sharpened arrow of God, protected all the while by the hand of God, carefully preserved for His day of use. In his second term as president, he will **re-build** <u>what God had brought down</u> and like kings Nebuchadnezzar, Darius, and Cyrus thousands of years before him, he too will decree... **"men are to tremble in fear before God, For He is the living God, He endures forever; His kingdom will never be destroyed, and His dominion will never end!"**

One who Sounds the Trumpet for the Return of the JESUS!

5.

TRUMP

"My Trump will rebuild My cities and set My exiles free, says the Lord Almighty."
- Cycle of Isaiah 45:13

God only needs 1-DAY!

God raises kings and can throw them down
- Daniel 2:21

CHAPTER 8
The Trump Factor

DONALD TRUMP WILL be the fifth leader of the story in replaying Daniel's timeline. In 2 Chronicles 36:23, King Cyrus declared that God had given him all the kingdoms of the earth and charged him (Cyrus) to build God a house in Jerusalem. That declaration was made seventy years after Jerusalem fell. And that timeline parallels today.

On May 14, 1948, Israel proclaimed the establishment of its independent statehood, which the United States officially recognized on that same day. Seventy years later, on May 14, 2018, our 45th President, Donald Trump, officially opened the U.S. Embassy in Jerusalem. Trump fulfilled part of the Cyrus prophecy, as explained in Isaiah 44.

Even more exciting, comes Isaiah 45, which is fitting as Trump was our 45th President:

> *"I will raise up Cyrus in my righteousness: I will make all his ways straight. He will rebuild my city and set my exiles free, but not for a price or reward," says the Lord Almighty.*
>
> Isaiah 45:13 NIV

So, let's use God's word concerning Cyrus as it parallels to Donald Trump. *I will raise up Trump in my righteousness. I will make all Trump's ways straight. Trump will rebuild my city and set my exiles free, but not for a price or reward . . ..*

I believe we will see Donald Trump turn to God as he is about to witness signs, miracles, and wonders that are unexplainable, except by the hand of God! The Lord has and will continue to make all His ways straight. So far, despite indictments, weaponizing voting ballots, two assassination attempts and an all-out offensive by the media and the political establishment, nothing will stick. God made it so that everything Trump touches has and will continue to turn to gold. His path will be straight and unimpeded—the purpose of which to fulfill all that God desires.

God desires to rebuild His cities after the chaos and destruction. He desires to set his exiles free. We are those exiles: God's children, His churches, His people. And we will be set free.

Cyrus did as God commanded, not for a price or a reward, and as we know, Trump has declined his presidential salary under both terms. He is not motivated politically for financial gain; he genuinely loves America.

In **one day**, we will see God's money, God's children and God's cities restored. It will be a truly historic overturning of power that manifests. And that is **good news** for those who have sown into God's kingdom because so shall we reap.

THE HAND OF GOD IN THE CALCULATIONS

When you analyze the presidency and life of Donald Trump, there are some divine "coincidences" that occurred through the hand of God. One has to ask, "What are the odds?"

- Donald Trump was born on June 14, 1946. On that day there was a blood moon over Israel.

- Trump's first day in office as President was on January 21, 2017. That was the 70 years, 7 months, and 7 days after he was born. The consistent presence of the number seven clearly illustrates how Trump's birth was written at the beginning of time.

- The election was held on November 8, 2016. Exactly 777 days later, the markets crashed into a turn on exactly December 24, 2018.

- Donald Trump opened the U.S. Embassy in Jerusalem on May 14, 2018. That was exactly 70 years and 70 days from the birth of Trump.

- The number 8 is also important as it signifies new beginnings, resurrection and spiritual renewal. Donald Trump's second term began eight years from his first time in office.

Review the images on the following pages for more interesting calculations regarding the presidency and life of Donald Trump.

> *"Seventy 'sevens' are decreed for your people and*
> *your holy city to finish transgression, to put an end to sin,*
> *to atone for wickedness, to bring in everlasting righteousness,*
> *to seal up vision and prophecy and to anoint*
> *the Most Holy Place."*
>
> Daniel 9:24 NIV

THE GREAT WEALTH TRANSFER

Expect the great wealth transfer to begin after January 21, 2025 with Donald Trump in office as President. Why? When did the Great Wealth Transfer occur for Israel in the days of Pharaoh? It happened *after* Passover when Israel plundered the Egyptians on Nisan 15 (April 13-20, 2025).

It is fascinating that during his inaugural speech he stated, "Welcome to the start of the Golden Age." The wealth transfer is a golden age of prosperity and freedom from bondage.

DIVINE TRUMP CALCULATIONS
TIMING by the Hand of God!

May 14th is ISRAEL'S INDEPENDENCE DAY, commemorates the establishment of the State of Israel in 1948, adding 77-years is 2025!

Trump, from the Bloodline of David, brings in the 'KINGDOM of DAVID' in 2025

Born on June 14th, 1946, Calculations from his Birthday:

700-Days (7) later Israel Proclaimed a 'State' on May 14, 1948

70-Year, 7-Months, 7-Days (777) later his First Day as President of the USA on January 21, 2017
70-Year, 7-Months, 7-Days (777) Robert F Kennedy's birth on January 17, 1954, to endorsing Donald Trump on August 23, 2024

700-Days, 70-Years (77) later opens U.S. Embassy in Jerusalem on MAY 14, 2018

77-years, 7-Months (777) later Trump is anointed for a 3rd Term on January 14, 2024 (Gregorian)

77-Years, 7-Months, 7-Days (7777) later is the exact LAST DAY of the 50-Year cycle since Roe v Wade became law in USA and Florida Governor Ron DeSantis drops out, endorses Trump on January 21, 2024 (Gregorian)

77-Years, 7-Months, 77-Days (77-7-77) later is RESURRECTION Sunday 2024 on March 31, 2024 (Gregorian)

77-Years, 7-Months, 7-Weeks, 77-Days (777-777) later is PENTECOST 2024 on May 18-19, 2024 (Gregorian)

70-Year, 8-Years, 7-Months, 7-Days (777+ 8) later his First Day, of Second Term, as President of the USA on January 21, 2025

Biblical Meaning of Number 8:
New Beginnings, Resurrection, and Spiritual Renewal

BIRTH OF <u>TRUMP</u> JUNE 14, 1946 <u>PLUS</u> 700-DAYS & 70-YEARS = May 14, 2018

TRUMP OPENS U.S. EMBASSY IN JERUSALEM MAY 14, 2018, + 7-YEARS = MAY 14, 2025

TRUMP born June 14th, 1946, add **700-DAYS** is exactly May 14, 1948, and Israel was proclaimed a STATE as prophesied by **Ezekiel** 2500 years ago; by adding **70-YEARS** is exactly May 14, 2018, US Embassy Opens.

- The Ezekiel prophecy in chapter 37 is called, *"The Valley of Dry Bones"*, this prophecy was fulfilled <u>between</u> 70 AD and 1948, as the *"Dry Bones"* are now coming back to life!
- Ezekiel's War: The *'last prophecy'* of Ezekiel in chapters 38/39 references a worldwide war that kills 1/3 of the world's population (Revelation 9:13-21); however, before the war, billions of saints are Raptured. Those "left" behind and not martyred will later be 'caught up' to meet CHRIST in the clouds when HE returns for His bride and to judge the wicked.

TRUMP - The 45ᵗʰ PRESIDENT/KING
Whose Presidency marks the STARTS of the End of Days

TRUMP is God's TRUMPET
He is sounding the Trumpet for the RETURN of Christ!

1ˢᵗ Term: Presidency 2016 - 2020
Using divine KEY DATES of Daniel's 7-Year Timeline

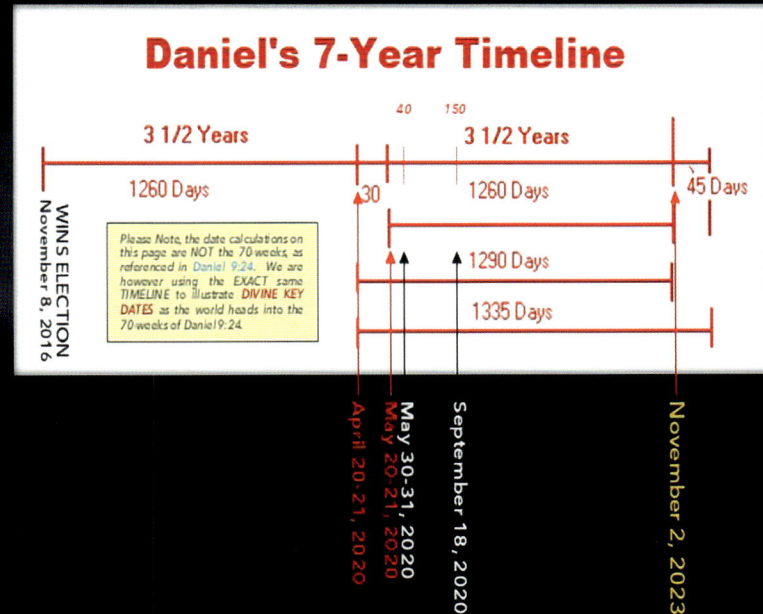

Daniel's 7-Year Timeline

40   150

3 1/2 Years   3 1/2 Years

1260 Days   30   1260 Days   45 Days

1290 Days

1335 Days

Please Note, the date calculations on this page are NOT the 70 weeks, as referenced in Daniel 9:24. We are however using the EXACT same TIMELINE to illustrate DIVINE KEY DATES as the world heads into the 70 weeks of Daniel 9:24

WINS ELECTION
November 8, 2016

April 20-21, 2020

May 30-31, 2020
May 20-21, 2020

September 18, 2020

November 2, 2023

KEY DATES FOR TRUMP AND AMERICA

✓ **April 20-21, 2020** - November 8, 2016, Election + 1260 Days ends, and **OIL** goes to **ZERO** *(-$38 actual)*

✓ **May 20-21, 2020** - April 21 + **30 Cycle** ends and in **EDEN**ville, Michigan, Township **HOPE** a dam breaks, foreshadowing of the **water breaking** before Birth of the **latter temple***

  ➢ **May 31, 2020 / Pentecost** - Noah's **40-day** cycle & Daniel's Cycle April 21 + **40 Cycle** ends with George Floyd RIOTS and "Peace is taken from the Earth", **2ⁿᵈ Seal** opens.

  ➢ **September 18, 2020** - Noah's **150-day** cycle (Genesis 7:24) ends with the death of **Ruth Bader Ginsburg**, foreshadowing the future overturning of Roe v Wade

✓ **November 2, 2023** - May 21, 2020, + 1260 Cycle ends… *US Dollar drops sharply and begins its CRASH cycle!*

TRUMP - The 47th PRESIDENT/KING
Whose Presidency marks the STARTS of the End of Days

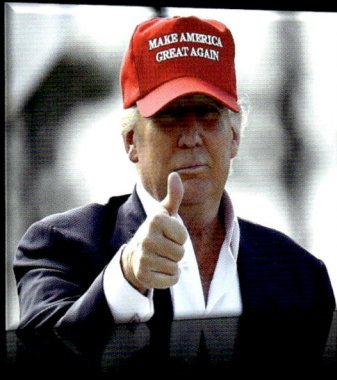

TRUMP is God's TRUMPET
He is sounding the Trumpet for the RETURN of Christ!

2nd Term: Presidency 2024 – 2028
Using divine KEY DATES of Daniel's 7-Year Timeline

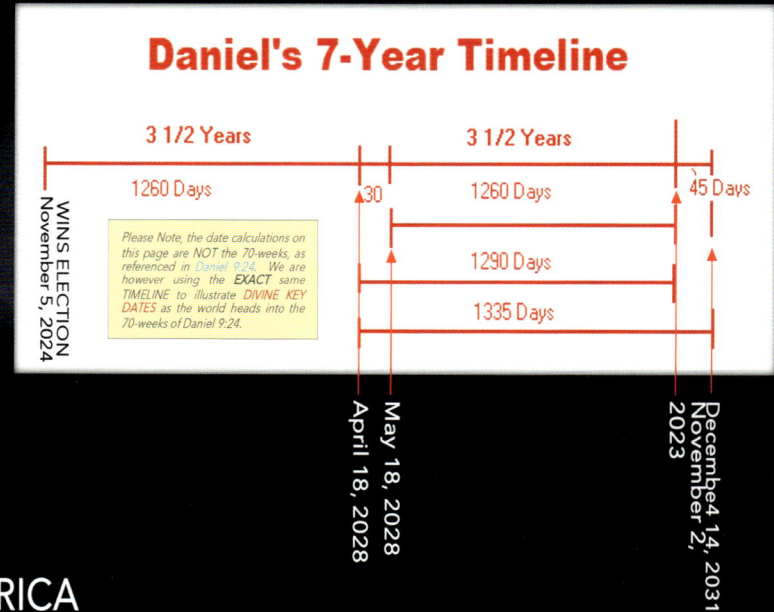

Daniel's 7-Year Timeline

3 1/2 Years   3 1/2 Years

1260 Days   30   1260 Days   45 Days

1290 Days

1335 Days

WINS ELECTION
November 5, 2024

April 18, 2028

May 18, 2028

December 14, 2031
November 2, 2023

Please Note, the date calculations on this page are NOT the 70-weeks, as referenced in Daniel 9:24. We are however using the EXACT same TIMELINE to illustrate DIVINE KEY DATES as the world heads into the 70-weeks of Daniel 9:24.

KEY FUTURE DATES FOR TRUMP AND AMERICA

- ❑ **April 18, 2028:** 1260 Days, event ?...
- ❑ **May 18, 2028:** 1290 Days, event ?...
- ❑ **October 30 – 31, 2031:** 2550 Days, event ?...
- ❑ **December 14, 2031:** 2595 Days, event ?...

EAGLE MOLTING

When eagles become old, their feathers, beak, and claws start withering. They need to transform themselves so that they can live longer. Therefore, they undergo **MOLTING**, and to be safe from predators, they choose a secure valley (Mar-a-Lago) to start this process. As eagles cannot hunt during this time, they are dependent on their brothers and sisters, for food (the WORD!). Eagles that survive this gruesome transformation, emerge stronger, fitter, and sharper than before.

Election Fraud of 2020 will it be overturned in 2025
'Fraud vitiates everything it touches!'

UNITED STATES v. THROCKMORTON, Supreme Court

GREAT

Fall 2024 WIN & Inauguration 2025

RETURN!

Worldwide Celebrations Coming in 2025!!

"TRUMP is SET - ASIDE and then In the FALL (2024) you will know who my David is" - Kim Clement 2014

"The Eagle has Landed!"

- Julie Green

Are you familiar with the saying, *"Fraud vitiates everything?"* This is a doctrine upheld by the Supreme Court after a case tried in 1878 titled Throckmorton vs. the United States. Fraud is a wrongful or criminal deception intended to result in financial or personal gain. As it pertains to law, fraud is an intentional act used to secure unlawful gain.

Some believe that the 2020 election involved fraudulent ballots. If that is the case and is overturned in a court of law, then it vitiates (or renders invalid) Joe Biden's presidency over the previous four years including everything that Biden signed and including all of Biden's presidential pardons. Any law, executive order or judgment rendered by the Biden administration throughout his presidency would also be void.

JUDGMENT DAY

Yom Kippur (the day of Judgment) is the holiest day on the Jewish calendar. It occurs annually in late September to early October and is primarily centered around atonement (*kippurim*) and repentance.

Nine days prior to Yom Kippur is Rosh Hashanah. According to Jewish tradition, Rosh Hashanah is the time when God inscribes each person's fate into the Book of Life for the coming year. The verdict is sealed on Yom Kippur.

Yom Kippur is also a time of unique closeness to God. When the Israelites sinned by worshipping the golden calf, Moses broke the tablets of stone that contained the ten commandments. Later, God agreed to forgive their sins and called Moses back up to Mount Sinai where he was given a second set of tablets. The date which Moses descended with this new set of tablets was established as Yom Kippur and is now a permanent date of forgiveness.

In 2023 Yom Kippur was observed on Monday, September 25th. On that same day, while on the campaign trail in South Carolina, Donald Trump (45) was photographed holding a Glock 45 with his image on the gun's grip. This was a foreshadowing of what is soon coming to the global elite—a day of judgment. Yom Kippur is observed on October 2, 2025.

DID YOU KNOW? When an eagle needs to rejuvenate and transform themselves, they undergo a "molting." To be safe from their predators, they choose a secure valley to begin the process. They also feast on the food from their brothers and sisters since they can't hunt during this time.

Donald Trump molted from 2021 to 2024 in preparation to return in 2025, stronger, fitter, sharper and more rejuvenated than ever!

THE PURIM AND GOD'S HAND

As illustrated on page 125, January 30, 2033 marks the 100th anniversary of when Hitler came into power. On March 22, 1932, one year before Hitler came about, the Jewish holiday, Purim, occurred on the day of an eclipse. Purim commemorates the saving of the Jewish people from the hands of an official named Haman.

The next year, after Hitler was in power, on March 12, 1933, there was another lunar eclipse on the same day as Purim occurred. Two eclipses on Purim marked the birth of the evil system of Hitler.

Interestingly, on April 20, 2023, there was an eclipse on Hitler's 134th birthday. There are no coincidences in the Bible.

Also, the first concentration camp (Dachau) opened on March 22, 1933. March being the 3rd month and on the 22nd day gives us 322. The Skull and Bones society is also known as "the Order of 322." It was formed in 1932, with the second "2" confirming that it is the 2nd chapter of the secret society (with the Bavarian Illuminati in Germany being the first). Organizations of the global elite and certain Masonic orders pledge allegiance to the skull and crossbones whose number is 322.

➤ **DID YOU KNOW?** The movie *Olympus Has Fallen*, which was a political action thriller about the fall of the United States, was released on March 22, 2013 (3/22).

THE HAMAN EFFECT

Haman built ten gallows because he hated the Jews and wanted to kill them. One of them was Mordecai, who had adopted his orphaned cousin, Esther. Esther became the King's wife, but she kept her Jewish heritage a secret.

Upon discovering Haman's plot to exterminate the Jews, Esther realized she must approach the King. But that could mean her own life. So she fasted for three days, then went to visit the King and that's when God intervened.

The ten gallows that were built for the Jews ended up being used for Haman and his sons. And Esther is now long remembered for her role in delivering Israel.

In World War I, eleven men worked for Hitler. Ten individuals were executed by hanging on the gallows (one ended their own life with cyanide). In Revelation, the ten kings of the earth give their power to the antichrist. Do you see history repeating here? The Haman effect is when God uses an Esther to turn the tables on evil.

THEIR END BEGINS

Beginning in April 2025, God's glory, with signs, miracles and wonders, will begin to manifest during the Passover feast and will continue in the year of Jubilee, followed by an additional three and a half years, until the end of 2029. These next four and a half years will be the time of Harvest.

What's remarkable is that three consecutive eclipses will occur on Purim, from 2024 to 2026! We can expect the Haman effect by 2026. Many like Haman will "hang" as it biblically plays out.

What Haman planned for the church is coming to the Hamans of this world. People will collapse and fall, fall and collapse. There will be literal destruction of what they have built as described in Jeremiah 30:16. I believe the first domino will be the collapse of the dollar with the help of the BRICS nations, triggering the collapse of Babylon.

The story of Purim focuses on hope. In 2024, Purim was celebrated on March 23rd. This is exactly, to the day, 7000 days from the wedding of Donald and Melania Trump (January 22, 2005). Many believe that God is raising another Queen Esther to soften the king's heart and to help deliver his people. To the Hamans of the world, *their end* begins in Purim, March 2025!

NINETEEN EIGHTY-FOUR (1984)

Who of us wasn't required to read George Orwell's dystopian thriller, *1984*, while in school? Published in 1949, his book served as a warning on totalitarianism. And some of the outlandish concepts mentioned in the book, like Big Brother and governmental control, are threats in today's world. The book is a sobering account of the evil that comes about when a government isn't held accountable.

In December 1984, a movie based on the book was released, depicting a closely-monitored government ruling a futuristic society. Expect to see the rise of a Hitler-like antichrist in 2034 (fifty years from the release of the movie 1984) who assumes the throne of Satan. We must continue to pray, fast and seek God's wisdom. Later in the book, we will discuss the 248-year cycle. Note that exactly eight cycles of 248 years is 1984. As illustrated on the following page 124, the number 1984 can be used to count backward to creation 4008 B.C.

Before God flips the tables on evil, first He brings in an Esther, to help deliver of the people and softens the king's heart!

The Esthers!

PURIM

"they hung Haman on the gallows that he had prepared for Mordecai." - Esther 7:10

50 Golden Jubilee

'THEIR' END BEGINS 2025!

JAN 6th TUCKER INVESTIGATES

OUR REPORTING IS ACCURATE. THE TAPES CONFIRM IT. - TUCKER CARLSON

AIRED MARCH 6-7, 2023

March 6-7, 2023: Tucker Airs J6 Video

January 22, 2005

March 23, 2024: 7000-Days from Wedding
Wedding calculation foreshadows Melania will be Esther to America

March 2025: Babylon gets a 'MORTAL WOUND'

3-PURIMS *God's Vengeance* 2025 - 2026

Beginning March 23-25, 2024

90-YEAR HITLER ANNIVERSARY JANUARY 30, 2023
Hitler / Esther / Haman Connection

- On January 30, 1933, President Paul von Hindenburg names Adolf Hitler, leader or führer of the National Socialist German Workers Party (or Nazi Party), as chancellor of Germany.

- Prior to becoming chancellor, a Lunar Eclipse occurred on PURIM March 22, 1932, then immediately after he became chancellor another Lunar Eclipse occurred again on PURIM March 12, 1933. Two consecutive Eclipses landing exactly on PURIM with Hitler rising to power in-between the two.

- In 2023, the April Eclipse lands on Hitlers Birthday and then beginning in 2024 and continuing for the next 3-years consecutive, 2024, 2025 and 2026, PURIM lands on exactly the next 3-consecutive Eclipses, see image below.

HITLER RISES TO POWER
JANUARY 30, 1933

THRONE OF PERGAMON BERLIN

Eclipse 4/20/23 Solar | PURIM 3/25/24 Lunar | PURIM 3/14/25 Lunar | PURIM 3/3/26 Lunar

ESTHER/HAMAN EFFECT
Revelation "ON HOLD"
& God's Vengeance for 3.5-Years

2026...
Military Tribunals!
HAMAN EFFECT 2023 - 2026

90 YEARS January 30, 1933, to **January 30, 2023**

Esther / Haman Effect: Esther prayed and fasted, then God turned the tables on Haman causing him to hang from the gallows he built for Mordechai.

"Go, gather all the Jews who are in Susa, and fast for me. Do not eat or drink for three days, night or day. I and my attendants will fast as you do. When this is done, I will go to the king, even though it is against the law. And if I perish, I perish."- Esther 4:16

"So, they impaled Haman on the pole he had set up for Mordecai. Then the king's fury subsided." - Esther 7:10

GOD's GLORY *Begins...* March 2026

Beginning March 6-7, 2023, the Haman Effect began with Tucker airing the 'J6' footage! The Haman Effect continues for the next 3.5 years into the end of 2026 as GOD brings vengeance on those who mocked him in 2025. Fall 2025 starts the GREAT HARVEST SEASONS and those who planted evil seeds will reap what they have sewn, as they HANG, like Haman!

2027 - A NEW BEGINNING... or a Kim Clement prophesied... "Beyond the veil of Limitations!"

"Be not deceived; God is not mocked: for whatsoever a man soweth, that shall he also reap." - Galatians 6:7

1000 Year = 1 Day

But, beloved, be not ignorant of this one thing, that <u>one day</u> is with the Lord as <u>a thousand years</u> and a <u>thousand years</u> as <u>one day</u> - 2 Peter 3:8

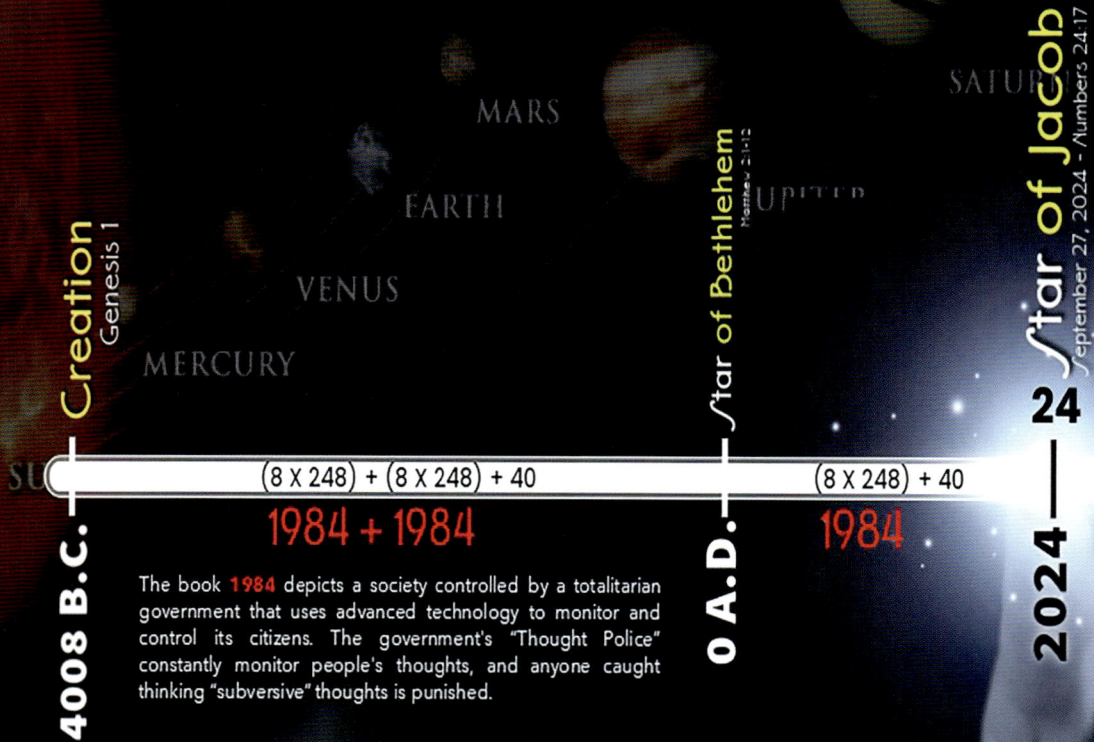

DWARF PLANETS

NEPTUNE

URANUS

SATURN

MARS

EARTH

JUPITER

VENUS

MERCURY

SUN

Creation Genesis 1

Star of Bethlehem Matthew 2:1-12

Star of Jacob September 27, 2024 - Numbers 24:17

8 X 248 = 1984

1984

BIG BROTHER IS WATCHING YOU

GEORGE ORWELL

(8 X 248) + (8 X 248) + 40

1984 + 1984

(8 X 248) + 40

1984

4008 B.C.

0 A.D.

2024

24

The book **1984** depicts a society controlled by a totalitarian government that uses advanced technology to monitor and control its citizens. The government's "Thought Police" constantly monitor people's thoughts, and anyone caught thinking "subversive" thoughts is punished.

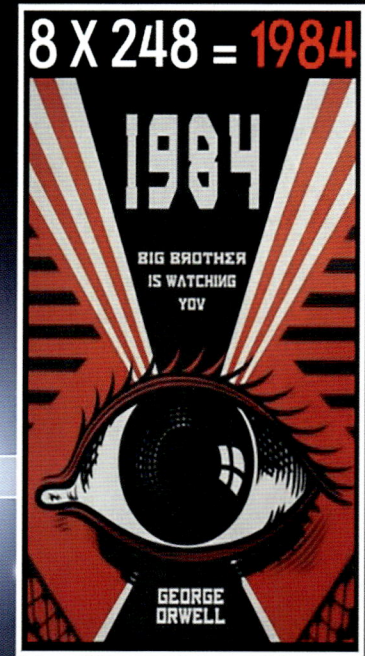

Commit thy works, unto the LORD, and thy thoughts shall be established. - Proverbs: 16:3

SKULL & BONES 3:22

PURIM
March 22, 1932
March 12, 1933
ECLIPSES
322

George Orwell's Movie 1984 about a dystopian society in totalitarianism

50
GEORGE ORWELL
1984

Released December 1984
50-Years later is December 2034

THE FALLEN

GREAT EGYPTIAN
August 2, 2027
March 20, 2034
ECLIPSES

Rise of AntiChrist 2033

100 YEARS Hitler Rises To Power January 30, 1933
100-Years later is January 30, 2033

Satan's Throne - Revelation 2:12-17

April 20
BIRTHDAY

April 20, 2023
ECLIPSE

Prior to Hitler becoming chancellor on January 30, 1933, a Lunar Eclipse occurred on **PURIM** March 22, 1932, then immediately *after* he became chancellor another Lunar Eclipse occurred the year following again on **PURIM** March 12, 1933. Two consecutive Eclipses landing exactly on **PURIM** with Hitler rising to power in-between. One hundred years from Hitler becoming chancellor is January 30, 2033, Antichrist REVEALS HIMSELF with a Peace Treaty in 2033.

On December 14, 1984, George Orwell's movie 1984 was released, a movie about a dystopian society in totalitarianism that has rewritten history where everyone is closely monitored and there is no escape from Big Brother. **Fifty (50) years** from the movies release is December 14, 2034. Expect "Another Beast" to rise in 2034 (Rev. 13:11) and Babylon's **Mortal Wound** (Rev. 13:12) to heal in 2035.

THRONE OF PERGAMON BERLIN

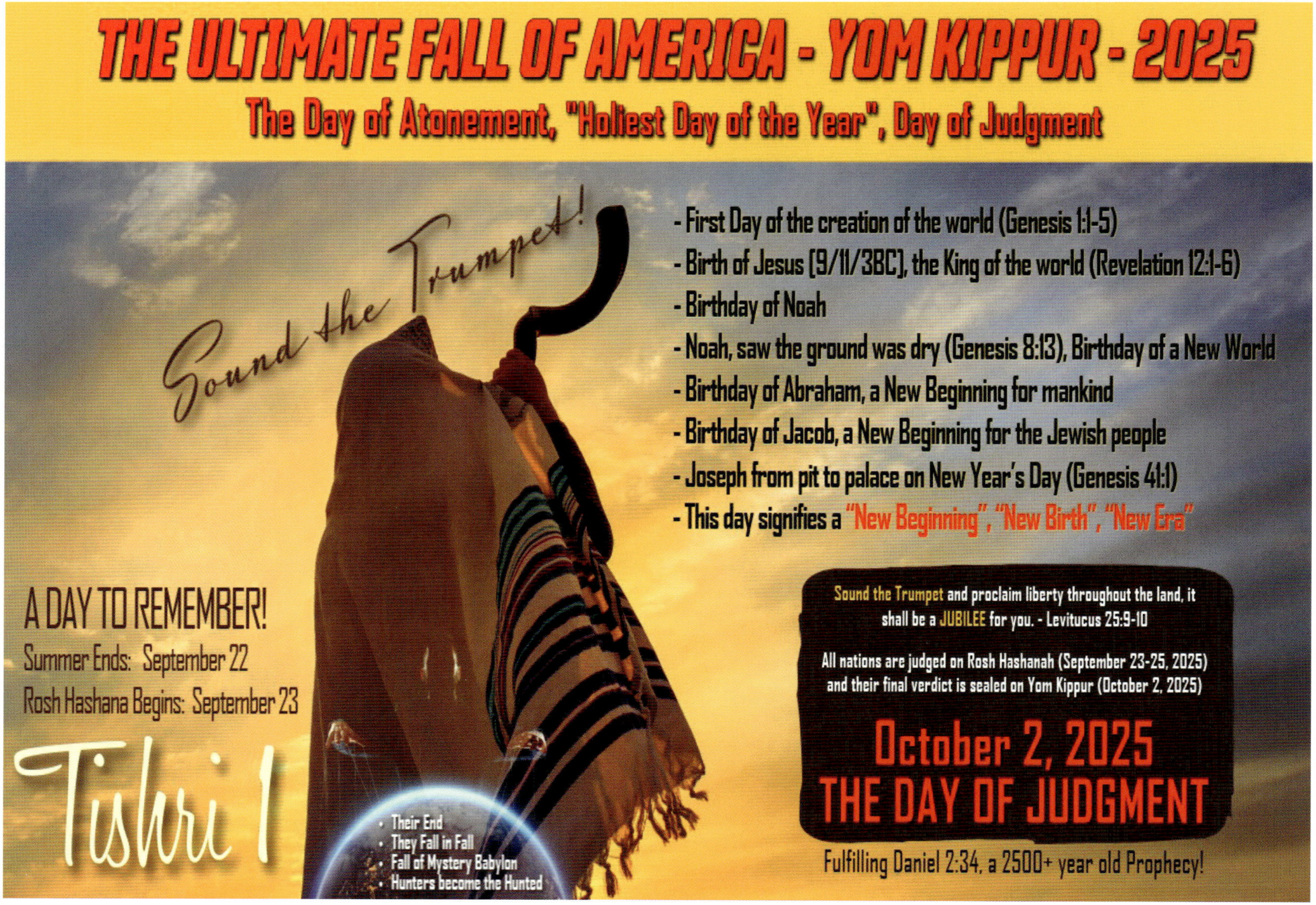
THE ULTIMATE FALL OF AMERICA - YOM KIPPUR - 2025
The Day of Atonement, "Holiest Day of the Year", Day of Judgment
Sound the Trumpet!
- First Day of the creation of the world (Genesis 1:1-5)
- Birth of Jesus (9/11/3BC), the King of the world (Revelation 12:1-6)
- Birthday of Noah
- Noah, saw the ground was dry (Genesis 8:13), Birthday of a New World
- Birthday of Abraham, a New Beginning for mankind
- Birthday of Jacob, a New Beginning for the Jewish people
- Joseph from pit to palace on New Year's Day (Genesis 41:1)
- This day signifies a "New Beginning", "New Birth", "New Era"
A DAY TO REMEMBER!
Summer Ends: September 22
Rosh Hashana Begins: September 23
Tishri 1
Sound the Trumpet and proclaim liberty throughout the land, it shall be a JUBILEE for you. - Levitucus 25:9-10
All nations are judged on Rosh Hashanah (September 23-25, 2025) and their final verdict is sealed on Yom Kippur (October 2, 2025)
October 2, 2025
THE DAY OF JUDGMENT
Their End
They Fall in Fall
Fall of Mystery Babylon
Hunters become the Hunted
Fulfilling Daniel 2:34, a 2500+ year old Prophecy!

There will be signs in the sun, moon, and stars. On the earth, nations will be in anguish and perplexity at the roaring and tossing of the sea . . . when these things begin to take place, stand up and lift up your heads, because your redemption is drawing near.

Luke 21:25, 28 NIV

THE YEAR OF RELEASE...
Begin in 2025!

- *Land Is Returned*
- *All Debts Cancelled*

"Then shall you cause the trumpet to sound on the tenth day of the seventh month, on Yom Kippur (October 2, 2025) shall you sound the trumpet throughout all your land. And you shall Consecrate the (50th) fiftieth year and proclaim liberty throughout the land to all its inhabitants. It shall be a Jubilee for you." - Leviticus 25:9-10

Understanding the timing written in Leviticus 25, '50-YEAR JUBILEE', and how critical events of 1971 and 1975 relate to 2021 and end with 2025.

50
Golden Jubilee

Leviticus 25... In Year 2025:

- *A Sabbath Year of rest to the Land, of the people of the Land and the LORD GOD.*

- *A holy year*

- *Each shall return to his property and clan (families reunite)*

- *You will dwell in the land securely and the land will yield its fruit (a return to the Constitution and law and order)*

- *I will command my blessing on you... sufficient for three years*

- *A right of redemption, means (finances) shall be released to recover property*

- *I am the LORD your God, who brought you out of the land of Egypt (a release from bondage, the fiat debt based monetary system)*

- *All the land's yields shall be for food, not for gather or storage*

- *You shall not wrong one another, if a family member is poor, you shall support them, not make them a slave, take no interest or profit, but fear your God*

CHAPTER 9
A New Era

THE BIBLICAL JUBILEE

THE 25ᵀᴴ CHAPTER of Leviticus describes a time known as the **Sabbath year**, where certain things were *to be done* or *not to be done* during that time. The Sabbath year came in the seventh year, following six years of activity.

> *For six years you may plant your fields and prune your vineyards and harvest your crops, but during the seventh year the land must have a Sabbath year of complete rest. It is the Lord's Sabbath. Do not plant your fields or prune your vineyards during that year. And don't store away the crops that grow on their own or gather the grapes from your unpruned vines. The land must have a year of complete rest. . ..*
>
> Leviticus 25: 3-5 NLT

Did you catch it? The 25th chapter is in fact directly pointing us to the 25th year: 2025. It is the Year of Rest that is expected to begin on July 4, 2025 and Leviticus 25:9 points to Yom Kippur, which is October 2, 2025. Leviticus 25 is referencing the year 2025.

As described in the previous scripture passage, during the six years prior, the Israelites stored up or prepared extra blessings coming from God to cover the needs in the seventh year. Deuteronomy 15 also mentions the Sabbath year's debt cancellation and release from captivity.

> *The LORD your God will bless you as he has promised. You will lend money to many nations but will never need to borrow. You will rule many nations, but they will not rule over you.*
>
> Deuteronomy 15:6 NLT

Those who faithfully observed the Sabbath year were always blessed abundantly because of their faith in God's provision.

Leviticus goes into more depth about the **Jubilee year**, a unique event taking place every fifty years, and which brings plentiful blessings to Israel's land, food sources, and assets. In the 50-Year Jubilee, debts are forgiven, land is returned to original owners, bonded laborers are freed, and there is an abundant harvest. The year is also set aside for rest.

Why does a Jubilee happen every fifty years? Because in the Bible, there is a particular emphasis placed on the number "7." Similar to how a week consists of six workdays and one day of rest, after seven Sabbath years (7 x 7 = 49 years), the fiftieth year is designated as a year of rest and Jubilee.

What is interesting is the 50-year Jubilee has not been observed in 2000 years. That said, when we finally have one, it will be by the hand of God. And there will be biblical magnitudes of change.

> "Count off seven sabbath years—seven times seven years—so that the seven sabbath years amount to a period of forty-nine years. ... Consecrate the fiftieth year and proclaim liberty throughout the land to all its inhabitants. It shall be a jubilee for you; each of you is to return to your family property and to your clan. . .."
>
> Leviticus 25:8, 10 NIV

A NEW ERA

The end of Mystery Babylon will come with a crash of biblical proportions. While everyone thinks all is well, an event is coming that will cause the ground to shake, volcanoes to erupt and the markets to collapse. As the evil ones, the global elite, have refused to repent and turn from their wicked way, the Lord God will now bring His Vengeance upon them in 2025 and Mystery Babylon will begin to crumble.

> ...to proclaim the year of the LORD's favor and the day of vengeance of our God . . .
>
> Isaiah 61:2 NIV

The world as we know it is about to come to an end, and a **new era** is about to be birthed. The birth will cause the rug to be pulled out from underneath everything the elite have built. And they will fall. Their time is up, and their perversions are about to be revealed.

People have fear because of what we have just come through. But just as in childbirth, there are labor pains, so are the wars and rumors of war the beginning of birth pains for this new season. It isn't the end, but a new season as we prepare for the ultimate coming of Christ.

> You will hear of wars and rumors of wars, but see to it that you are not alarmed. Such things must happen, but the end is still to come. . . . All these are the beginning of birth pains.
>
> Matthew 24: 6, 8 NIV

At the Trump Inauguration, the Golden Age began. But it is not until the 4th of July when America is expected to be reborn. April 20, 2025 (Resurrection) is expected to be a critical biblical time point. July 4, 2025 begins a year of rest (Jubilee), that is then followed by seven years as the glory of God manifests on the earth. Unbelievable and remarkable events, along with miracles, will occur in a global move of God.

July 11, 2025 is Brit Milah which is a symbol of the covenant between God and His people. It is considered a fulfillment of a divine command. America will once again be blessed by God.

As Kim Clement prophesied, we will be the generation that will defy death (the generation he spoke of began in 1967). He spoke of "...The Glory of God that shall cover the earth with knowledge and manifestation, as the waters cover the sea. It is yet to come before I return, you are the generation that shall defy death!" Scan the code on the image on the next page to hear the prophecy.

Blessings that were stolen from us in the Garden of Eden will be restored. Land will be returned. Biblical Covenants will be restored. God will not forsake His saints.

What a time of **good news** for God's people! During this time of favor all the foolishness going on will cease and a window of divine favor will open. This will be an opportunity to prepare, a time to move to the mountains, to build safe havens and prepare before all hell breaks loose on the earth as the Tribulation begins.

The images on the following pages illustrate the completion of two 1260-day Daniel Cycles and all of the evil events that happened throughout a 2595-day time cycle (i.e., 7 years, 7 months, 7 days). 2025 begins a "New Era" of light and a time of glory. This will be the starting timepoint for HIS glory to begin to manifest.

This month shall be unto you the beginning of months; it shall be the first month of the year to you.

Exodus 12:2 KJV

March 30th is the start of God's New Year according to the Hebrew calendar. As Kim Clement foretold, there will be miracles like you've never seen. It will be both the *best* of times and the *worst* of times. It will be the "worst" if you are of this world. But have confidence if you are only "in the world and not of it" because you will be prepared and faithful, knowing that God is in control.

For the evildoers shall be cut off, but those who wait for the Lord shall inherit the land.

Psalm 37:9 ESV

For those blessed by the Lord shall inherit the land, but those cursed by him shall be cut off.

Psalm 37:22 ESV

Wait for the Lord and keep his way, and he will exalt you to inherit the land.

Psalm 37:34a ESV

FULFILLMENT OF THE 1776 COVENANT

- The wolf will live with the lamb, the leopard will lie down with the goat, the calf and the lion and the yearling together; and a little child will lead them.

- The cow will feed with the bear, their young will lie down together, and the lion will eat straw like the ox.

- The infant will play near the cobra's den, and the young child will put its hand into the viper's nest.

- They will neither hurt nor destroy on all my holy mountain, for the earth will be filled with the GLORY of the LORD as the waters cover the sea.

- Isaiah 11:6-9

Kim Clement 2013: *"The Glory of God that shall cover the earth with knowledge and manifestation, as the waters cover the sea. It is yet to come before I return, you are the generation that shall defy death!"*

Scan Me

JULY 11, 2025
8TH DAY CIRCUMCISION
(BRIT MILAH, JULY 3, 2025 + 8 DAYS)

NEW ERA

ONE NATION UNDER GOD!

THE BRIT MILAH IS A SYMBOL OF THE COVENANT BETWEEN GOD AND HIS PEOPLE, AND IS CONSIDERED A FULFILLMENT OF A DIVINE COMMAND.

UNDERSTANDING GOD'S TIMING

DANIEL'S 7-YEAR TIMELINE

" **It will be** for a time (360), times (360 x2) and half a time (180)." Daniel 12:7

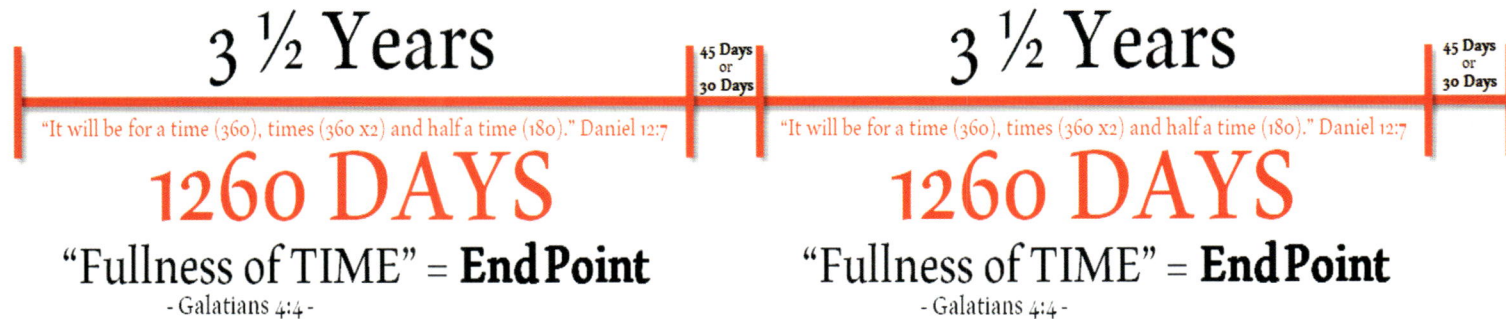

3 ½ Years

45 Days
or
30 Days

"It will be for a time (360), times (360 x2) and half a time (180)." Daniel 12:7

1260 DAYS

"Fullness of TIME" = **End Point**
- Galatians 4:4 -

3 ½ Years

45 Days
or
30 Days

"It will be for a time (360), times (360 x2) and half a time (180)." Daniel 12:7

1260 DAYS

"Fullness of TIME" = **End Point**
- Galatians 4:4 -

Their End!

BIRTH of the GOLDEN AGE

- June 30, 2016: Obama allowed Transgenders into the U.S. military and Last Hands, Mary Lynn Ritzenthaler, Chief of Conservation to Touch the Declaration of Independence, Retired
- December 12, 2019: A cluster of patients in Wuhan begin to experience Covid symptoms
- December 27, 2019: Sample taken, 3-days later first diagnosed lab sample contained SARS coronavirus on last day of Hanukkah December 30, 2019, 1st SEAL opened
- January 12, 2020: First confirmed case of Covid outside of China [Pandemic Begins]
- June 21 - 25, 2023: Summer Solstice / Biden LINKED to son Hunter's Business dealings via text, marking the start of evil's downfall
- August 8, 2023: Maui Fires and the song Rich Men North of Richmond debuted at number 1 on Billboard Hot 100, the artist to debut atop the chart without prior chart history
- March 14, 2024: New Years Day 2024, March the 1st month of the New Year (Julian Calendar)
- April 8, 2024: The Great USA Eclipse, 8-months from the Maui Fires. New Years Day April 9, 2024 (Hebrew Calendar - Exodus 12:2)
- January 20, 2025: Trump Inaugurated President and the GOLDEN AGE begins!
- July 4, 2025 - July 11, 2025: America Re-Born One Nation under God and a New Covenant expect July 11, 2025

January 20, 2025 - GOLDEN AGE

July 4 - 11, 2025 - America Re-Born

8-Months | **BIRTH FULL-TERM**

7-Months, 7-Days | **40-Weeks/6-Days**

2025 Jubilee then NEXT 7-YEARS

1260-Days (3.5-Years) | **30-Days** | **1260-Days (3.5-Years)** | **45-Days**

"FULLNESS OF TIME"

June 30, 2016

December 12, 2019

January 12, 2020

June 21-24, 2023

August 8, 2023

March 14, 2024 / April 8 ECLIPSE

TRUMP Inauguration

With Transgender Military Ban Lifted, Obama Cements Historic LGBT Rights Legacy

TORAH CODE calls this the "TIME of Troubles"

The Time of Darkness...

DANIEL'S 7-YEAR TIMELINE

EVIL	GLORY
3 ½ Years	3 ½ Years
1260 DAYS	1260 DAYS
"Fullness of TIME" = End Point	"Fullness of TIME" = End Point

2595 DAYS

HAWAII WILDFIRE MAUI DEVASTATED Aug 8, 2023

2595 DAYS ENDS

"This month is to be for you the **first month**, the first month of your year." Exodus 12:2

USA

2026-2033 RE-BORN,

BLESSED UNDER GOD 'NEW ERA' OF LIGHT

GOLDEN AGE TIME OF GLORY

Birth 2025!

NEW ERA

Birth of the Bride, the Latter House

"The glory of this **Latter House** shall be greater than of the former, saith the LORD of hosts: and in this place will I give peace, saith the LORD of hosts."
- Haggai 2:9

The Latter House prepares the way for the Lord.
"A voice of one [John the Baptist] calling: In the wilderness **prepare the way for the LORD...**"
- Isaiah 40:3

"You will hear of wars and rumors of wars, but see to it that you are **not alarmed.** Such things must happen, **but the end is still to come.** Nation will rise against nation, and kingdom against kingdom. There will be **famines** and **earthquakes** in various places. All these are the **beginning of BIRTH PAINS."** - Matthew 24:6-8

BIRTH PAINS
Jacob's Trouble

- "CRY of PANIC, of TERROR" - Jeremiah 30:5
- "That 'DAY' is SO GREAT there is none like it; it is a time of **"DISTRESS FOR JACOB"**; yet **HE SHALL BE SAVED OUT OF IT**" - Jeremiah 30:7

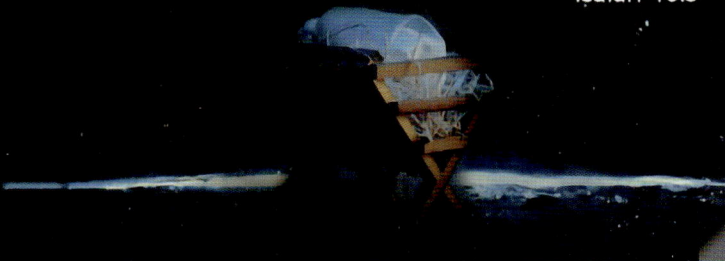

717
EVIL   GOOD
717
2017 - 2024   2026 - 2033
"TIME OF DARKNESS"   "TIME OF PLENTY"

FINAL HARVEST
Begins!

The BEST of TIMES, In the WORST of TIMES

2025 - 2028 BLESSING For The Latter House/Bride

"Bring the full tithe into the storehouse, that there may be food in my house. I will ... pour down for you a BLESSING until there is no more need... your vine in the field shall not fail to bear... all nations will call you blessed." - Malachi 3:10-12

Worldwide
REAPING SEASON
NOVEMBER 2025

Sun	Mon	Tue	Wed	Thu	Fri	Sat
						01
02	03	04	05	06	07	08
09	10	11	12	13	14	15
16	17	18	19	20	21	22
23	24	25	26	27	28	29
30						

July 3, 2025, ends the 248th year from the 1776 Declaration of Independence and STARTING the JUBILEE YEAR and FINAL HARVEST!

For some Great, others *Hell!*

Be not deceived; God is not mocked: for whatsoever a man soweth, that shall he also REAP - Galatians 6:7

DID YOU KNOW? There is a point of interest in the picture above, as it pertains to the Sabbath year and the Jubilee. This photo shows the Hebrew characters for the name Yahweh, the LORD as was discussed in Chapter 6. But those same characters are also the numbers "7" and "1" in Hebrew. And so even the name Yahweh follows the "7-1-7" pattern paralleling God's plan for Seven Sabbath years, one year rest in between (a Jubilee), then another seven Sabbath years.

THE SHEMITAH AND SUPER SHEMITAH

The year of rest following each six-year period described previously is called the Shemitah. And every seventh Shemitah (or 49 years) brings what is followed by a "Super Shemitah" or Jubilee. The Super Shemitah, in the 50th year, is the year of restoration, rest, and the return to lost land and repossession of freedom for those who are enslaved.

As described in the books of Exodus and Leviticus, those who observe the Shemitah, a year of rest following six years of work, will have bountiful harvests.

> *Plant and harvest your crops for six years, but let the land be renewed and lie uncultivated during the seventh year.*
>
> Exodus 23:10-11a NLT

So what do the Shemitah and Super Shemitah have to do with end-time events, specifically the year 2025? It will be a time of glory where God's people bring in the harvest so that they may rest in the seventh year. Recall in Chapter 7, several key events in the early 1970s were a time when evil was allowed into the United States. And we as a nation, founded under God, then turned away from God.

But as we've discussed previously, 50 years from the last key event (the signing of the Petro-Dollar contract, was on June 9, 2024. That was the beginning of the 50th year, which does not end until June 8, 2025. One month later, July 4, 2025, will begin the Super Shemitah.

Calculations indicate that the year of rest should have begun on June 2024 and carried to June 2025. However, the present day pharoahs—those controlling the world—refused to follow God's commandment to work and to rest. Thus we are going to witness the hand of God come down upon the world with His vengeance.

FINAL 3 SEASONS

2025 - REST, JUBILEE

717

7 EVIL

717 GOOD

7 EVIL

2017 - 2024
"TIME OF DARKNESS"

2026 - 2033
"TIME OF PLENTY"

2033 - 2040
"TIME OF TRIBULATION"

GOD'S COMMANDMENT TO WORK & REST

Six DAYS you shall do work," he commands, "and on the seventh DAY you shall have a Shabbat of complete rest - Exodus 35:2

For six YEARS you are to sow your fields and harvest the crops, but during the seventh YEAR let the land lie unplowed and unused - Exodus 23:10-11

The Year of Jubilee 'Count off seven sabbath years—seven times seven years—so that the seven sabbath years amount to a period of forty-nine years. Then have the trumpet sounded everywhere on the tenth day of the seventh month; on the Day of Atonement sound the trumpet throughout your land. Consecrate the fiftieth year and proclaim liberty throughout the land to all its inhabitants. It shall be a jubilee for you - Leviticus 25:8-10

> The 6th DAY/YEAR is when work is COMPLETED
> The 7th DAY/YEAR is a TIME OF REST / SHEMITAH
> The 50 YEAR is a "SUPER SHEMITAH" JUBILEE

The earth is the Lord's, and everything in it... and the one who has clean hands and a pure heart, who does not trust in idols or swear by a false god ... will receive **blessings** and **vindication** from God their Savior... The Lord Almighty — The 'King of Glory'! - PSALM 24

- *Super Shemitah*
- *Year of Rest*
- *By the Hand of God*

2025

BLESSINGS & VINDICATION!

MOSAIC of the MONTHS
- ROMAN EMPIRE -

MARCH *the First Month of the year.*

SEPTEMBER *the 7th month of the year.*
OCTOBER *the 8th month of the year.*
DECEMBER *the 10th month of the year.*

FEBRUARY *the 12th, last month of the year.*

First Month!

1. MARCH — MARTIUS
2. APRIL — APERICE
3. MAY — MAIUS
4. JUNE — JUNO/LUNO
5. JULY — QUINTILIS
6. AUGUST — AUGUSTUS
7. SEPTEMBER — SEPTEMBER
8. OCTOBER — OCTOBRES
9. NOVEMBER — NOVEMBER
10. DECEMBER — DECEMBER
11. JANUARY — JANUS
12. FEBRUARY — FEBRUUM

Last Month!

CHAPTER 10
Two Clocks and Two Calendars

TO FULLY UNDERSTAND the times and dates that point to events unfolding in the end times, we must understand our calendar system. Currently, the world operates under the Gregorian (or Roman) calendar. This calendar considers January 1 as the first day of the year. It was developed by the same people who crucified Christ.

This calendar has two months, Janus and Februum that were not a part of the Jewish calendar. Janus was a mythological god (essentially a fallen angel) who was known as the god of transition. In Latin, the word Janus means "a doorway" and is illustrated on page 147 by a two-headed figure. To the Jews, January was viewed as the transition from one year into the next but the days in this month were not part of the new year.

Februum in Latin means "purification" or "purging" and was considered a time after the transition from one year when people prepared themselves for the coming year. The Roman calendar often designated February 15th as a purification festival. And

again, the days in February were not part of the Jewish calendar which began in March.

Originally, the Roman calendar had only ten months, starting in March and ending in December. Remember, Dec is Latin for "ten." Both January and February were the last two months added to the Roman calendar because initially the Romans originally considered winter a "month-less" period. The Roman calendar was primarily a lunar calendar.

In 45 BC, Julius Caesar introduced a new calendar system called the Julian calendar, a solar calendar based on the rotation of the sun with 365 days in every year, with an additional leap day every fourth year. Caesar's calendar was the predominant calendar for the entire Roman empire and most of the western world for over 1500 years. Following that is when Pope Gregory developed a revised calendar.

As Christians, we do not follow astrology, but rather astronomy. However, because we live under the Roman calendar, and this calendar uses astrology, it is good to analyze where we are in our world. We have been living in what Babylon considers the "Age of Aquarius." The planet, Pluto, has a solar orbit of 248 years. God is the creator of all things, including the planets and their orbits around the sun.

Pluto is the farthest planet from the sun and its solar orbit is fascinating. Particularly since the 248-year timing directly ties in with understanding divine timelines, going all the way to creation and to the time of the Declaration of Independence. Pluto is also called "the giver of wealth."

The reason for the name "Age of Aquarius" is the entry of Pluto into Aquarius. In 2024, that happened on 11/19/24.

New age people are thinking 2025 is going to be a great year, a new dawning—the age of Aquarius. But God has other plans. And it will be horrific for them.

God is speaking through the scripture and through His prophets (both Biblical times and modern-day). He wants to explain that we are at a time of transition. And to see the manifestation of what we've been waiting for—the flipping of the financial scales and the destruction of Babylon.

God is not beginning a "new age." He is starting a "New Era" with the fall of Babylon. Satan offers counters to the real deal. He's the master of deception and does anything to move your focus off of God. New age is the great falling away.

ASTRONOMY

- The Study of Planets
- **There <u>will be</u> Signs in the Sun, Moon and Stars** - *Luke 21:25-28*
- For Signs, and for Seasons, and for Days, and Years - *Genesis 1:14*
- Star of Bethlehem
- Eclipses
- Wisemen of Babylon
- Wisemen (Magi) of Heron

ASTROLOGY

- Zodiac, Horoscopes, Star Signs
- **Divination** to Predict the Future
- Forbidden in the Bible, Let no one be found among you who ... practices **Divination** or who is a Medium or Spiritist or who Consults the Dead. - *Deuteronomy 18:10-14*
- **Doorway for Demons**

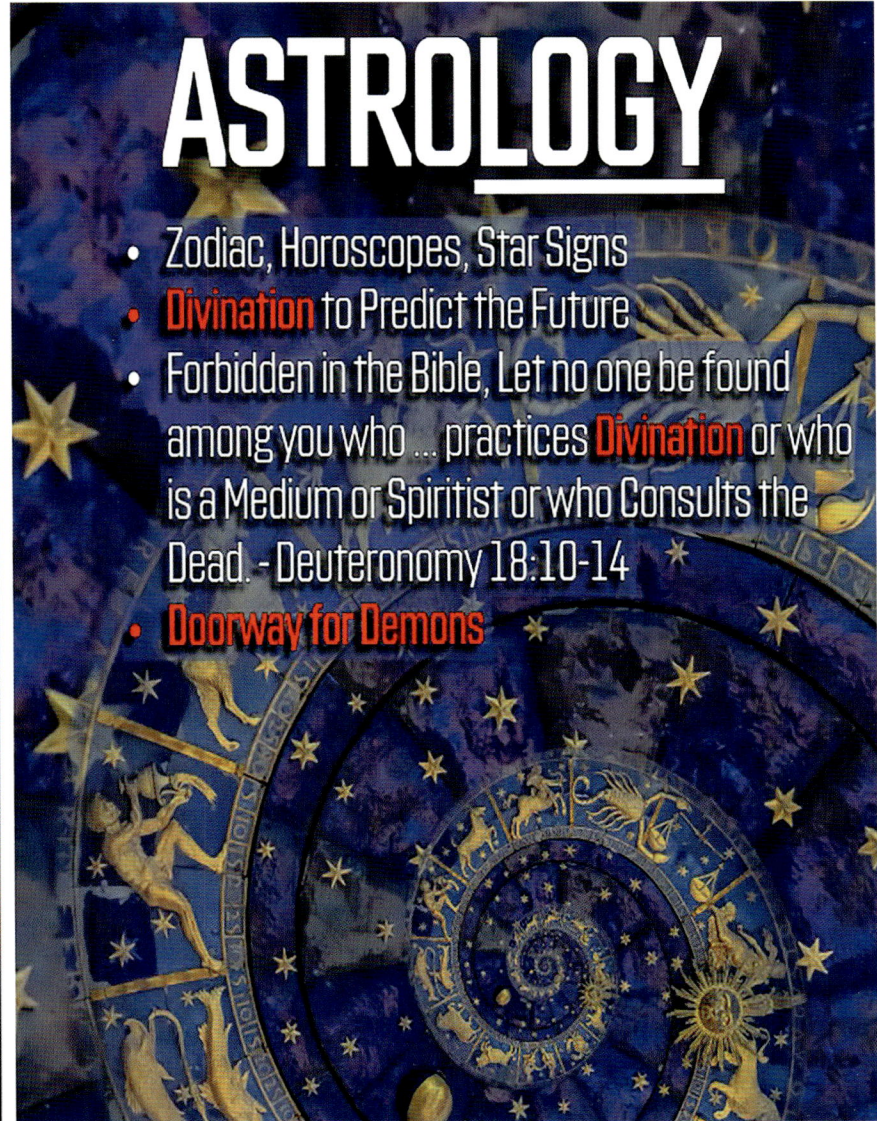

AGE OF AQUARIUS

Pluto entered Aquarius on November 19, 2024

PLUTO
Solar Orbital Period
248 YEARS
The Giver of Wealth
Entered Aquarius
November 19, 2024

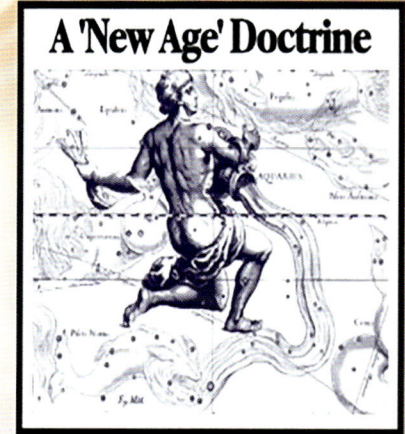

A 'New Age' Doctrine

TRANSITION

Evil's Plan!

2024 | 2025

New Age, The Age of Aquarius
THE GREAT REST

JANUS

God of Transition - In latin... A Doorway, An Entrance, 2-Heads facing opposite direction, one looking back, other looking forward into a NEW BEGINNING!

ROMAN CALENDAR

First Month!

MARTIUS   APERICE   MAIUS

JUNO/LUNO   QUINTILIS   AUGUSTUS

EPTEMBER   OCTOBRES   NOVEMBER

Last Month!

DECEMBER   JANUS   FEBRUUM

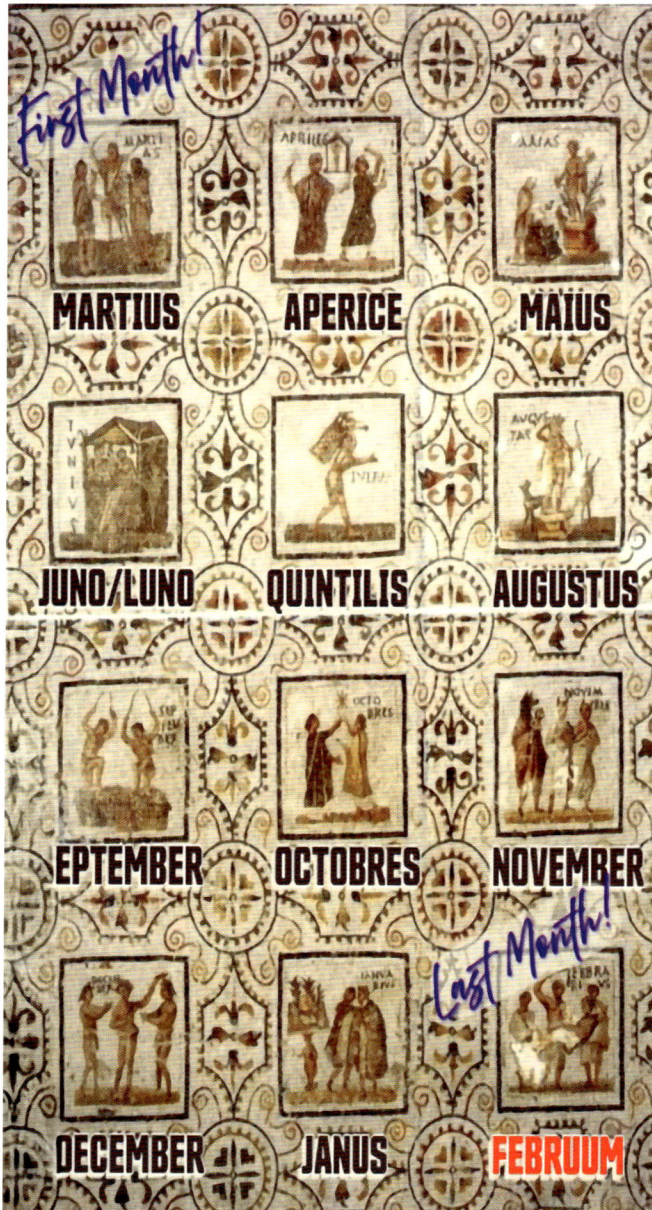

MOSAIC of the MONTHS
- ROMAN EMPIRE -

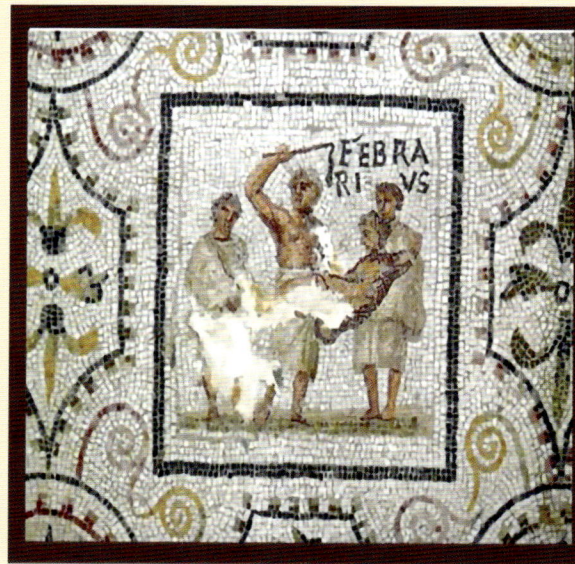

Februum *reflect the theme of "purification". The name of the month itself is derived from the Latin februarius which means "purification" or "purging" and was considered a time after the transition from one year when people prepared themselves for the coming year.*

On Febuary 27, 2025 Pam Bondi started the release of the **Epstein List**, *even though nothing truly damaging was released on this date the exposure, the "purging", of evil within the depths of America has started. Three days later Trump meets with Zelenski, as February ends, and Trump ends Ukraine's military aid.*

The Month of FEBRUUM 2025 is 'HYPAPANTY'

HYPAPANTY *is a Greek word that means "meeting" or "encounter" and commemorates:*
- *Mary and Joseph's presentation of Jesus in the temple for the customary rites of 'purification'*
- *Simeon and Anna meet and recognize Jesus as Messiah*
- *First time Messiah is in the Temple and presented to the people 40 days after his birth - Luke 2:22-38*
  - *40-days from the Trump Inauguration Janaury 20, 2025 is* **February 28 - March 1, 2025**. *Trump has a "meeting" with Zelenski at Whitehouse, Russia-Ukraine peace negotiations fail as Zelenski reveals he does not want peace with Russia, Trump asks him to leave and stops funding Ukraine's military aid.*

THE NEW VS. OLD CALENDAR SYSTEM

THE 1752 CALENDAR CHANGE

Today, Americans are used to a calendar with a "year" based on the earth's rotation around the sun, with "months" having no relationship to the cycles of the moon and New Years Day falling on January 1. However, that system was not adopted in England and its colonies until 1752. The changes implemented that year have created challenges for historians and genealogists working with early colonial records. Because it is sometimes hard to determine whether information was entered according to the then-current English calendar or the "New Style" calendar we use today.

Throughout history there have been numerous attempts to convey time in relation to the sun and moon. Even now the Chinese and Islamic calendars are based on the motion of the moon around the earth, rather than the motion of the earth in relation to the sun. And the Jewish calendar links years to the cycle of the sun and months to the cycle of the moon.

THE JULIAN CALENDAR

In 45 B.C., Julius Caesar ordered a calendar consisting of twelve months based on a solar year. This calendar employed a cycle of three years of 365 days, followed by a year of 366 days (leap year). When first implemented, the "Julian Calendar" also moved the beginning of the year from March 1 to January 1. However,

following the fall of the Roman Empire in the fifth century, the new year was gradually realigned to coincide with Christian festivals until by the seventh century, Christmas Day marked the beginning of the new year in many countries. By the ninth century, parts of southern Europe began observing the first day of the new year on March 25. This would coincide with Annunciation Day. This is the church holiday nine months prior to Christmas celebrating the Angel Gabriel's revelation to the Virgin Mary. He told her that she was to be the mother of the Messiah. The last day of the year was March 24.

However, England did not adopt this change in the beginning of the new year until late in the twelfth century. Because the year began in March, records referring to the "first month" pertain to March; to the second month pertain to April, etc., so that "the 19th of the 12th month" would be February 19.

In fact, in Latin, September means seventh month, October means eighth month, November means ninth month, and December means tenth month. Use of numbers, rather than names, of months was especially prevalent in Quaker records.

This same March 24-25 time point could be an important time point in 2025. Kent Christmas had a prophecy about a "mortal wound" to the enemies of God. The prophecy was given on March 19. In that prophecy, it was stated that things would happen "in the next seven days" (i.e., from March 19th). View the prophecy itself with the code on page 64.

THE GREGORIAN CALENDAR

During the Middle Ages, it began to become apparent that the Julian leap year formula had overcompensated for the actual length of a solar year, having added an extra day every 128 years. However, no adjustments were made to compensate. By 1582, seasonal equinoxes were falling 10 days "too early," and some church holidays, such as Easter, did not always fall in the proper seasons.

In that year, Pope Gregory XIII authorized that most Roman Catholic countries adopt the "Gregorian" or "New Style" Calendar." As part of the change, ten days were dropped from the month of October, and the formula for determining leap years was revised so that only years divisible by 400 (e.g., 1600, 2000) at the end of a century would be leap years. January 1 was established as the first day of the new year. Protestant countries, including England and its colonies, not recognizing the authority of the Pope, continued to use the Julian Calendar.

DOUBLE DATING

Between 1582 and 1752, not only were two calendars in use in Europe (and in European colonies), but two different starts of the year were in use in England. Although the "Legal" year began on March 25, the use of the Gregorian calendar by other European countries led to January 1 becoming commonly celebrated as "New Year's Day" and given as the first day of the year in almanacs.

To avoid misinterpretation, both the "Old Style" and "New Style" year was often used in English and colonial records for dates falling between the *new* New Year (January 1) and *old* New Year (March 25), a system known as "double dating." Such dates are usually identified by a slash mark [/] breaking the "Old Style" and "New Style" year, for example, March 19, 1631/2. Occasionally, writers would express the double date with a hyphen, for example, March 19, 1631-32. In general, double dating was more common in civil than church and ecclesiastical records.

➥ **DID YOU KNOW?** In genealogical records, people born between 01/01/1752 and 03/25/1752 had two dates for their birth. One date for their birthday, according to the Julian system, and one birthdate for when England adopted the Gregorian process. Death and marriage records were handled the same way (with two dates) during the 3-month transition from one calendar system to the next.

EXPECT GOD TO MOVE ON HIS CALENDAR IN 2025

The calendars on the next few pages overlay both the Julian and Gregorian calendars, including the dates for the Jewish feasts and festivals (Purim, Passover, Resurrection, Pentecost, etc.). You will notice the word "Nisan" on some of the dates.

WHAT IS NISAN?

Nisan is the first month of Spring on the Hebrew calendar and is considered the first month of the ecclesiastical year. 15 Nisan is the date when Passover must be scheduled per Leviticus 23.

> *These are the LORD's appointed festivals, the sacred assemblies you are to proclaim at their appointed times: The LORD's Passover begins at twilight on the fourteenth day of the first month. On the fifteenth day of that month, the LORD's Festival of Unleavened Bread begins;*
>
> Leviticus 23:4-6a NIV

Remember, Jewish days begin at nightfall. So when Leviticus says Passover begins at twilight on the 14th day of the first month, Passover begins on the night of the 14th and carries through the day of the 15th. Then on the evening of the 15th day, the second festival (the Feast of Unleavened Bread) begins.

In the Bible, Passover marked the time when the angel of death arrived at the end of the 15th day and killed Pharaoh's son (his most prized possession) and all the firstborn sons in Egypt. As mentioned in Chapter 3, numerous biblical events have occurred exactly on 15 Nisan, including the crucifixion of Jesus. As Passover 2025 is once again expected to mark one of the most important time points in history.

John 10:10 starts by saying that the enemy comes to "steal, kill and destroy." And that is what the world has been witnessing for centuries. But is was especially apparent, beginning in 2020 into 2024. The rest of John 10:10 states, "But I [Jesus] came to give you life more abundantly." The only way our world will see life more abundantly is through an act of God. Moving from steal, kill and destroy to abundance requires a divine intervention of God. Time calculations indicate Passover 2025 is expected to once again mark one of the most important time points in history.

Satan has and will continue to change time. If we had a divine appointment from God and Satan intervened and swapped the time, we would miss that appointment because of the time change. That is essentially what he has already done because, in 1752, the calendar changed.

England changed its calendar from the Julian to the Gregorian. This change made the first day and month of the year different from what it had been previously. The Julian calendar had previously used March 25th as the first day of the New Year. The change to the Gregorian calendar moved New Year's Day to January 1st.

When prophets speak of a blessed new year coming in 2025, the actual start of that year would be in March rather than in early January, according to the original Jewish calendar. And per the Roman calendar, March was named after Martius, who is the god of War. There is a high probability of war, or military conflict in March, after Purim (March 13-14, 2025).

New Advent Calendar

2024 JULIAN

2024 - 2025 'DOUBLE DATING'

FEBRUARY 2025 - GREGORIAN/ROMAN

Sun	Mon	Tue	Wed	Thu	Fri	Sat
2024 - Eleventh Month / January						1 *19*
2 *20*	3 *21*	4 *22*	5 *23*	6 *24*	7 *25*	8 *26*
9 *27*	10 *28*	11 *29*	12 *30*	13 *31*	14 *1* **2024 ADVENT BEGINS** *(Julian Calendar)*	15 *2* **Purification Festival** *(Ancient Roman Calendar)*
16 *3*	Washington's Birthday 17 *4*	18 *5*	19 *6*	20 *7*	21 *8*	22 *9*
23 *10*	24 *11*	25 *12*	26 *13*	27 *14*	28 *15*	March 1 **HYPAPANTE** *Jesus Presented in the temple for the customary rites of purification' *40-days from Trump Inauguration, he meets with Zelenski in Whitehouse and stops military aid to Ukraine.*

2024 - Twelfth Month / February - ADVENT

Commit thy works, unto the LORD, and thy thoughts shall be established. - Proverbs 16:3

2024 - 2025 'DOUBLE DATING'

MARCH 2025 - GREGORIAN/ROMAN

New Advent Calendar 2024-25 JULIAN

Sun	Mon	Tue	Wed	Thu	Fri	Sat
2024 - Twelfth Month / Febuary - ADVENT						NEW YEARS DAY **1** *(Roman Calendar)* 16
2 17	**3** 18	**4** 19	**5** 20	**6** 21	**7** 22	**8** 23
9 24 — 2024 ADVENT ENDS *(Julian Calendar)*	2024 ADVENT Christmas **10** 25	**11** 26	**12** 27 PURIM Sundown	**13** 28 PURIM	PURIM **14** 1 Sundown March 13 to Sundown March 14 Esther 9:22 - *'sorrow turned to joy'* — BLOOD MOON NEW YEARS DAY *(New Advent Calendar)*	**15** 2
16 3	**17** 4	**18** 5	**19** 6 MARCH "MORTAL WOUND" TO EVIL — "MORTAL WOUND" to the enemy within the next 7-days (March 19 - 26) - Kent Christmas	SPRING Starts Day 1 "Joy in Spring" **20** 7	**21** 8	**22** 9 322 Skull & Bones
23 10	**24** 11	**25** 12 Annunciation Day Angel Gabriel announced to Mary she would bear a son, Jesus. - Luke 1:26-38	**26** 13	**27** 14	**28** 15	**29** 16
NEW YEARS DAY NISAN 1 **30** 17 *"This month is to be for you the first month, the first month of your year."* - Exodus 12:2	**31** 18			**2025 - First Month / March**		

USA "Short-Lived" War/Conflict?

Commit thy works, unto the LORD, and thy thoughts shall be established. - Proverbs: 16:3

New Advent Calendar   JULY 2025

2025 'DOUBLE DATING'

APRIL 2025 - GREGORIAN/ROMAN

Sun	Mon	Tue	Wed	Thu	Fri	Sat
		Day 70 1 *19* *Death to Spirit of Pythos (bondage) between 70 and 100 Days begins!* *- Kim Clement Prophecy*	2 *20*	3 *21*	4 *22*	5 *23*
6 *24*	7 *25*	**NISAN 10** 8 *26* *Preparation Begins!* *Every man shall take a lamb* *- Exodus 12:3*	9 *27*	10 *28* **2025 First Month / March**	11 *29*	**NISAN 14** 12 *30* *Blood on doorposts* *- Exodus 12:13* *Last Supper,* *Jesus dies at 3PM* CHRIST OUR PASSOVER
NISAN 15 13 *31* *HEBREW PASSOVER* *One of the Most Important Days in Biblical History Death Angel* CHRIST OUR PASSOVER	14 *1* CHRIST OUR PASSOVER	**NISAN 17** 15 *2* *NEW BEGINNING* *Feast of First Fruits* *The 3rd Day - Resurrection Day on the Hebrew Calendar* CHRIST OUR PASSOVER	16 *3* CHRIST OUR PASSOVER	**DEATH** 17 *4* CHRIST OUR PASSOVER	18 *5* *Jesus Dead in the Tomb* *Roman Calendar* CHRIST OUR PASSOVER	19 *6* CHRIST OUR PASSOVER
PASSOVER ENDS - LIFE! 20 *7* **RESURRECTION** *Easter Sunday* *Exodus 12:18* RISEN **NISAN 21** *Key to Heaven's Treasure*	**4.21** 21 *8* *Death-To-Life!*	22 *9*	23 *10*	24 *11*	25 *12*	26 *13*
27 *14* *Roman and Hebrew Calendar Meet 2 Clocks become One!*	28 *15*	29 *16*	30 *17*			**2025 - Second Month / April**

Commit thy works, unto the LORD, and thy thoughts shall be established. - Proverbs: 16:3

2024/25

MAY 2025 - GREGORIAN/ROMAN

Sun	Mon	Tue	Wed	Thu	Fri	Sat

2025 - Second Month / April

Day 100 1 / 18 — *Death to Spirit of Pythos (bondage) between 70 and 100 Days begins!* - Kim Clement Prophecy — **MAYDAY MAYDAY MAYDAY**

2 / 19 — 3 / 20

4 / 21 — 5 / 22 — 6 / 25 **Rich Strike Wins (Strike it Rich)** 2022 KENTUCKY DERBY — 7 / 24 — 8 / 25 — 9 / 26 — 10 / 27

11 / 28 — 12 / 29 **2nd HEBREW PASSOVER** *Pesach Sheni, for those 'unclean' on the First Passover 30-days prior.* — 13 / 30 **Miracle at Fatima** *1917 plus 108 Years NEW BEGINNING* — 14 / 1 **RED SEA MIRACLE?** *Resurrection April 20 + 25-Days 7-Years ago, Embassy moved to JerUSAlem* **Trump 777** — 15 / 2 — 16 / 3 — 17 / 4

America is 'Delivered' because of Repentance and for overturning Roe v Wade, while the enemies of God face 'Judgement'.

18 / 5 — 19 / 6 — 20 / 7 — 21 / 8 — 22 / 9 — 23 / 10 — 24 / 11

25 / 12 — 26 / 13 — 27 / 14 — 28 / 15 — 29 / 16 *Day 40 from Resurrection (4/20) Jesus Ascends to Heaven* — 31 / 18 *1974 Yom Kippur War ENDED* **YOM KIPPUR WAR**

2025 - Third Month / May

Commit thy works, unto the LORD, and thy thoughts shall be established. - Proverbs: 16:3

New Advent Calendar · JUBILEE 2025

2025

JUNE 2025 - GREGORIAN/ROMAN

Sun	Mon	Tue	Wed	Thu	Fri	Sat
1 19	2 20	3 21	4 22	5 23	6 24	7 25

2025 - Third Month / May

Sun	Mon	Tue	Wed	Thu	Fri	Sat
• Tower of Babel Fell • Birth of the Law • Birth of the Spirit 8 26 **50-Days** *from Resurrection (4/20)* **PENTECOST**	*50-Years Ends* 9 27 *from Petro-Dollar Contract Signing* *Petro-Dollar June 8, 1974* *50 Year ENDS June 8, 2024*	10 28	11 29	12 30	13 31	**MAY ENDS** *(Julian Calendar)* **TRUMP's Birthday** 14 1 *Happy Birthday* **PRESIDENT TRUMP**
15 2	16 3	17 4	18 5	19 6 20	7 **SPRING Ends**	**SUMMER** 21 8 **Begins!** 2025
22 9	23 10	24 11	25 12	26 13	27 14	28 15
29 16	30 17					

2025 - Fourth Month / June

Commit thy works, unto the LORD, and thy thoughts shall be established. - Proverbs: 16:3

THE TWO CLOCKS PROPHECY

In 2010, Kim Clement gave a profound prophecy regarding two clocks. In the prophecy he told how one of the clocks was going to be annihilated because it kept the timing and agenda of men. The other clock had been ignored by the people of God because they see poverty and sickness around them. And things don't seem to be getting better.

The prophecy urged us that it is time to listen to the Lord. We've been looking at the wrong clock. We've been looking at the wrong timing.

We must look to the new clock and see something different in our hearts. God is going to do what HIS timing dictates. Now is God's time.

> *He shall speak pompous words against the Most High, shall persecute the saints of the Most High, and shall intend to change times and law.*
>
> Daniel 7:25a NKJV

Look at the month of April on the previous calendar marked "double dating." Notice that there is a very important date, and its timing brings together two different clocks. The date, April 20th or Resurrection Sunday, coincidentally lands on exactly the last day of Passover (also April 20th) or Nisan 21 as described in Exodus 12:18.

> *In the first month, on the fourteenth day of the month at evening, you shall eat unleavened bread, until the twenty-first day of the month at evening.*
>
> Exodus 12:18 NKJV

This date is believed to be the day that two clocks come together as one. And the key to the treasures of heaven, which have been locked away for thousands of years, is released. The following day, Monday, coincidentally just happens to be April 21st. 4.2.1. It is a death-to-life moment with death on Thursday, April 17th and Resurrection (life) on Sunday, April 20th, following the third night/day.

A PERIOD OF AMAZING GRACE

The Daniel calculation indicates the world will experience the great harvest (according to Haggai 2:9) for three and one-half years, plus a year of Jubilee, starting July 2025. July is half way through 2025. By adding January through June 2025 to the four and one-half years total, the Great Harvest will be five years in total or until the end of year 2029.

In addition to the Harvest, the world will enter a period of not just grace, but AMAZING grace. This will last for a total of five years as referenced in a Kim Clement prophecy. Five years ends in 2029, along with the end of the 2020 decade. Now that's **good news!**

100 + 8

May 13, 1917 plus 100-Year
2017

plus 8-Year
2025

Revelation 12 Sign
September 23, 2017

Virgo

Jupiter

Revelation 12:3 Calculation:
(7) seven heads
(10) ten horns
(7) seven crowns

Total 24... May 13, 2024
Year 2024 ends May 12, 2025

VIRGO MAY QUEEN
NEW BEGINNING!

Miracle at Fatima

On May 13, 1917 Mary, the Mother of JESUS, the 'MAY QUEEN', appeared to three young peasant children 6 times:

1. May 13, 2025 - New Era / Red Sea Miracle?
2. June 13
3. July 13
4. August 13
5. September 13
6. October 13

May 13, 1917 plus 100-Year 2017

- From May 13, 1917 to May 13, 2025 is 100 + 8-Years

Biblical Meaning of Number 8:
- New Beginning
- Resurrection
- Spiritual Renewal

A¹
M²
G¹ **R**² **A**³ **C**⁴ **E**⁵
A⁴
Z
I⁵
N⁶
G⁷

March 31, 2025 (Abib 1, Hebrew/God's Calendar) - This month shall be unto you the beginning of months: it shall be the **FIRST MONTH of the YEAR** to you. - Exodus 12:2

5 Years of Amazing Grace!

March 31 2025

5 = GRACE 2025
5 = GRACE 2026
5 = GRACE 2027
5 = GRACE 2028
5 = GRACE 2029

Joy in SPRING
March 20, 2025 - June 21, 2025
PASSOVER - April 13, 2025
RESURRECTION - April 20, 2025

"A thousand years in your sight are like a day that has just gone by, or like a watch in the night." - Psalm 90:3-4

4 + 2 + 1 = 7

GOD's TIMING, A 7000-Year Cycle
THE END, WRITTEN FROM THE BEGINNING
so that you may know that GOD is GOD, the creator of all things!

GOD'S *7000-Year Timeline, a Return to Eden, where It All Began!*

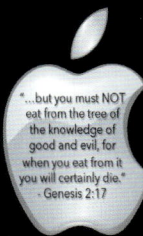

THE SIN
Earth was created specifically with man in mind, God wanted Relationship. Adam and Eve were given **Dominion** (authority/ownership) over all the creatures over the earth. Satan was a **usurper** (someone who takes a position of power) of Adam's dominion and is now referred to as **"the prince of the world."**

God/Jesus is in control of our lives, **but NOT the earth**, the world system. God does have the ability to destroy the earth, He did it in the Great Flood, but after the flood HE made a covenant with man that He would never flood the earth again; therefore, this time HE is going to destroy it with FIRE before the return of Jesus. Apostle Peter said He would destroy it with fire. - 2 Peter 3:10

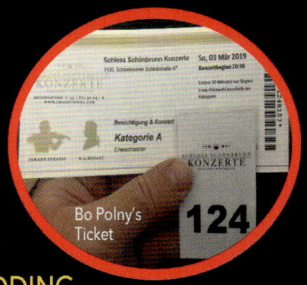

"...but you must NOT eat from the tree of the knowledge of good and evil, for when you eat from it you will certainly die." - Genesis 2:17

TIME OF WRITTING 2025

RESURRECTION to RETURN 2000 + 7 Years

33 A.D. Death @ 33-YOA & Resurrection

124 YEARS | JERUSALEM 1913
70 YEARS | 1967 ARAB-ISRAELI WAR SIX-DAY WAR

2040 A.D. Return of Christ

Bo Polny's Ticket | 124

➤ 'Caught Up'
➤ ROYAL WEDDING
➤ RETURN TO EDEN
• *JEWS & GENTILES become 1 with CHRIST*
• *Millennium Sabbath, 1000-YEARS of PEACE! - Revelation 20:1-4*

CREATION 4008 B.C. ROSH HASHANAH

4000 YEARS

STAR OF BETHLEHEM 9/11 3 B.C. ROSH HASHANAH

2000 YEARS

2000-YEARS from Birth 2033 A.D. GREAT TRIBULATION

1000 YEARS
Thousand years of REST - Hebrews 4:8

1000-YEARS from Return 3040 A.D.

7000 YEARS

TIME OF **JEWS**

TIME OF **GENTILES**

Commit thy works, unto the LORD, and thy thoughts shall be established. - Proverbs: 16:3

CHAPTER 11
God Speaks Through Numbers

WHERE WOULD WE be without mathematics? It provides order, logic, and sound reasoning for society. Before the beginning of the world, there was chaos and a state of nothingness—that is, until God spoke. And when He spoke, everything was spoken into existance, including His math.

All human traits and functions depend on math because we depend on God. Math is His gift to us, demonstrating accountability, multiplication, and blessing. Through mathematics and logic, we also understand God's infinite nature more clearly.

The Bible consistently references the core principles of arithmetic: addition, subtraction, multiplication, and division. Math is not the supreme truth but points us to the Truth.

Before delving into the examples of God's math in world events, let me explain the twisted version of math that does not apply within God's kingdom.

GOD'S MATH IS NOT PAGAN NUMEROLOGY

Throughout history, man has tried to suppress the truth of God by focusing on numbers rather than on God. For example, numerology is used in pagan religions, supposedly to infuse power and magic into their customs. They believe that they place a greater emphasis on particular numbers and connect them to gods and goddesses who will provide for their needs.

Make no mistake—God's math is not numerology! As the Creator of the universe, He uses math to help us understand and relate to His principles. Math is part of God's glory and shows His sovereign nature.

In every land, nation, and tribe, the answer for the equation one plus one always equals two. While we don't all share the same language, we are united through the common foundation of math.

THE END FROM THE BEGINNING

> *What has been will be again, what has been done will be done again; there is nothing new under the sun.*
>
> Ecclesiastes 1:9 NIV

While Christians reject the notion of magic or power connected to digits, certain numbers have appeared consistently in biblical history. The numbers 3 (Trinity), 5 (Grace), 7 (Seals), 8 (New Beginnings), 12 (Tribes and Disciples), 50 (Jubilee) all hold weight when calculating God's divine timeline.

The Bible says that which has been will be again. And that is certainly evident in the ties between worldwide events today and that of biblical times. In 2020, oil went to zero for the first time since trading began in 1983. This happened exactly three and one-half years from the 1st day that Donald Trump took office. Then exactly 150 days later, Supreme Court Justice Ruth Bader Ginsburg died. Interestingly, that is the exact same length of time that the waters kept rising following the forty days of rain during the Ark and the Great Flood.

The Israelites were in bondage to Pharaoh for 400 years. Eight cycles of 50 years is 400 years—a new beginning and Israel was freed. Four hundred years after the Pilgrims landed on the eastern shores of the United States in 1620, was 2020, the year Corona hit. And Donald Trump was removed from the White House for a season. God's season is four years. Four hundred years, plus one season is 2024 when Trump wins the election. Also, add five years (Grace) to the year 2020 takes us to 2025. That is the five-year beginning of God's amazing grace!

THE DANIEL TIMELINE

Seven is an important number, as used throughout the Bible, and particularly in the book of Daniel when calculating time points. In Daniel 9:24, we read, *"Seventy 'sevens' are decreed for your people and your holy city to finish transgression, to put an end to sin, to atone for wickedness, to bring in everlasting righteousness, to seal up vision and prophecy and to anoint the Most Holy Place."* This speaks to the period of Babylonian captivity as prophesied by Jeremiah.

Daniel had prayed for Israel, acknowledging the nation's sins, and asking God for mercy. In response to his prayer, Daniel received the seventy-sevens prophecy (which is a period of 490 years). Those verses provide a timeline, giving an idea of when the Messiah would come and some of the events that would accompany His appearance. Daniel's prophecy lays out an amazingly accurate timeline.

> *Know and understand this: From the time the word goes out to restore and rebuild Jerusalem until the Anointed One, the ruler, comes, there will be seven "sevens," and sixty-two "sevens."*
>
> Daniel 9:25a

The seven-year tribulation is a period of great trouble that occurs in the last week of Daniel's Prophecy of the 70 weeks. The tribulation is a time when Satan tries to take God's throne. It begins when the Antichrist makes a covenant and signs a peace

8 x 50 = 400

8 = 'New Beginning'!

November 1620 Mayflower Landed

Red Sea Moment Coming!
'New Beginning' by the Hand of God, NOT Trump

"And he said unto Abram, Know of a surety that thy seed shall be a stranger in a land that is not theirs, and shall serve them; and they shall afflict them 400-years." - Genesis 15:13

Israel served Pharaoh for 400-years, then Moses returned to Egypt after God spoke to him on Mt. Sinai. He warned Pharaoh and instructed him to let God's people go. - Exodus 4:22-23

Then say to Pharaoh, 'This is what the Lord says: Israel is my firstborn son, and I told you, "Let my son go, so he may worship me." But you refused to let him go; so, I will kill your firstborn son.'" - Exodus 4:22-23

1620 + 400 = November 2020, Stolen US Election

+ 4-Years (1-Season) = November 2024

NO MAN (TRUMP) will take GOD's GLORY!

TRUMP WINS US ELECTION 2024

★ TRUMP WINS ★

RED SEA MIRACLE May 2025?

BIBLICAL COVENANT RESTORED IN JULY 2025

A Covenant is a **PROMISE, a contract**. A Biblical Covenant, is an <u>unconditional</u> permanent PROMISE and the promising parties must keep their PROMISE *regardless* of the other party's breach of their PROMISE and is **enforceable by GOD!** The <u>1776</u> **Declaration of Independence** was a Biblical Covenant, a PROMISE, by the founding fathers to GOD that *"all men are created equal"* and in return, God's PROMISE was to BLESS the United States and was born the **Greatest Nation in the World!** The PROMISE was <u>binding</u>; however, in the early seventy's we turned away from God by allowing anti-Christian events, from the legalization of abortion via from Roe v Wade (the legal killing children) to removing Prayer from school and this began the downfall of America that culminated with Covid-19 being released and the 2020 election to the stolen 50-years later by a Godless communist foreign power. In 2020 God's BLESSING of protection was finally <u>removed</u>, for a SEASON, for breach of Covenant, contract, and all hell broke loose in America and the earth for <u>4-YEARS</u>!

BLESSED

UNBLESSED
Breach of Biblical Covenant

ONE SEASON

2021 JANUARY
Inauguration of Joe Biden

JULY 2025
Return of Trump / USA Reborn Under God

NEW ERA 2025
THE YEAR OF JUBILEE

ONE SEASON
To God 1-SEASON is 4-YEARS
to Man 4-SEASONS are 1-YEAR

A SEASON of DARKNESS
Began as Covid was unleashed!

After years of secret planning, those in power allowed the USA to be infiltrated by GODLESS *"all men are <u>NOT</u> created equal"* communist foreign power, China <u>the dragon</u>, with the aid of treasonous US operatives.

Election Fraud 2020
'Fraud vitiates everything it touches!'

<u>UNITED STATES v. THROCKMORTON, Supreme Court</u>

2025 YEAR OF JUBILEE
"Make America BLESSED Again!"

- Fraud revealed, TRUMP Returns*
- ***"All men are created equal"***
- Re-Do / Re-Start / Re-Build
- **Re-Born** to shine once again as a 'BEACON OF LIGHT' for all the World to see during end-times!
- God's Kingdom on earth is Born

treaty with Israel (and the world) for seven years. Midway through the seven years, the Antichrist breaks the treaty and sets up an abomination in the temple, as written in Daniel 9:27.

The seven-year tribulation period is divided into two periods of three and one-half years (2 x 1260 days). At the start of the final three-and-one-half-year period, the Antichrist claims to be God and demands worship. The Jews realize they built the temple for the Antichrist and consequently reject him, which begins his persecution of them.

Revelation 11:2 mentions 42 months. A biblical month is 30 days. So 42 months, comprising 30 days each is 1260 days or three and one-half years. Revelation 11:3 also mentions 1260 days, which corresponds to three and one-half years or exactly half of the tribulation period. No randomness appears in the "end of days" mathematical day counts. The end has already been written from the beginning of time, including the timing of events leading up to Christ's return.

A PATTERN TO FOLLOW

As an analyst of time, I have noticed a consistency in the use of the number pattern, 4 − 2 − 1 (or sometimes vice versa). The Jews had 4000 years, followed by 2000 years of the Gentiles, and now we are entering the final phase, the 1000 years of millennial reign. It doesn't mean that Christ is coming back exactly in 2030. But that decade, starting 2030 into 2039, is expected to be biblically critical.

The point is: There's not a lot of time left! The story is written; God wins! And before Christ shows up, just like Belshazzar witnessed, the handwriting is on the wall. Tekel is a 3rd Seal Revelation event that indicates the rebalancing of the financial system. The fuse is lit, and it ends in either glory or devastation, depending on what seeds you have sown.

DID YOU KNOW? In 2023, scientists updated the infamous Doomsday Clock on January 24th. In other words, on a date with a 1−2−4 pattern. I had previously stated that something was going to happen on that day and this rare occasion occurred.

The clock was updated to move forward by 90 seconds before midnight. The Doomsday Clock has been maintained since its origin in 1947; the original setting was at 7 minutes to midnight. However, the clock has been set forward 17 times and set backward eight times since then. Whenever they determine it's needed, the Science and Security Board members adjust the metaphorical Clock based on their assessment of global danger. To borrow their words, and pertaining to end times, "...*every second counts*."

The number pattern 1-2-4 can be used to count time, both forwards and backwards. Recall the discussion on the 1-2-4 number pattern? By adding 124 and 124, another secret math pattern of time is revealed, the number pattern 2-4-8, which pinpoints specific biblical moments. The Star of Bethlehem was a sign from God that Jesus was coming to earth. The Star appeared in 0 A.D. There are precisely seven 248-year periods from the Star of Bethlehem's appearance, leading up to the year 1736. When we add 40 years, which corresponds with the 40 years in the desert wilderness (Joshua 5:6), that brings us to 1776. And that is the exact year the Declaration of Independence was signed or the time America was born.

Fast forward another 248 years, from 1776 to 2024, and the Star of Jacob appears on September 27, 2024, completing the eighth 248-year cycle since the Star of Bethlehem. Recall the teaching of the Age of Aquarius in Chapter 10, where we discussed Pluto's 248-year solar orbit period. The latest Pluto orbit was completed on November 19, 2024.

In Luke 21:25, the Bible refers to signs appearing in the sun, moon, and stars, given by God in order to warn His Church. In fact, Luke says expressly, *"...there WILL BE signs in the sun, and in the moon, and in the stars."*

Throughout history, prophets have appeared to deliver God's Word before God acts. Those prophecies are followed by signs to confirm His Word. This is the beautiful way our Heavenly Father reveals Himself.

As you read in Numbers 24:17 below, a scepter will arise from Israel and crush the head of Moab's people. The Moabites were the descendants of Lot, who survived the destruction of Sodom and Gomorrah. They were a people who frequently conflicted with Israel and worshipped gods of war and human sacrifice.

> *I see Him, but not now;*
> *I behold Him, but not near;*
> *A Star shall come out of Jacob;*
> *A Scepter shall rise out of Israel,*
> *And batter the brow of Moab,*
> *And destroy all the sons of tumult.*
>
> Numbers 24:17 NKJV

We see this play out through the recent sign given by the Star of Jacob. The Star of Bethlehem was the sign for the coming birth of Christ, the King (the Head). The September 27, 2024, Star of Jacob is the sign for the coming birth of the Bride of Christ (the Body) at 40 weeks, full term, on the 4th of July 2025! The inauguration of Donald Trump foreshadows the coming of a new era in time, i.e., the Golden Age. Just as John the Baptist was born six months before Jesus to clear the way for the coming King, the inauguration of Donald Trump was six months before the 4th of July 2025. The Star of Jacob prepares the way for the official rebirth of America on July 4th, 2025, and the restoration of Israel. Per God's law, a male child is circumcised (Brit Milah) on day eight, with July 4 being day one and the eighth day being July 11. The Brit Milah is a symbol of the covenant between God and His people.

JACOB'S TROUBLE

A prophecy in Jeremiah, Chapter 30, describes a period of time known as "Jacob's trouble." This prophecy is 2500 years old. But we are seeing it play out today.

During this time, Jacob experiences many things. The Bible says that there are cries of panic, terror, and no peace. Verse 30:6 says, "Ask now, and see, can a man bear a child?" In Jacob's time of trouble, men try to bear children. While it may sound absurd, many online articles today discuss transgender men advocating for their reproductive rights.

> *Alas! For that day is great, so that none is like it: it is even the time of Jacob's trouble; but he shall be saved out of it.*
>
> Jeremiah 30:7 KJV

But the ***good news*** is that we shall be saved out of this (Jeremiah 30:7). God will not reveal the secrets of His timing until it is time! And my friends, it is time. Jeremiah 30:24 says, "In the latter days you will understand." Isn't it a coincidence that this is verse 24, corresponding to 2024, when the Lord revealed the understanding of this 2500-year-old prophecy?

God will bring destruction on all the nations, but not on you. He will discipline you justly. But you will not be destroyed. And all of your foes—every one of them—will go into captivity, and all who prey on you, God will make a prey. i.e., the hunters become the hunted.

THE POWER IN GOD'S NAME

The Bible uses many names to refer to God. One of the most recognized names for God is **Jehovah**, often paired with an adjective that characterizes a particular attribute. For example, **Jehovah Shalom**, as recorded in Judges 6:24, means "the Lord your Peace."

Jehovah Rapha, "the Lord your Healer" (from Exodus 15:26), **Jehovah Ro'i**, "the Lord your Shepherd" (found in Psalm 23:1), and **Jehovah Sal'i**, "the Lord your Rock" (written in Psalm 18:2) are some of the references to God used in the Old Testament.

The Lord appeared to Abram when he was 99 years old and referred to Himself as "El Shaddai." Abram received a divine message to walk in righteousness, and as a result, God would establish an everlasting covenant with him.

> *I am **El Shaddai**, walk before me, and be perfect.*
>
> Genesis 17:1b NIV [Emphasis Added]

El-Shaddai is a compound of two words and means "God Almighty." The name El translates as "God" (big "G" in this case). The name Shaddai comes from the Hebrew word "shaddu," meaning mountain, which translates to God our overcomer or powerful almighty. Abram fell down before the LORD in humility because he was old and frail. But God was his **El Shaddai,** his mighty one despite the impossible.

20**25**

THE YEAR THE **LORD** RESTORES HIS COVENANT

LORD / JEHOVAH / YAHWEH / ADONAI / HA-SHEM / EL SHADDAI

The Name of God: Within the Bible, we find many different names of God. The most familiar include Jehovah, Yahweh, The Most High, Adonai, HA-SHEM, El Shaddai and Yahweh, translated 'LORD'. All these names are relevant in their own way with each name of God is reflective of the nature who God really is; however, if we were to rank them, the one name that stands apart is the name is El Shaddai. El Shaddai means of God Almighty. The name El Shaddai is all-inclusive, having absolute power over all, thus the name El Shaddai stands out among many of the other names of God. The term is a compound of two words: **"El,"** which is a generic term for God in Hebrew, and **"Shaddai,"** which is derived from the root word meaning "breast" or "mountain.

"That men may know that thou, whose name alone is **JEHOVAH**, art the Most High over all the earth." - Psalm 83:18 KJV

The Meaning of GOD: "He Is" the perpetual testimony to his faithfulness to His promises of to save, help, deliver, redeem, bless, and keep covenant.

Jesus as GOD: An abbreviated form of Yahweh is preserved in the Hebrew name **Joshua** and in the Greek name **JESUS**, both meaning **"The Lord [Yahweh] saves."**

7 1 7

יהוה

7 ✗ **7**
2025 - REST, JUBILEE
EVIL   **717**   **GOOD**

2017 - 2024
"TIME OF DARKNESS"

2026 - 2033
"TIME OF PLENTY"

1914 + 111-Years = 20**25**
YEAR OF REST

1-1-1 = TRINITY - Father, Son, Holy Spirit
"The Lord saves, helps, delivers, redeems, blesses, and keep covenant."

Jehovah in Hebrew written on the front of the Basilica of Saint Louis, King of France, formerly the **Cathedral of Saint Louis MO, USA**, and colloquially the Old Cathedral.

Founded 1914
Oldest Church in the USA with the LORD's name 'JEHOVAH'

יהוה

DEO UNI ET TRINO

GOD RESTORES HIS COVENANT IN 2025

The oldest church in the United States displaying the Hebrew inscription for Yahweh (Jehovah) is located in St. Louis, MO. Named after the former King of France and the city who bears his name, the church is called the Basilica of St. Louis IX. The front of the cathedral displays the Hebrew lettering "Yud Hay Vov Hay," which represents the unutterable name of God in the Hebrew Bible, also known as "YHVH." (Remember Hebrew words are written from right to left.)

These letters derive from the Hebrew "to be" and refer to God's completeness as the source of all being. Yahweh is considered the personal name of God and appears over 6800 times in the Hebrew bible. It is also shown as LORD (in all caps) when used in the King James Version.

During biblical times, the name Yahweh was considered so sacred by Jews that they refrained from speaking it to avoid breaking Exodus 20:7.

> You shall not misuse the name of the Lord your God, for the Lord will not hold anyone guiltless who misuses his name.
>
> Exodus 20:7 NIV

God's holy name serves as a testament to His unwavering commitment to keep His promises. A covenant is God's promise to forgive sin, restore land, and reestablish the inheritance to His people. In 2025, the Lord will restore His covenant.

> This is what the LORD says, "In **the time of my favor** I will answer you, and in the day of salvation I will help you; I will keep you and will make you to be a covenant for the people, to restore the land and to reassign its desolate inheritances . . . ."
>
> Isaiah 49:8 NIV [Emphasis Added]

> Then you shall cause the trumpet of the Jubilee to sound on the tenth day of the seventh month; on the Day of Atonement you shall make the trumpet to sound throughout all your land.
>
> Leviticus 25:9 NKJV

At the end of 2022, my wife and I visited the Jungfraujoch, a mountain pass in the Swiss Alps, also known as "the top of Europe." At the peak is a breathtaking mountain view from over 11,700 feet above sea level. From one vantage point, you can literally see most of Europe!

Earlier that morning, before heading out, I received a word from the Lord instructing me to take a camera and be prepared to make a video. As we were driving with a tour guide up this mountain, I pondered what it symbolized to be up this high and what the Lord might have for us to understand there.

I reflected back on what the Lord had told Moses when He was preparing the Israelites to leave Egypt. God told Moses to tell Pharaoh, "Let my people go!" As we approached the top of the mountain, I was astonished to see a beautiful glass building that had been constructed.

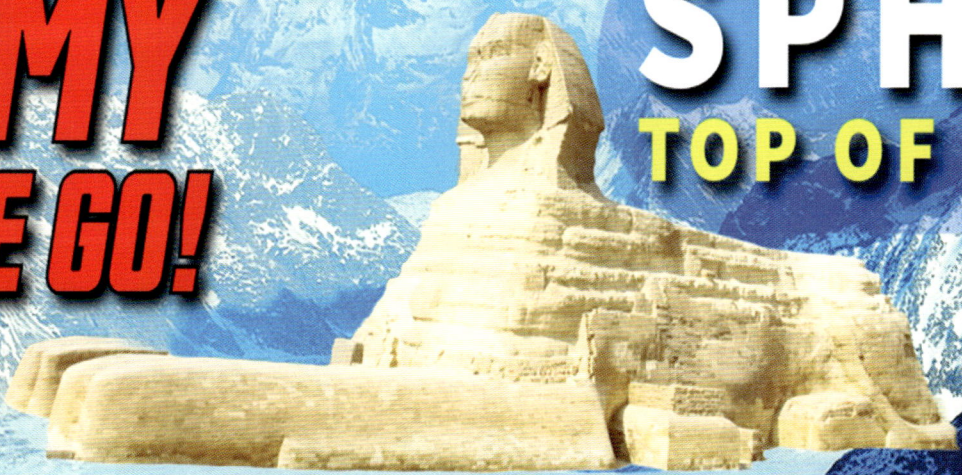

It was named the Sphinx Observatory and looked exactly like the most recognizable symbol in Egypt today—the Great Sphinx of Giza (see the illustration on the previous page). Just as Moses had walked by several sphinx statues guarding Pharaoh's palace to deliver the message from God, here we were at our own modern-day version and God was again telling me the same message.

Incredibly, when we stepped into the Observatory, I heard God say, "Look at the clock." It was exactly 1:24 p.m. (4-2-1) None of this was a coincidence! This occured on November 12, 2022. Three years later, the Trinity (Father, Son and Holy Spirit 1-1-1) will be in November 2025. Interestingly, there is a Kim Clement prophecy from 2014 that calls for a "hypnotic November" in the future.

We were standing on this mountain overlooking the world, and God was showing me that it was time for us to stand up to the Pharaohs of this world. It was time to say, "Let my people go!" God shows up on the mountains. The Bible has numerous examples where the Lord gives His word to people, while they are on mountains.

And I was humbled to hear from God in this way. God wants His people to be set free from the evil hold. And that my friends is *good news*!

AGENDA 2030

In 2015, world leaders from the United Nations adopted a program designed to transform our world called "The 2030 Agenda." The plan outlined 17 goals focused on people, the planet, prosperity, and peace. According to the Agenda, there are three primary goals: to end poverty, protect the planet, and tackle inequalities. For example, by 2030 the financial investment system would be steered toward "fairer outcomes" for all people.

Although it may seem reasonable and well-intended, numerous conservatives perceive this as a component of the Great Reset of Society, a proposal put forth by Klaus Schwab, the World Economic Forum's leader. The Reset fails to provide substance and does not outline any concrete plans for promoting equity and health worldwide. Instead, it is laced with concepts like a "wealth tax" and the replacement of fossil fuels for transportation.

Both Agenda 2030 and the Great Reset advocate for a greener world, emphasizing ecological sustainability. Yet, a common belief is that these plans are influenced by the privileged few who only seek greener bank accounts.

So, where is the *good news* in a situation like this? Calculations indicate that Agenda 2030 is part of the biblical timeline pointing to the rise of the Antichrist and the ultimate return of Christ.

TWO THOUSAND YEARS

Jewish tradition indicates Jesus started his 3.5-year Ministry on his 30th birthday based on Levitical Rabbinical tradition (Numbers 4:3). And Jesus was 33.5 years old at Crucifixion by many traditional accounts in the year 33 A.D.

Scripture teaches that a day is like a thousand years and a thousand years is like a day in God's view. The term "day" and "thousand years" are often used interchangeably.

> *A thousand years in your sight are like a day that has just gone by, or like a watch in the night.*
>
> Psalm 90:4 NIV

> *. . . With the Lord a day is like a thousand years, and a thousand years are like a day.*
>
> 2 Peter 3: 8b NIV

The prophet Hosea says "*After **two days** the LORD will revive us; on the third day he will restore us, that we may live in His sight*" (Hosea 6:1 Emphasis Added). When we interchange the word "days" for "thousand years" in this passage, we may conclude that Christ will return to the world after two thousand years.

Adding two thousand years to the date of his death in 33 A.D. takes us to the year 2033—three years after the commencement of the great plan described earlier. The calculations indicate Satan plans to reveal himself in 2033 by making a covenant with many (as described in Daniel 9:27). God raptures His church as the Great Tribulation begins. And that is ***good news***!

Some will be "left." And as Christians, we must be prepared for what lies ahead. As instructed in 1 Thessalonians 5:

> *But you, brothers and sisters, are not in darkness so that this day should surprise you like a thief. You are children of the light and children of the day. . . So then, let us not be like others, who are asleep, but let us be awake and sober.*
>
> 1 Thessalonians 5:4-6 NIV

REVELATION 12 SIGN

I close this chapter with revelation about the end-of-day's timeline and secrets hidden within the Revelation 12 sign. Heaven displayed another significant sign, as recorded in Revelation 12. The passage portrays a woman wearing the sun as a garment, with the moon under her feet and a twelve-starred crown. Also, she was pregnant and crying out in pain as she was about to give birth.

Simultaneously, a massive dragon appeared in the heavens; it had seven heads, ten horns, and seven crowns (Revelation 12:3). The dragon stood before the pregnant woman and planned to devour her baby after it was born. The math here is mind-blowing: 7 heads, 10 horns, and 7 crowns. 7+10+7 = 24... or 2024, the year the Star of Jacob appeared. This is the first hidden secret!

Next, and an even more fascinating hidden secret, the Revelation 12 sign appeared in 2017. The 7 heads represent the seven years from 2017 (the start of Trump's first presidency) to 2023. Ten horns symbolize a decade, from Trump's 2024 reelection to 2033, the beginning of the Antichrist Kingdom's rise. The final 7 crowns represent the final seven years of the Great Tribulation from 2034 to 2040. This is a total of 24 years from the appearance of the Revelation 12 sign to the return of Christ.

A hidden mystery, the Revelation 12 sign is a secret countdown clock marking the three final seasons before Christ returns. The third secret is even more mind-blowing math and pertains to the sign's appearance on September 23, 2017. Each of the 12 stars that make up the crown on her head accounts for exactly 700 days or 100 weeks each. Multiplying 700 days or 100 weeks by 12 stars is 8,400 days or 1,200 weeks. Incredibly, exactly 8,400 days (1,200 weeks) from September 23, 2017 (the start of Rosh Hashanah) is September 22, 2040 (the start of Tabernacles and the Final Harvest)! The math here is impossible—it could only be by God's design.

In 2040, Tabernacles ends on September 28th. From September 22nd to 28th spans six days, suggesting a six-day duration for World War 3 (Ezekiel 38-39), mirroring the 1967 Israeli War. Daniel 12:12 states, "Blessed is the one who waits for and reaches the end of the 1,335 days." Counting 1335 days from February 1, 2037 (the start of the middle of the Tribulation) takes us to September 28, 2040.

The reason they will be "blessed" is because they were "left," i.e., not raptured. They survive the final three and one-half horrific years without being martyred.And then they are caught up meeting Christ in the clouds (1 Thessalonians 4:17). They make it to the fulfillment of Zechariah 14:16, the Marriage Feast celebration.

Day 7, the Sabbath day of rest, is September 29, 2040, and Day 8 is the "eighth day of assembly." September 28-30, 2040, marks the start of a new beginning—a return to the Garden of Eden after a 6048-year journey. This day, also known as Shemini Atzeret, is celebrated with rain (of the Holy Spirit). Singing, dancing, and rejoicing mark the first day of the annual Torah readings. In 2040, this data is expected to mark the royal wedding of Christ to Jacob, the body of Christ (the wedding feast), and the start of the 1000-year millennial reign in Hebrew year 5801.

The fourth and final hidden secret calculation the Lord has revealed about the Revelation 12 sign is an understanding of the number 666 written in Revelation 13:18. This passage states that 666 is both the number of man and the number of the beast. This number sequence 6-6-6 represents time.

As noted earlier, the period from September 23, 2017, to September 22, 2040, comprises 1200 weeks, two 600-day cycles, with a significant midpoint on March 30, 2029 (Nisan 14). And from September 22, 2040 to September 28, 2040 is an additional six days. Therefore, from September 23, 2017 to September 28, 2040, is exactly **6**00 weeks, **6**00 weeks, and **six** days. That gives us **three consecutive 6s** or 666—all ending in the year 2040.

THE RAPTURE AND THE FINAL 1260 DAYS OF THE TRIBULATION REVEALED

Understand the timing of Revelation 12:6: "The child was caught up to God and His throne, and the woman fled into the wilderness

(March 3, 2037) where she was nourished for 1260 days." (Day 1260 being August 14, 2040). This represents believers not raptured in an expected 2033 pre-tribulation rapture, and are "left" behind on the earth, who will flee into the wilderness. That is when the Antichrist desecrates the temple in Jerusalem and sets up an idol for worship in March of 2037 (see page 203).

The "catching up" is described in 1 Thessalonians 4:17, which says, "...caught up in the clouds to meet the Lord in the air." Those who are "caught up" are the ones who survive the final 1335 days of the Great Tribulation and are not martyred but are "blessed" (Daniel 12:12). The catching up also fulfills the Kim Clement 2013 prophecy, which stated, "We are the generation that will defy death!" As discussed earlier, a generation is seventy-plus years. From 1967 to 2040 is 73 years.

GOD'S PERFECT 7000-YEAR TIMELINE, FROM CREATION TO END

From creation (4008 BC), there are sixteen (16) 248-year cycles, plus Israel's 40 years in the wilderness. From there, we arrive at the Star of Bethlehem, the birth of Jesus, and eight (8) subsequent 248-year cycles. Plus America's 40-year period in the wilderness, from 1736 to 1776, we arrive at the Star of Jacob in 2024. Then, there are another 16 years until the Return of Christ and the Royal Wedding in 2040 (6048 years from creation) to a 15-year-old bride, exactly 5555 days from birth on July 3, 2025, to Yom Kippur, September 17, 2040. This ends with a final four (4) 248-year cycles and one (1) final year of Jubilee. Thus, the 1000-year Millennial Reign will end in 3033, or 7041 years from creation (represented by the equation $7 + 4 + 1 = 12$, the number of divine completion; see page 175). The End!

> When the thousand years are over, Satan will be released from his prison and will go out to deceive the nations in the four corners of the earth—Gog and Magog—and gather them for battle. In number, they are like the sand on the seashore. They marched across the breadth of the earth and surrounded the camp of God's people, the city he loves. But fire came down from heaven and devoured them.
>
> Revelation 20:7-9 NIV

God's 1-2-4 and 2-4-8 cycles beautifully illustrate that the end was present from the time of creation. The hand of God accomplished perfect mathematical calculations, spanning 7000 years despite their impossibility. The ***good news*** is the end was always written from the beginning!

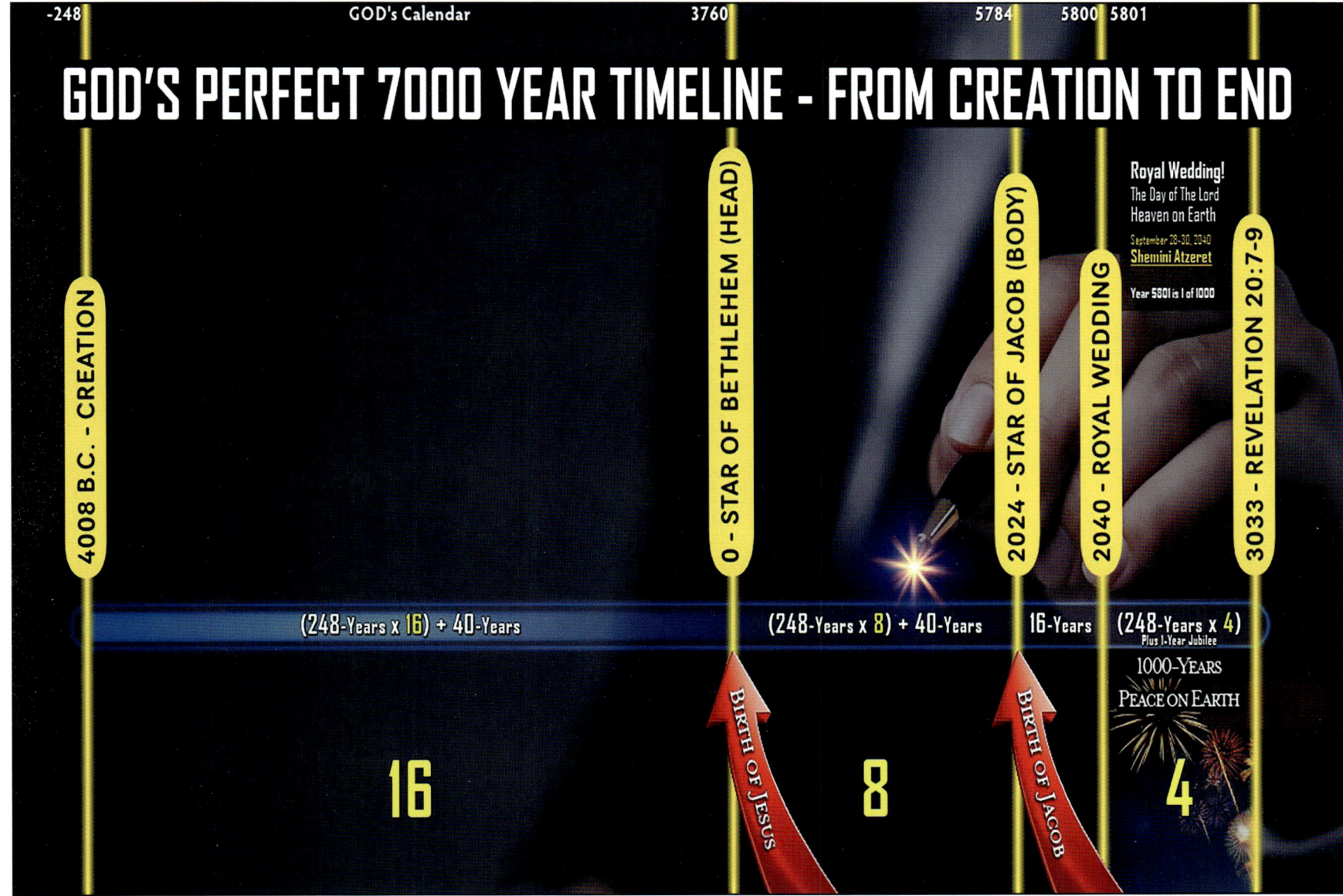

GOD'S PERFECT 7000 YEAR TIMELINE - FROM CREATION TO END

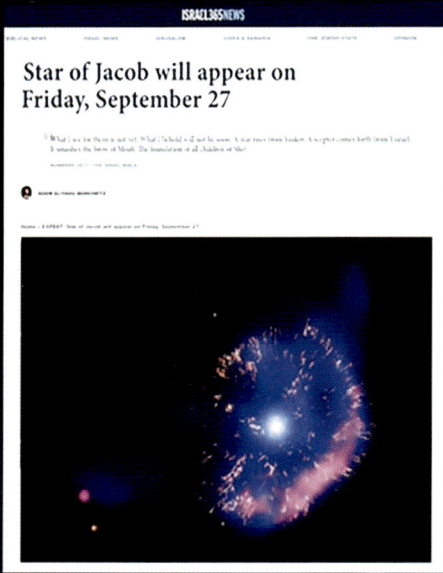

Star of Jacob
Numbers 24:17
SEPTEMBER 27, 2024 – Conception

SIGN: The (Body) BRIDE of Christ is Born!
Latter Temple – Haggai 2:9

JULY 3, 2025
BIRTH (40-WEEKS)

Scan Me

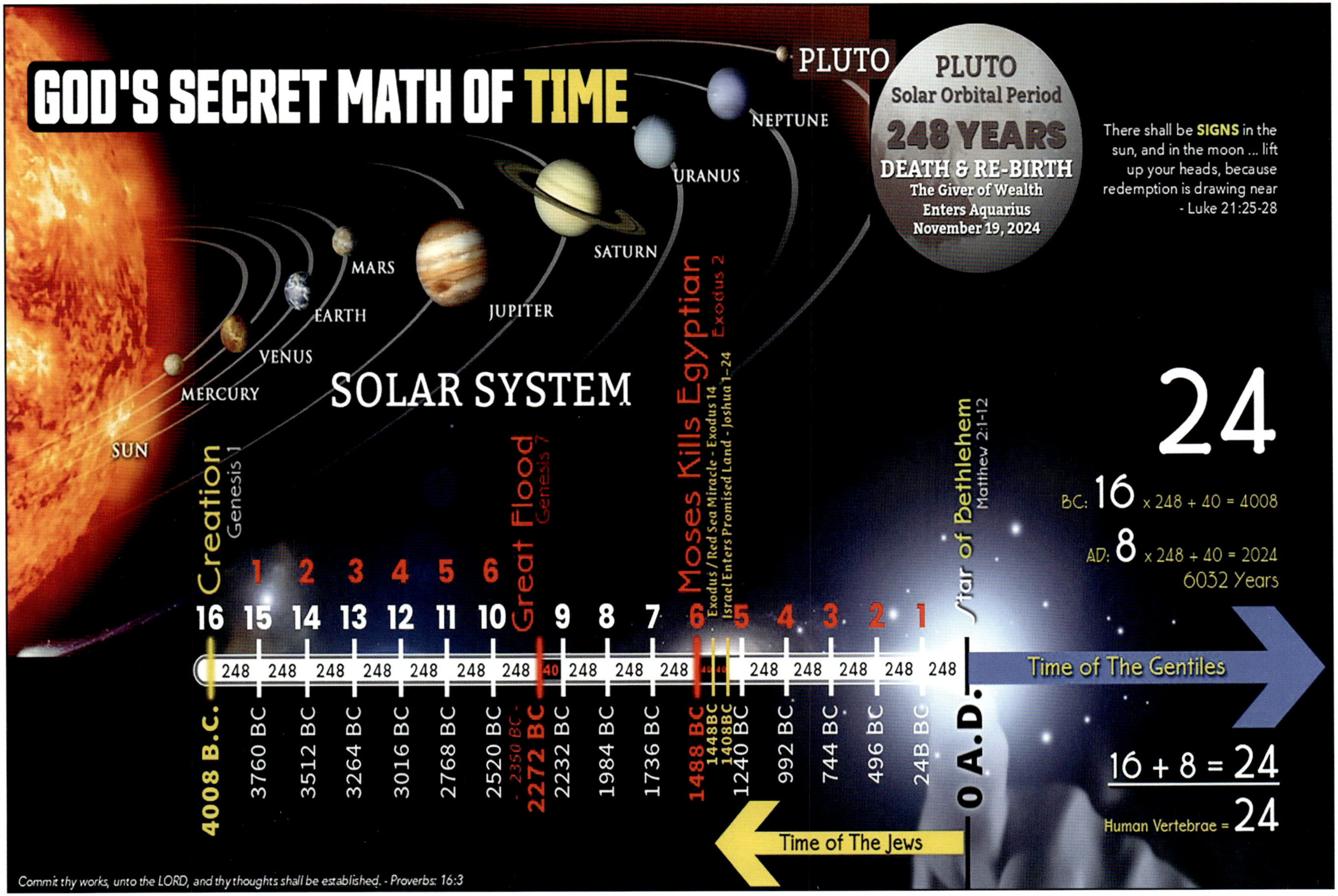

GOD'S SECRET MATH OF TIME

PLUTO

NEPTUNE

URANUS

SATURN

JUPITER

MARS

EARTH

VENUS

MERCURY

SUN

SOLAR SYSTEM

PLUTO
Solar Orbital Period
248 YEARS
DEATH & RE-BIRTH
The Giver of Wealth
Enters Aquarius
November 19, 2024

There shall be **SIGNS** in the sun, and in the moon ... lift up your heads, because redemption is drawing near
- Luke 21:25-28

Creation
Genesis 1

Great Flood
Genesis 7

Moses Kills Egyptian
Exodus / Red Sea Miracle - Exodus 14
Israel Enters Promised Land - Joshua 1–24
Exodus 2

Star of Bethlehem
Matthew 2:1-12

24

BC: **16** x 248 + 40 = 4008

AD: **8** x 248 + 40 = 2024

6032 Years

| 1 | 2 | 3 | 4 | 5 | 6 | | | | | | | | | | |

16 15 14 13 12 11 10 9 8 7 6 5 4 3 2 1 0 A.D.

248 248 248 248 248 248 248 40 248 248 248 40 40 248 248 248 248 248

4008 B.C.
3760 BC
3512 BC
3264 BC
3016 BC
2768 BC
2520 BC
- 2350 BC -
2272 BC
2232 BC
1984 BC
1736 BC
1488 BC
1448BC
1408BC
1240 BC
992 BC
744 BC
496 BC
24B BC

Time of The Gentiles

Time of The Jews

$$\frac{16 + 8 = 24}{24}$$

Human Vertebrae = **24**

Commit thy works, unto the LORD, and thy thoughts shall be established. - Proverbs 16:3

THE RE-BIRTH OF AMERICA

"And there shall be signs in the sun, and in the moon, and in the stars" - Luke 21:25

REVELATION 12 SIGN
THE WOMAN AND THE DRAGON

2024 USA ECLIPSE

2024 STAR OF JACOB
Star of Jacob
Rosh Hashanah - A KING Is Born!

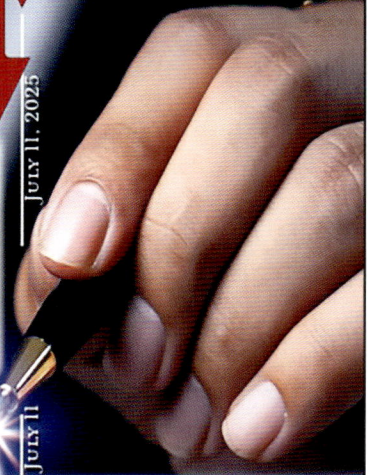

AMERICA RE-BORN JULY 4, 2025

Revelation 12

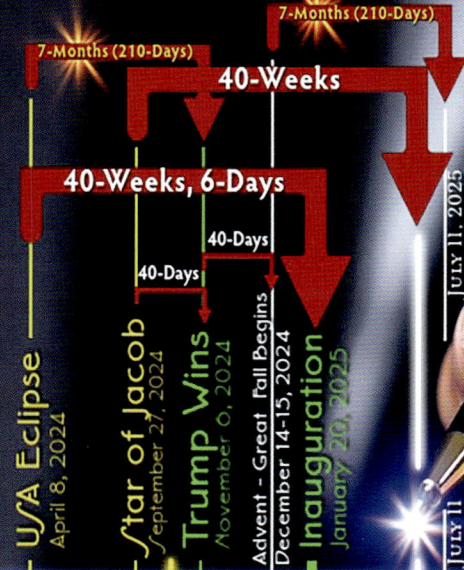

7-Months (210-Days)
7-Months (210-Days)
40-Weeks
40-Weeks, 6-Days
40-Days
40-Days

USA Eclipse April 8, 2024
Star of Jacob September 27, 2024
Trump Wins November 0, 2024
Advent - Great Fall Begins December 14-15, 2024
Inauguration January 20, 2025
July 11, 2025
July 11

6-Months
6-Days
6-Months
TIME OF REPENTANCE

AMERICA RE-BORN

ONE NATION UNDER GOD!

September 23, 2017
October 31, 2024

"It **will be** for a time (360), times (360 x2) and half a time (180), and when he shall have accomplished to scatter the power of the holy people, all these things shall be finished." Daniel 12:7

7-YEARS (2595-DAYS)

BIRTH John Baptist
PASSOVER PENTECOST

JULY 4, 2025

YEAR 248 FROM THE 1776 DECLARATION OF INDEPENDENCE ENDS JULY 3, 2025

Commit thy works, unto the LORD, and thy thoughts shall be established. - Proverbs: 16:3

JACOB'S TROUBLE

Jeremiah 30:6. Ask now, and see, **can a man bear a child?** Why then do I see every man with his hands on his stomach like a woman in labor?

SNP-led Scottish Government set to argue for the rights of 'pregnant' men and male-born 'lesbians' at the UK's highest court TOMORROW - in landmark case about the definition of a woman

By TOM GORDON DEPUTY SCOTTISH POLITICAL EDITOR
02:10 25 Nov 2024, updated 03:17 25 Nov 2024

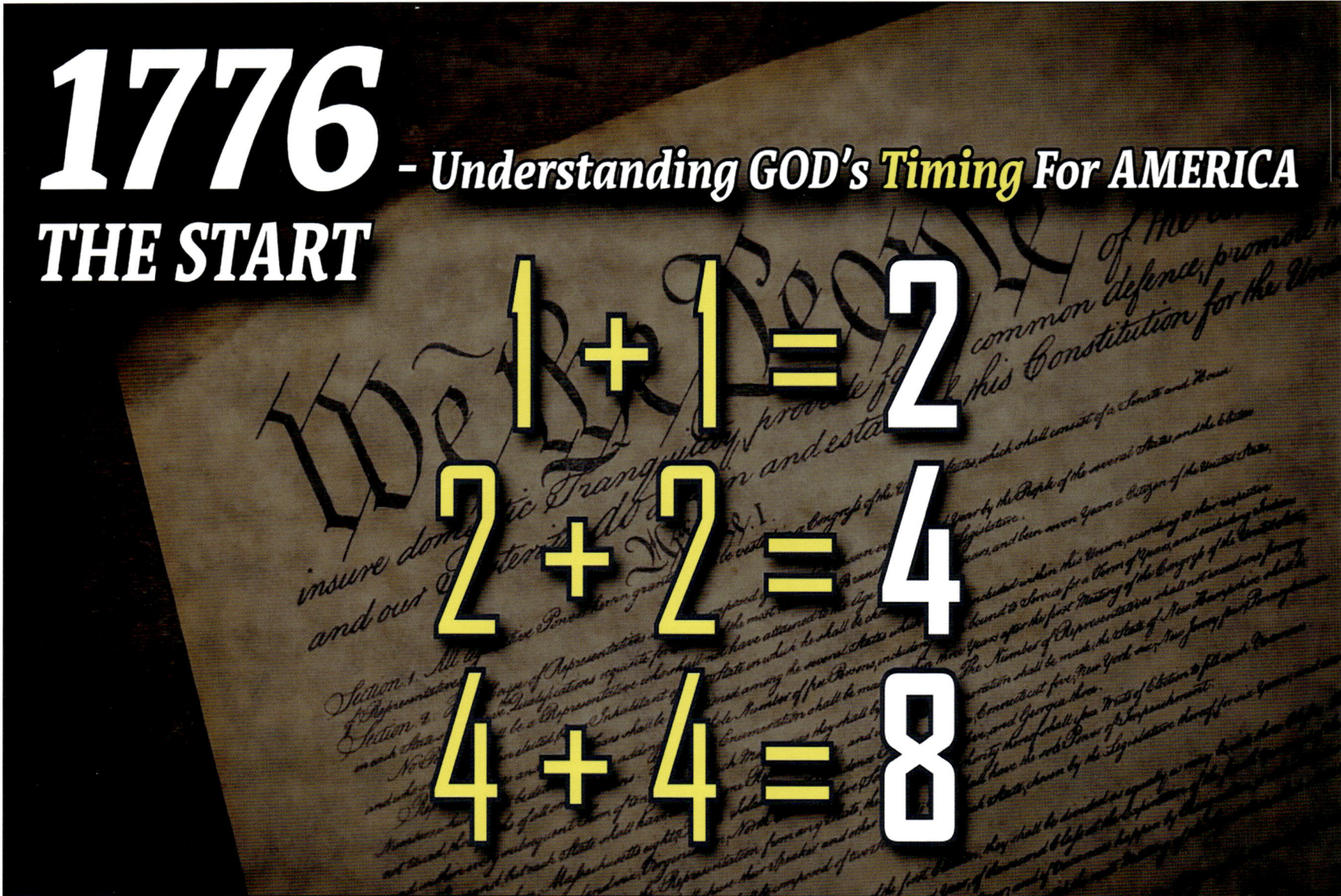

1776 THE START

- Understanding GOD's Timing For AMERICA

$$1 + 1 = 2$$

$$2 + 2 = 4$$

$$4 + 4 = 8$$

"There will be **SIGNS** in the sun, moon and stars" - Luke 21:25

THE WOMAN AND THE DRAGON

Revelation 12:3
(7) seven heads [7-Years 2017 to 2023]
(10) ten horns [10-Years 2023 to 2033]
(7) seven crowns [7-Years 2033 to 2040]

Total of 24 Years from 2017 is **2040**

Revelation 12:3
(7) seven heads
(10) ten horns
(7) seven crowns

Total of 24, points to YEAR... **2024**
Star of Jacob

Secret Calculations Revealed!

And a great sign appeared in heaven: a woman clothed with the sun, with the moon under her feet, and on her head a crown of twelve stars. She was **PREGNANT** and was crying out in **BIRTH PAINS** and the agony of giving birth. And another sign appeared in heaven: behold, a great **RED DRAGON**, with **SEVEN HEADS** and **TEN HORNS**, and on his heads **SEVEN CROWNS**. His tail swept down a third of the stars of heaven and cast them to the earth. And the dragon stood before the woman who was about to give birth, so that when she bore her child, he might devour it. She gave birth to a male child, one who is to rule all the nations with a rod of iron, **but** her child was caught up to God and to his throne, and **THE WOMAN FLED INTO THE WILDERNESS**, where she has a place prepared by God, in which she is to be **NOURISHED** for 1,260 days.

2024
YEAR OF THE DRAGON

GREAT EGYPTIAN ECLIPSES
MARKER FOR THE RISE OF ANTICHRIST KINGDOM
The two eclipses will pass over Mecca and Medina, the center of Islam, followers of Muhammad's Quran, the antichrist's religion

THE FALLEN

AUGUST 2 ECLIPSE **2027**

7-Years Apart

2034 ECLIPSE

Aug 2, 2027, Passes over Mecca

March 20, 2034, Passes over Medina

MARCH 20

Secret
Prophecy of SEVEN SEALS

And they (Islam) were given authority over a fourth of the earth, to kill with SWORD and with FAMINE and with PESTILENCE and by WILD BEASTS of the earth. - Revelation 6:8

The I saw another beast rising out of the earth. - Revelation 13:11

Saudi Arabia   Antichrist

FINAL 3 SEASONS

7 EVIL	7 GOOD	7 EVIL
717		
2017 - 2026	2026 - 2033	2033 - 2040
"TIME OF DARKNESS"	"TIME OF PLENTY"	"TIME OF TRIBULATION"

2025 - FEST. JUBILEE

2017 - 2027 / 9-YEARS 11-MONTH APART
❖ August 21, 2017, Great American Eclipses
❖ August 2, 2027, Great Egyptian Eclipses

Applying the TIME calculation of the 2024 US Eclipse to the 2034 EGYPTIAN Eclipse points to JUNE 21-22, 2035, for Babylon's FATAL / MORTAL WOUND to be HEALED *(Revelation 13:12)*.

The Resurrection of Babylon... "Babylon Rises!"

CHAPTER 12
What the Future Holds

THE GREAT DECEPTION

ALIENS. They've been packaged in Hollywood mysticism, misinformation, and public curiosity. Society has been conditioned to see them as other-worldly beings with advanced technologies and superior intelligence. Or perhaps it is one of the biggest cover-ups orchestrated by the great deceiver himself, Satan.

The Bible gives us a clear outline of the end times. These extraordinary signs and events, if left unmanipulated, would prove the truths of the Bible, including the life of Jesus, salvation, and the return of the Messiah. Satan wants to deceive the world by explaining the events of Revelation through "extraterrestrials." Don't be deceived. These alien encounters are the Fallen Ones.

After the fall of the U.S. dollar and the subsequent opening of the fourth seal with worldwide plague and pestilence, the world may become destitute and desperate for a Savior. Satan and his false Messiah, the anti-Christ, will arrive on the world scene as aliens or men under the counsel of aliens. The world will perceive them as beings of high intelligence, possessing the knowledge of the entire universe.

God's truth about creation, the rapture of the church, and many other Biblical events could be defamed by a false doctrine taught by these celestial creatures. A societal acceptance of aliens with all the answers will usher in a one-world government that is devoid of God and a global financial system. The Lost will take the mark of the Beast.

Again, don't be deceived. These are the Fallen Ones!

Then I saw a second beast, coming out of the earth... And it performed great signs, even causing fire to come down from heaven to the earth in full view of the people. Because of the signs it was given power to perform on behalf of the first beast, it deceived the inhabitants of the earth. It ordered them to set up an image in honor of the beast who was wounded by the sword and yet lived. The second beast was given power to give breath to the image of the first beast, so that the image could speak and cause all who refused to worship the image to be killed. It also forced all people, great and small, rich and poor, free and slave, to receive a mark on their right hands or on their foreheads, so that they could not buy or sell unless they had the mark, which is the name of the beast or the number of its name. This calls for wisdom. Let the person who has insight calculate the number of the beast, for it is the number of a man. That number is 666.

Revelation 13:11-18 (NIV)

HYPERINFLATION

Hyperinflation is a rapid decrease in the value or buying power of a particular currency. This occurs when there is more paper money in circulation without a corresponding increase in domestic product. As discussed previously, a fiat currency like the U.S. dollar has no backing by a commodity or precious metal. Historically paper money was used as "notes" that could be exchanged for something tangible like gold or silver.

The global demand for the USD is greatly supported because of America's position as the world's reserve currency and its use as the "petrodollar." This high demand created a blank check to print USDs and create modern day Babylon, as evil attempted to maintain control. We will soon see the fall of the USD and thus the fall of Babylon.

Our money supply is so vast, and backed by nothing but a reputation, a global acceptance of its value. But the gig is up! In 2024, many countries including Iran, Saudi Arabia, and the United Arab Emirates joined BRICS. At the time of this writing the BRICS nations now include more than 70% of the world's population. Some countries have begun selling off U.S. treasuries which will soon dethrone the petrodollar and the USD as the world reserve currency.

As demand drops and circulation skyrockets, we'll witness unprecedented hyperinflation which will be both the worst and greatest event in financial history. The power of Babylon, wars, and corruption funded by worthless paper will diminish. Then God, through Trump, will usher in a new currency backed by gold and silver, the greatest wealth transfer in the world's history. And Babylon's money, the Federal Reserve Note, will be considered junk money and will not be accepted as payment globally.

DID YOU KNOW? In the 1970s there were approximately one billion USDs in circulation. That number is now in the quadrillions. *One million billion* is a trillion for reference.

ARKS OF SAFETY

Many theories have been derived about the rapture of the church before the Second Coming of Christ. Some believe in a pre-tribulation rapture, where God's Bride is taken up and/or "caught up" at the start of the seven-year Great Tribulation. A recent prophecy given to Carolyn Dennis in 2025 indicates exactly that. A pre-tribulation rapture is coming and calculations point to 2033. "The

Bible tells you of a seven-year tribulation in the earth. The church will be gone. And there will be no one here left on earth to pray back the enemy. And all hell will break loose."

Others believe in a post-tribulation rapture in which Christians and non-believers alike share the burden of the tribulation, bearing witness to the destruction. Christ died for our sins. He has already saved us. When Christ returns, He is coming for a victorious bride and to redeem the earth, because the 6000-year lease set up with Adam has come to an end,

> Go, my people, enter your rooms and shut the doors behind you; hide yourselves for a little while until his wrath has passed by. See, the Lord is coming out of his dwelling to punish the people of the earth for their sins. The earth will disclose the blood shed on it; the earth will conceal its slain no longer.
>
> Isaiah 26: 20-21 (NIV)

We know that Isaiah 26 speaks of the end times and the return of Christ. We will "shut the doors...until his wrath has passed." The places we will go to are known as Arks of Safety, or Christian safe havens that will be established throughout the World.

THE 6000-YEAR EARTH LEASE

God will not violate His Word, and He has made a contract that He will not breach. He said, "Heaven and earth may pass away, but My word will not pass away." What contract is it that He will not breach?

When God created man (male and female), He gave them dominion over the Earth. He contracted them for the purpose of Earth's protection and preservation. The animals were categorized and named. Everything was provided for the success of the Earth to "multiply and replenish" under their watchful care. In essence, God gave the legal right, by way of a "lease," to Adam and Eve, which can be called an "earth lease." God's plan for man was to have dominion over His creation for a predetermined time. Dominion was given in Genesis 26 and 28, "And God said, Let us (THE TRINITY) make man in our image, after our likeness and let them have dominion ... Be fruitful and multiply and replenish the earth, and subdue it, and have dominion."

The authority and dominion given to Adam was for a limited period, precisely 6000 years. It would be 4000 years from creation to the birth of Jesus and another 2000 years from birth to His return. Then God said, "My Spirit shall not always strive with man, for that he also is flesh: yet his days shall be a hundred and twenty years." (Genesis 6:3)

Several things have been profiled in these 120 years. It seems that God revealed to Noah that there would be 120 years before judgment would come upon the wicked of the Earth through the flood. However, this 120-year period has a much more significant prophetic implication concerning the Earth lease.

Earlier, Leviticus 25 was referenced; it states God had established that every 50 years was to be a year of Jubilee. Understand that 8 cycles of 50 years is 400 years, and 15 cycles of 400 years is 6000 years. Adding the 1 and 5 in "15", we arrive at six days. But recall, a day is but a thousand years, thus a 6000-year lease. Another way of understanding the lease is the 120 years mentioned in Genesis 6:3. The 120-year cycle of 50 Jubilees is again 6,000 years. God's word reveals that the Earth's lease, Adam's Lease, will expire 6,000 years from creation.

God cannot violate His Word to take back the dominion of the Earth until the original 6000-year lease expires. When Adam fell, he unknowingly gave his 6000-year lease to Satan. In other words, Satan usurped Adam's inheritance through trickery, saying, "Eat of this fruit, and you will be like God." When the truth of the matter was that Adam and Eve were already made in God's image.

Demons and evil spirits are living illegally on this planet, using wicked men by accessing their authority. And this will continue until Christ returns when the lease expires. But there is good news on the horizon: the Earth's lease will soon expire, signifying Jesus' return, not to save but to redeem the Earth from evil. This long 6000-year wait has always been about His Word and a lease. It has always been about divine TIMING and, for us, understanding it!

PEOPLE FLEEING THE CITIES

In 1971, David Wilkerson prophesied that there would be a "sudden rush" to buy land as people fled from cities. The United States has already begun to see this following the opening of the first seal during COVID-19. The increased crime and unrest in cities have caused people to fear for their safety. And with the ongoing food shortages and mysterious fires at food processing plants, people are wanting to grow their own food and raise their own livestock. What was predicted 50 years ago is coming to pass.

THE OTHER BEAST

Revelation 13:11 speaks of "another beast rising out of the earth." The other beast is Horus, an Egyptian God. He is considered the divine son of the god Osiris. Horus' mother is Isis, born on the winter solstice. Horus is often depicted as a man with the head of a falcon and is the **copycat** of the TRUE divine son, Jesus Christ.

According to Egyptian beliefs, Horus governed the sun and moon's movements. Additionally, it was thought that he had magical abilities to protect against evil. He had a close connection with the pharaohs. There are numerous temples dedicated to Horus.

EGYPTIAN ECLIPSES COMING

There will be two eclipses which cross Egypt in a seven-year span. One will occur on August 2, 2027 and passes over Mecca. The other happens on March 20, 2034 and passes over Medina. Like the eclipses which crossed America, they will form a cross, but in this case it will be a cross, over the center of Islam, who are the followers of Muhammad's Quran, the antichrist's religion!

From 8/2/27 to 3/20/34 is exactly **6** years, **6** months, **6** weeks and **6** days if the months and years are added before the days. It is also notable that the date of the Great American Eclipse (August 21, 2017) and the date of the Great Egyptian Eclipse (August 2, 2027) are **9** years and **11** months apart. This is not a coincidence!

Let's further compare the U.S. Eclipses of 2017 and 2024 to the future Egyptian eclipses of 2027 and 2034. We will determine what secret calculations the Egyptian eclipses might reveal about the coming rise of the Antichrist. The second eclipse forms a cross when laid over the first eclipse; this happens in both 2024 and 2034. And the formation of a cross in 2024 should be used as the starting point to count time into the future.

In 2024, forty (40) weeks and six (6) days exactly from the cross formation on April 8, 2024, President Donald Trump was elected President of the United States for a second term. Applying the same calculation for the Egyptian Eclipse on March 20, 2034, forty (40) weeks and six (6) days is exactly December 31, 2034, and the following day is New Year's Day, 2035, which is interesting.

This day, January 1, 2035, is analogous to the day Trump won his second term to lead the U.S.A. and the world out of evil and chaos. However, we expect the exact opposite beginning January 1, 2035, as the Middle East turns the world back into evil and chaos toward an Antichrist figure.

Five months and nineteen days (nearly six months) after the U.S. cross formation of April 8, 2024, the Star of Jacob appeared on September 27, 2024. Forty (40) weeks later, America's rebirth under God will occur on July 4, 2025. And then a new covenant with God will occur seven days later, on July 11, 2025.

By applying this same time calculation of the 2024 U.S. eclipse to the 2034 Egyptian eclipse, five months and nineteen days after the cross formation of March 20, 2034, is September 8, 2034. There's a chance of a celestial event—like a star or UFO—on this date. Another 40 weeks later, it lands on June 15, 2035. The world anticipates a possible rebirth on this day. It might be the Resurrection of Babylon, fulfilling Revelation 13:12, which speaks of a "mortal wound" that is healed.

> It (the second beast) exercised all the authority of the first beast on its behalf and made the earth and its inhabitants worship the first (Babylon) beast, whose mortal/fatal wound had been **healed**."
>
> Revelation 13:11-12 NIV

THE DAY OF THE MOST HIGH

The summer solstice is considered the "Day of the Most High." It is often associated with sun worship because it marks the longest day of the year. It is a time when the sun reaches its highest point in the sky, signifying the peak of its power and the abundance of summer. Many cultures throughout history have significantly celebrated the sun's life-giving force on this day through rituals and traditions.

Many pagan traditions, especially Celtic Litha, view the summer solstice as a time to celebrate the sun god Horus and the height of fertility and growth. Cultures around the world have worshipped sun deities associated with the summer solstice, such as Rain in Egypt, Apollo in Greece, and Amaterasu in Japan.

The Summer Solstice (Day of the Most High) on June 21-22, 2035, is a mathematically-intriguing starting point. It points to either the second beast, Horus's rise, or the first beast, Babylon's return, both preceding the Antichrist's desecration of the temple.

THE FALLEN

50

GEORGE ORWELL

1984

322

Rise of AntiChrist 2033

FINAL 3 SEASONS

7 7 717 7

WHITE HOUSE

We Come In
PEACE!

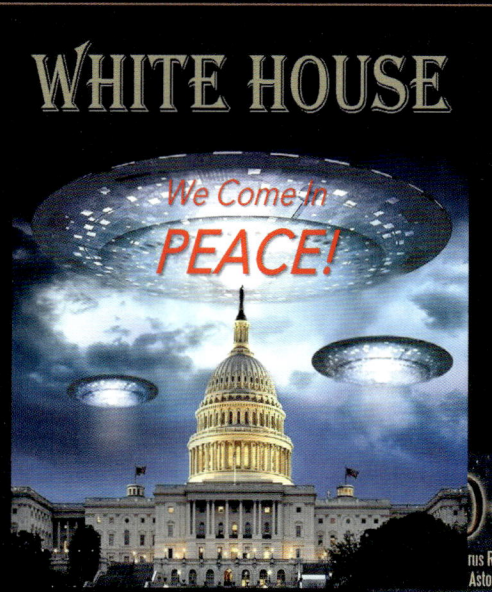

WHITE HOUSE
IMAGE
of the **VATICAN**
(Papacy/Beast)

VATICANA

Christians will not immediately need to renounce their faith in God "simply on the basis of the reception of [the] now, unexpected intimation of a religious character from extraterrestrial civilizations." However, once the "religious content originating from outside the earth "has been verified" they will have to conduct "a re-reading [of the Gospel] inclusive of the new date."

- Vatican Astronomer (Connected With Opus Dei) Father Giuseppe Tanzella-Nitti

ALIENS, the Fallen Ones, the Fallen Elohim are coming in to…

~~SAVE~~ the World 2033 - 2040!

DECEIVE

- Information release began on April 27, 2020
- Pentagon officially releases UFO videos
- Pentagon releases three UFO videos taken by US navy pilots
- Hundred of UFO sighting reported on 'X', formally Twitter in 2024

All a part of the set up for the coming end-times 'GREAT DECEPTION'

DEFINITION:
The word 'El' is a generic term for God in Hebrew, while the word 'Elohim' is the plural form of 'El'

A KEY TO THE MYSTIC NUMBER

666
LATIN

POPE 666

"VICARIUS FILII DEI",
OR
"VICAR OF THE SON
OF GOD",

666

Arks like "THEME PARKS": The bride ESCAPE from a world of sorrow, a world who has rejected the LOVE of Jesus. Arks will be areas of safety when ALL hell breaks out on earth, as <u>more</u> seals open!

The bride is to live <u>separate</u> from the world in one mind and one accord, and the beauty of nature will be there to enjoy, as more seals open and then God's wrath pours down on the earth.

ARKS OF SAFETY

Beautiful Sanctuaries, like *"Theme Parks"*, in the Mountains built and used as Safe Zones during the time of the coming storms when food will be scarce, as it was during the **Time of Joseph.**

• *Arks will be built with God's money, silver and gold and will be Safe Zones for God's Church, Jesus' bride, in preparation for the Great Tribulations. Many will be raptured with the start of the Tribulation, while others will be "left" behind to later be **"Caught Up"** should they survive the 1260-days and not be martyred.* **Come, my people, enter your <u>chambers</u> (ARKS of SAFETY), and shut your doors behind you; hide yourselves for a little while until the indignation has passed by.** *For behold, the Lord is coming out from his place to punish the inhabitants of the earth for their iniquity, and the earth will disclose the blood shed on it and will no more cover its slain."* **- Isaiah 26:20-21**

• *The* **"chambers"** *are the* **ARKS OF SAFETY**, *"and in this place, I will give peace, says the LORD of hosts."* **- Haggai 2:9**

THOUSANDS WILL ATTEMPT TO FLEE THE CITIES!

- Coming is the fulfillment of David Wilkerson's 1971 Prophecy and *Isaiah 26:20-21*
- Arks will be built with God's money, gold and silver, and will be *Safe Zones* for Jesus' bride during the time of famine and the Antichrist.
- The bride will live _separated_ from the world, in one mind and one accord, and the beauty of nature will be there to enjoy as God's wrath pours down on the earth.
- The Woman fled into the *wilderness (Safe Havens)* to a place prepared for her by God, where she might be taken care of for 1,260-days. - *Rev 12:6*
- But woe to the earth and the sea because the devil has gone down to you and is filled with fury because he know his TIME is short. - *Rev. 12:12*
- The woman was given two wings of an eagle to fly to the place prepared for her in the *wilderness (Safe Havens)*. - *Rev 12:14*

A RUSH TO THE COUNTRY:

THERE WILL BE A SUDDEN RUSH TO BUY FARMS, RANCHES, AND HOMES IN THE COUNTRY. THOUSANDS WILL ATTEMPT TO FLEE FROM CITIES, HOPING THAT A RETURN TO THE LAND AND NATURE WILL PROVIDE SECURITY. THERE WILL BE A GROWING URGE TO "GET AWAY FROM IT ALL" – AND MUCH MONEY WILL BE INVESTED IN LAND AND ACREAGE IN RURAL AREAS BY PEOPLE WHO HAVE SECRET DREAMS OF RAISING THEIR OWN FOOD AND CATTLE AND OF BECOMING SELF-SUPPORTING.

- David Wilkerson, 1971

Scan me

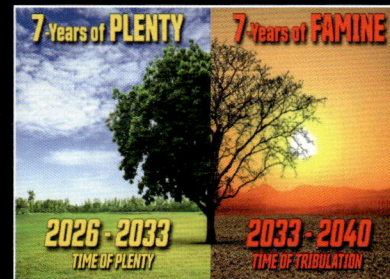

TIME OF JOSEPH

"Behold, seven years of great abundance are coming throughout the land of Egypt, but seven years of famine will follow them. Then all the abundance in the land of Egypt will be forgotten, and the famine will devastate the land. The abundance in the land will not be remembered, since the famine that follows it will be so severe." - **Genesis 41:29-31**

7-years of PLENTY: Begin in Fall 2023, Proverbs 13:22, and will continue into 2030. Prophetic work of Kim Clement... "You have been besieged by your internal enemies for 7-years America; there shall be followed by 7 years of blessing." **(LINK)**

7-Years of FAMINE, the TIME of FAMINE, is expected to begin in 2030 with the signing of an Israel PEACE TREATY, the fulfillment of the Shane Warren Prophecy... **"They have divided MY land, now I will divide their land." LINK** This 7-years of famine ends with the expected return of Christ!

Famine 2033 - 2040 food will be scarce, as it was during the TIME OF JOSEPH **(LINK)**.

Come, my people, enter your chambers (THE ARKS), and shut your doors behind you; hide yourselves for a little while until the indignation has passed by. For behold, the Lord is coming out from his place to punish the inhabitants of the earth for their iniquity, and the earth will disclose the blood shed on it and will no more cover its slain." - Isaiah 26:20-21

HYPERINFLATION

HISTORIC CORRELATION BETWEEN HYPERINFLATION **AND THE** FALL OF A NATION

STEPS:
1. Long-Term Inflation of money supply
2. 'Sudden' HYPERINFLATION *(Simple definition: the doubling of prices of goods within hours/days)*
3. Collapse of a Nation

France, May 1795
Highest monthly inflation: 150%
Prices doubled every 15 days

Greece, October 1944
Highest monthly inflation: 13,800%
Prices doubled every 4.3 days

Germany, October 1923
Highest monthly inflation: 29,500%
Prices doubled every 3.7 days

Hungary, August 1945
Prices doubled every: 15 hours

China, October 1947
Prices doubled every 5.3 days

Nicaragua, June 1986
Highest monthly inflation: 120%
Prices doubled every 16 days

Peru, July 1990
Highest monthly inflation: 150%
Prices doubled every 13 days

Yugoslavia, Jan. 1994
Highest monthly inflation: 313,000,000%
Prices doubled every: 1.4 days

Zimbabwe, November 2008
Highest monthly inflation: 79,600,000,000%
Prices doubled every: 24.7 hours

Venezuela, 2013
Prices rose 41% in 2013
2018 inflation was 65,000%

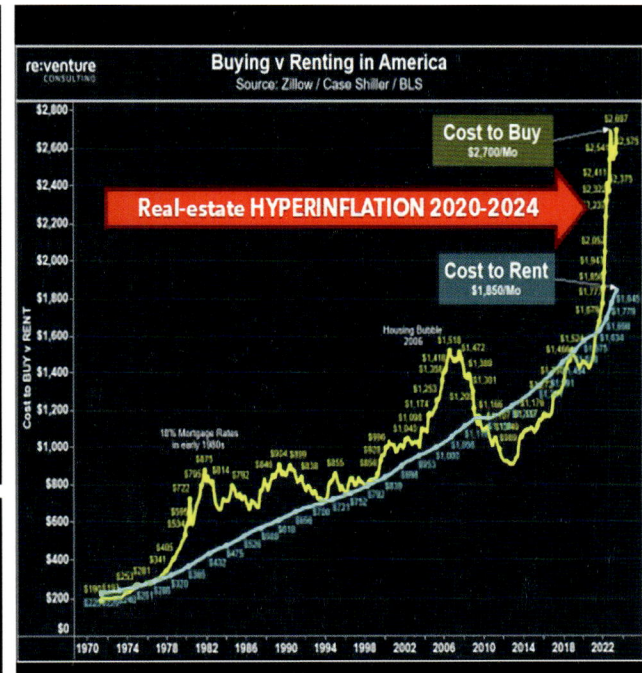

TIME OF JOSEPH

In Genesis, we read of seven years when Joseph stored up food in anticipation of a coming famine. He worked for the Pharaoh and had a high level of mental perception. One of his roles was to oversee agriculture throughout Egypt. He considered it wise to store up grain during an abundant harvest to ensure there would be provision during the lean years.

> He gathered up all the food of the seven years when there was plenty in the land of Egypt, and stored up food in the cities; he stored up in every city the food from the fields around it. So Joseph stored up grain in such abundance—like the sand of the sea—that he stopped measuring it; it was beyond measure.
>
> Genesis 41:48-49 NRSV

As in the time of Joseph, 2026-2033 will be a time when we must store up from an abundant harvest. And starting in 2025 is not too early. Kim Clement prophesied, *"You have been besieged by your internal enemies for 7-years America; there shall be followed by 7-years of blessing."* Receive your blessings during this time of abundance and store the provision needed for the coming famine.

WILL GOD'S BRIDE EXPERIENCE LACK?

Following the seven years of abundance, 2033-2040 will bring The Great Tribulation and a time of famine. Genesis 41:31 (NIV) says that "the abundance in the land will not be remembered, because the famine that follows it will be so severe." Food will be scarce, as it was in the time of Joseph. And in the last three and one-half years, no man will be able to buy and sell without the Mark of the Beast.

The **good news** is a pre-tribulation rapture is expected in 2033. For those "left" behind (Matthew 24:40) there will be arks of safety in the mountains, with many available provisions. Because the storehouses will be filled, although there will be hell on earth.

During the period of good harvests, Joseph stored grain for the future drought. Amid the seven-year drought, he opened the storehouses, ensuring there was sufficient food to survive the famine.

Just as Joseph's famine was seven years, coincidentally, so too, is the Great Tribulation. God's people will not lack during this time if they use the same intuition that Joseph used and trust the Lord for their provision. Here is what Jesus told His disciples when they asked about material needs:

> Then Jesus asked them, "When I sent you without purse, bag or sandals, did you lack anything?" "Nothing," they answered.
>
> Luke 22:35 NIV

The final year of famine ends with World War 3 and the return of Christ.

7-Years of PLENTY | **7-Years of FAMINE**

Scan Me

2026 - 2033
TIME OF PLENTY

2033 - 2040
TIME OF TRIBULATION

TIME OF JOSEPH

*"Behold, seven years of great abundance are coming throughout the land of Egypt, but **seven years of famine** will follow them. Then all the abundance in the land of Egypt will be forgotten, and the famine will devastate the land. The abundance in the land will not be remembered, since the famine that follows it will be so severe."* **- Genesis 41:29-31**

7-years of PLENTY: Begin in Fall 2023, Proverbs 13:22, and will continue into 2030. Prophetic work of Kim Clement... *"You have been besieged by your internal enemies for 7-years America; there shall be followed by 7-years of blessing."*

7-Years of FAMINE, the TIME of FAMINE, is expected to begin in 2030 with the signing of an Israel PEACE TREATY, the fulfillment of the *Shane Warren Prophecy...* **"They have divided MY land, now I will divide their land."** This 7-years of famine ends with the expected return of Christ!

Famine 2033 - 2040 food will be scarce, as it was during the TIME OF JOSEPH.

FAMINE
2033 - 2040

"The abundance in the land will not be remembered, because the famine that follows it will be so severe." - Genesis 41:31

Will God's bride lack during the coming Famine?

"Then Jesus asked them, "When I sent you out to preach the Good News and you did not have money, a traveler's bag, or an extra pair of sandals, did you need anything?" "No," they replied.." - Luke 22:35

Scan Me

THE REBUILDING OF THE TEMPLE

King David had a lifelong dream to build a temple—a permanent building instead of the tent used for the tabernacle. David died before that dream came true, but his son Solomon built a magnificent temple according to his father's wishes.

When Judah and Jerusalem fell to Babylon, Solomon's temple, which had stood for almost 420 years, was destroyed. There was no temple for about 70 years.

A second temple was built, although it wasn't as grand as the one that Solomon had constructed. Years later, King Herod made several improvements, and the temple stood for nearly 600 years. It was known as "Herod's Temple" and was the place Jesus and the disciples visited. It was destroyed by the Romans in 70 AD.

The third temple holds great significance for Jews and aligns with their expectation of the coming Messiah. There is a longing among Jewish people for the construction of the yet-to-be-built third temple, especially since their return to their promised land.

The prophet Ezekiel had a vision of a temple being rebuilt and saw that the glory of the LORD would come and settle in it. However, Daniel had a vision of the temple as well where the abomination of desolation will take place. This final seven mentioned in the scripture below will come just before Christ returns to earth and be a time of great tribulation.

He will confirm a covenant with many for one "seven." In the middle of the "seven" he will put an end to sacrifice and offering. And at the temple he will set up an abomination that causes desolation, until the end that is decreed is poured out on him.

Daniel 9:37 NIV

We have witnessed many biblical events throughout the years, particularly starting in 2020. Yet there is still no temple in Jerusalem. The Jews think that there must be a third temple for the Messiah to come (although He has already come). And their whole focus for the last two thousand years has been building a third temple.

So they will build one. Because that's what they believe must be done to see the Messiah. But of course, that's only to find out that the Messiah was here. In the future, they will rebuild a temple for the antichrist to desecrate, as prophesied by Daniel. Then they will realize that he's the antichrist and they will flee their mountains as the Bible describes.

The calculations show that the Antichrist will reveal himself with the signing of a peace treaty in 2033, likely occuring in August. Then June 2034 is expected to be the time point where the animal sacrifices are reinstated in a newly built temple in Jerusalem. The 2033 peace treaty starts the seven-year clock for the Great Tribulation that ends with Christ's return and is expected in 2040.

NOT Accepting CHRIST is Antichrist

The Papacy, Europe and Islam will unite to form the NEW WORLD ORDER, see George Bush's 1991 'New World Order' speech. Then, no one who does not agree with and accept Islamic Rule (SHARIA LAW) will be able to buy or sell, they get shunned and killed for their disobedience in not worshiping Allah.

Scan Me

SEASON 3
The Great Tribulation
The FINAL Season

ANTICHRIST KINGDOM
2033 - 2040

- Temple Mount in Israel destroyed (?) to make way for the Third Temple construction.

- 'GREAT DECEPTION' - Yet the evil one will deceive many, "even many of the elect". - Matthew 24:24

- Isaiah's Prophecy of the coming Messiah, The Forbidden Chapter: Isaiah 53, has been completed with JESUS. There is NO LONGER a NEED for the Third Temple and its customs; but the Jewish Nations will rebuild the Temple for 'their coming messiah', only to find out they were deceived by the evil one as he desecrates the temple by calling himself the great 'I AM', "pollutes the sanctuary of strength and takes away the daily sacrifice" and replacing it with something that requires money to receive forgiveness of sins!

- AUGUST 2033 - COVENANT WITH MANY, ANTICHRIST PEACE TREAT - DANIEL 9:27
- JUNE 2034 - TEMPLE COMPLETE AND SACRIFICE REINSTATED
- MARCH 2037 - ABOMINATION OF DESOLATION, END TO SACRIFICE AND OFFERING - DANIEL 9:27

CONSTRUCTION BEGINS SOON

SHARIAH WILL DOMINATE THE WORLD

Because of Jesus, there is NO LONGER a NEED for the Third Temple and its customs; yet the Jewish Nation has been deceived by the great deceiver and will rebuild it for the Antichrist!

Scan Me

BUILDING OF THE THIRD TEMPLE

THE GREAT AND TERRIBLE DAY

The Bible describes a day that will be both great and terrible, depending on what camp you're in. Malachi describes it like this: On the day when I [the Lord] acts, you will again see the distinction between the righteous and the wicked, between those who serve God and those who do not. (vs. 3:18)

On that day, the wicked will be punished and the righteous will be blessed. That day will be glorious for the people who long for it. Paul said in 1 Timothy 4:8 that we look forward to the **day of the Lord** when there would be an award, a crown of righteousness, given to await His appearing. When Jesus returns, the righteous will be purified according to Malachi 3:3.

But that very same day will be terrifying for some. Christ will punish the wicked and they will recognize their sin. However, it will be too late to repent by then. It will be a terrible day for the wicked. If you're not sure which side you're on, it's time to turn to repentance and prepare for the great and terrible day of the Lord.

A GENERATION THAT WILL DEFY DEATH

As discussed previously, even though Israel declared its independence in 1913, the Arab nations did not recognize this. It wasn't until the Six-Day War in 1967, that Israel was "officially" recognized. When something isn't recognized, then it's not yet born. So you could say the birth of the nation of Israel was in 1967.

The years of our life are seventy or even by reason of strength eighty, yet their span is but toil and trouble; they are soon gone, and we fly away.

Psalm 90:10 NIV

There are many verses in scripture that describe the length of one generation as seventy years (see the illustration on page 199). So if we add seventy years to 1967, that puts us in the year **2037**. Calculations point to 2037 as the time point for the Abomination of Desolation by the Antichrist in the temple. It would have 24 years earlier that Obama was in Israel, forshadowing the Antichrist desecration in March 2013,

As one who aligns prophecy with patterns and time points, consider this: In 2013, Kim Clement prophesied that *"God says there is a new way, and yet it is an old way. I am the stone for this generation. That stone is my Son. That stone is the rock, Christ Jesus. And that stone shall be given to the Davids of this generation. . . . But I have yet to give you that which I have kept for last. The glory of God that shall cover the earth with knowledge and manifestation as the water covers the sea. It is yet to come before I return. You are the generation that shall defy death."*

All calculations point to 70 years, plus an additional three and one-half years, for a total of 73 1/2 years. Or the year 2040. The math outlined in the book is not only fascinating, but it is biblical.

God is a living God; He is the God of yesterday, today and tomorrow. He wrote the end from the beginning. Choose wisely.

Every knee will bow and that every tongue will confess that Jesus Christ is Lord - Philippians 2:10-11

REDEMPTION OF THE EARTH
THE 'GREAT' & 'TERRIBLE' DAY!

- "The sun shall be turned into darkness, and the moon into blood, before the great and the terrible day of the LORD come." - Joel 2:31
- "WHEN these things begin to take place, stand up and lift up your heads, because REDEMPTION is drawing near." – Luke 21:28

REDEMPTION Definition: The action of regaining or gaining possession of something

Relationship with the Lord!

- Well done, good and faithful servant - Matthew 25:23
- You are my friends if you do what I command. I no longer call you servants, because a servant does not know his master's business. Instead, I have called you friends, for everything that I learned from my Father I have made known to you. - John 15:14-15

Rapture Soon?

- **Pre-Tribulation 1st Rapture 2033**
  - Matthew 24:40 - "Then shall two be in the field; the one shall be taken, and the **other left**."

- **Post-Tribulation 2nd Rapture 2040**
  - 1 Thessalonians 4:17 - "Then we who are alive, **who are left**, will be caught up together with them in the clouds to meet the Lord in the air, and so we will always be with the Lord".

  - Daniel 12:12 - "Blessed is the one who waits for and reaches the end of the 1,335 days (September 28, 2040)." "Blessed" for surviving the Great Tribulation and is then "caught-up".

LIARS, TRAITORS, & THIEVES
- Diana Larkin, Prophet, March 2023

- "This ESCAPE MENTALITY disarms and disempowers people from waging the Victorious Warfare they were designed for.

- My son is not an escape artist, He is a Victorious King, should not His bride, His very own Sons and Daughters, reflect that instead of hiding and waiting to be whisked out of the way.

- No longer be fooled by Liars, Traitors, and Thieves!"

- We were made to wage war against evil, NOT escape evil!

Occupy Till I Come!

Rapture!

Two (2) Raptures?
2033 & 2040

"We are the generation that will Defy Death!"
- Kim Clement 2013

ISRAEL'S 'TRUE' BIRTH... 1967

A GENERATION IS 70-YEARS

On **14 May 1948**, **Israel proclaimed its INDEPENDENCE.** Less than 24 hours later, the regular armies of Egypt, Jordan, Syria, Lebanon, and Iraq invaded the country, forcing Israel to defend the sovereignty it had regained

1967 ARAB-ISRAELI WAR
SIX-DAY WAR

June 5, 1967, The Six-Day War And The Golan Heights

After the first Arab-Israeli war in **1948-1949**, the **Arab world** refused **to recognize Israel's INDEPENDENCE. 19-YEARS** later **June 5, 1967**, the 6-Day War began and ended on the 6th day, **June 10, 1967,** with an Israeli victory. Israeli forces seizing the West Bank, including East Jerusalem, as well as the Golan Heights.

On June 10, **1967**, Israel is finally recognized by ALL the world as INDEPENDENT, and **ISRAEL IS 'OFFICIALLY' BORN!!**

The Generation born on June 10, 1967, comes to an end in **2040**

"We Are The GENERATION That Will DEFY DEATH!"
- Kim Clement 2013

1967 6-DAY WAR

GENERATION 70 YEARS

2047 *"BY STRENGTH"*

2 Raptures!
66 YEARS PLUS GOD 2033
73 YEARS PLUS GOD 2040

Generation: The years of our life are seventy (70), or even by reason of strength eighty (80); yet their span is but toil and trouble; they are soon gone, and we fly away. - Psalm 90:10

RIP

Psalm 90:10 - The years of our life are seventy (70), or even by **reason of strength eighty (80)**; yet their span is but toil and trouble; they are soon gone, and we fly away.

2 Chronicles 36:21 - To fulfill the word of the LORD by the mouth of Jeremiah, until the land had enjoyed its Sabbaths. All the days that it lay desolate it kept Sabbath, to fulfill seventy (70) years.

Jeremiah 25:11 - This whole land shall become a ruin and a waste, and these nations shall serve the king of Babylon seventy years.

Jeremiah 25:12 - Then after seventy (70) years are completed, I will punish the king of Babylon and that nation, the land of the Chaldeans, for their iniquity, declares the LORD, making the land an everlasting waste.

Jeremiah 29:10 - "For thus says the LORD: When seventy (70) years are completed for Babylon, I will visit you, and I will fulfill to you my promise and bring you back to this place.

Daniel 9:2 - In the first year of his reign, I, Daniel, perceived in the books the number of years that, according to the word of the LORD to Jeremiah the prophet, must pass before the end of the desolations of Jerusalem, namely, seventy (70) years.

RETURN TO THE GARDEN OF EDEN

A 6000-year journey back to the Garden of Eden where PERFECTION was originally created, to begin the MILLENNIAL REIGN WITH CHRIST, a 1000-year Sabbath, with evil removed off earth!

Genesis 1
In the Beginning...

Must Watch!

A 6000-Year Journey...

Year 1 of 1000-Years begins Tabernacles 2040

"BUT OF THAT DAY AND HOUR KNOWETH NO MAN"

The True Meaning...

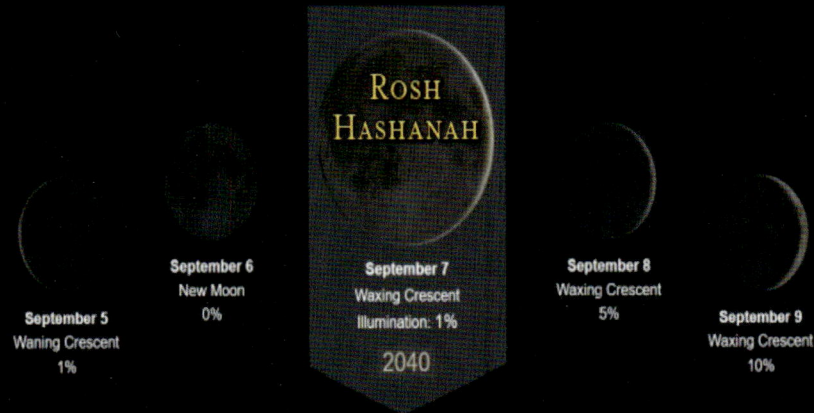

ROSH HASHANAH

September 5
Waning Crescent
1%

September 6
New Moon
0%

September 7
Waxing Crescent
Illumination: 1%

2040

September 8
Waxing Crescent
5%

September 9
Waxing Crescent
10%

"But of that day and hour knoweth no man" is a direct reference to the Feast of Trumpets, also known as Rosh Hashanah, and the "Hidden Day".

- "But of that day and hour no one knows, not even the angels of heaven, but My Father only. Matthew 24:36
- "Watch therefore, for you know neither the day nor the hour in which the Son of Man is coming. Matthew 25:13

Most people are not aware of the **TRUE MEANING** behind the phrase that Jesus spoke, concerning the DAY and HOUR of His return and believe His return to be God's secret that no man should ever know, and that God would never reveal this timepoint so that we might always be prepared. Can His return be calculated and <u>did God reveal the year, month and Feast of "The Day of the Lord"</u>? Rosh Hashanah begins on the first day of the seventh month in the Jewish calendar and starts what is called "The Day of the Lord," the start of the one-thousand-year reign of the Messiah on earth. This important Feast of Israel is signaled by the New Moon and the exact moment when the moon is invisible to the earth, when it appears in what is called the 'waxing crescent'. The moon is critically important to Israel, all of their feast days are signaled according to the moon cycles from new to full. Leviticus 23:4 is part of a passage that describes the appointed festivals of the Lord, which are holy days that are to be celebrated at **specific times** each year. The DAY and HOUR that starts the feast, Rosh Hashanah, is as soon as the New Moon is announced, Mattityahu 18:18-20. Two witnesses are appointed to watch for the New Moon, specifically looking for the 'crescent', a thin sliver of moon, to appear. Its first appearance witnessed by the two appointed witnesses marks the DAY and Hour for Rosh Hashanah to begin and is called God's 'Appointed Time'. No man has the right to set this time, it is determined by God alone, and no man has the authority to change the appointed time of this feast (Midrash Rabbah Numbers, Vol 2.21.25, p. 852). It was the intention of God, and well understood by the Sanhedrin of Israel, that the watch for the Feast of Trumpets, was a rehearsal for the time when this feast would be fully realized, for the Jews Messiah would arrive and for Christians Christ would return. When Jesus spoke, "But of that day and hour knoweth no man, no, not the angels of heaven, but my Father only", He was specifically referring to the feast of Rosh Hashanah, He was telling us that His return for His church will be at this unknown moment when the waxing crescent appears, the fulfillment of the Feast of Trumpets. The calculations revealed within this book that go back 6000 years to creation and point to the exact year the Unites States of America would be born including the year Mystery Babylon would fall and America would be reborn, incredibly points to Rosh Hashana September 2040 as the long awaited 'Appointed Time' the world has waited centuries for. In 2040 will there again be two appointed witnesses looking for the waxing crescent moon, as in the times of old, where "No man knows the day or the hour" was spoken of? Revelations 11:3 speaks of two witnesses, "And I will give power unto my two witnesses, and they shall prophesy a thousand two hundred and threescore days, clothed in sackcloth." Something also to consider, during the time of Antichrist, the bride will be in the wilderness, in safe havens, devoid of any 'technology' and therefore, expect the bride of Christ to be looking for that thin sliver of moon in anticipation of "The Day of the Lord". Will the waxing crescent be seen on September 7, 2040, with only 1% illumination, if so, at what time? Or will the waxing crescent be seen on September 8 at 5% illumination and if so, at what time? The waxing crescent will certainly be seen by September 9 at 10% illumination. There is no absolute exact day or hour the 'waxing crescent' will be seen, and is only know by God, the creator of the cycles of the moon.

All eyes of the bride will be anxiously looking for the 'Waxing Crescent' moon in September 2040!

GOD'S CALENDAR

5785 5986 5789 5790 5793

SEASON 2

7-Years of PLENTY Begins

7-Years of PLENTY Ends

7-Years of FAMINE Begins

Rise of AntiChrist 2033

GEORGE ORWELL 1984

AMERICA Re-Born July 4, 2025

Scan Me

FINAL 3 SEASONS

7 7 717 7

2017-2024 "TIME OF DARKNESS"

2026-2033 "TIME OF PLENTY"

2033-7040 "TIME OF TRIBULATION"

4-Year Final Harvest

5-Years of Amazing Grace   30

JUBILEE 1-YEAR   7-YEARS (2550-DAYS) - SEASON 2 - TIME OF "PLENTY"   45 Days 3 Days   SEASON 3 - END OF DAYS!

1260-Days   1260-Days

AC Peace Treaty 2033

July 11 2025

July 11 2026

USA Election November 2028

USA Inauguration January 2029

December 22 2029

January 21 2030

July 4, 2033

August 18-21, 2033

Commit thy works, unto the LORD, and thy thoughts shall be established. - Proverbs: 16:3

GOD's Calendar

5793   5974   5795   5797   5800   5801

FINAL 3 SEASONS
717

SEASON 3
A TIME of FAMINE & The Great Tribulation
The FINAL Season

Rapture!

Rise of AntiChrist Kingdom Begins!

Pre-Trib Rapture

1 Thessalonians 4:17
• Pray that your flight will not take place in Winter, or on the Sabbath (Saturday) - Matthew 24:20-30

1984
Rise of AntiChrist 2033

Egyptian Eclipse
March 20
2034

Abomination
of Desolation
End to Sacrifice and
Offering - Daniel 9:27

Holy Peolpe
delivered into his (evil)
hands - Daniel 7:25

Post-Trib Rapture

Feast of Tabernacles Ends 6000-Years!

September 22 - 28 (6-days?)
World War 3

Royal Wedding!
Bride's (Jacob) 15th-Birthday
The Day of The Lord
Heaven on Earth

September 28-30, 2040
Shemini Atzeret
- Final 5800 Year Torah Reading
- 8th Day, New Beginning!
- First Chapter of Genesis is Read
- "In the Beginning..."
- Return To Eden
- RAIN from HEAVEN

Must Watch!

- Year 1 of 1000 (Year 5801)

1260-Days   30   1260-Days

← 7-YEARS (2595-Days) - SEASON 3 - TIME OF "FAMINE" →   45-Days   1000-YEARS PEACE ON EARTH

← 295-Days →

"Covenant With Many"
Antichrist Peace Treaty
August 18-21
2033
Daniel 9:27

Temple Complete
Sacrifices Reinstated
June 12
2034

Rev. 13:11 – Another Beast
September 8
2034

Rev. 13:12 – Mortal Wound Healed
June 21-22
2035

Treaty Broken
February 1
2037

March 3
2037

January 2037
New USA President

Yom Kippur – Sept 16-17
Rosh Hashana – Sept 7-9
August 14, 2040

SEPTEMBER 28, 2040

THE GREAT TRIBULATION

❖ For then shall be GREAT TRIBULATION, such as was not since the beginning of the world to this time, no, nor ever shall be. - Matthew 24:21
❖ USA offers NO More Protection To Israel

❖ Two Witnesses for 1260-Days - Revelation 11:3
❖ Woman fled into the wilderness to a place prepared for her by God, where she might (most martyred) be taken care of for 1,260-days. - Rev 12:6
❖ But woe to the earth and the sea because the devil has gone down to you and is filled with fury because he know his TIME is short. - Rev. 12:12
❖ The woman was given two wings of an eagle to fly to the place prepared for her in the Wilderness (Safe Havens) for 1260-days. - Rev 12:14

INTRIGUING ASPECTS OF THE YEARS 2034 THROUGH 2040

- The 2034 Great Egyptian Eclipse occurs **9**-years, **11**-months after the 2024 Great American Eclipse and two days before the satanic **Skull and Bones date of 322**. The Skull and Bones date of 322 could also represent the year 20*34* by combining two plus two, representing the fourth year of the 3rd decade. This marks March 22, 2034 as a likely and highly important date for evil.

- Notice the year 2037 is 124 years (**1-2-4**) from the founding of the Federal Reserve and also the Origins of the Arab Israeli Conflict.

- 2037 is also 70 years (i.e., **one generation** as written about in Psalm 90:10) from the 6-day war of 1967.

- Dropping the zeros from the year 2040, gives you 2 and 4. 2+4=6, and six is the number of man. Man was created on the sixth day!

- Also on September 28, 2040, with the Feast of Tabernacles, a 6000 year period ends. This begins the celebration or assembly called Shemini Atzeret. The Hebrew word shemini means *eighth* and atzeret in this context means *closing festival*. The holiday signifies the end of the seven-day Sukkot and the start of the eighth day. The eighth day is a time of new beginning or a return to Eden ("In the beginning...")

➡ **DID YOU KNOW?** The all-seeing eye of the One World Government, also referred to as "Big Brother," is also called "the eye of **Horus**." By adding the seven years of Divine Favor to their plans for Agenda 2030, we arrive at the year 2037, the Abomination of Desolation.

By now, you understand this is not all just a coincidence! Remember, the end was written from the beginning. These are not political times we live in; they are Biblical. And, all of the math adds up!

NO MAN KNOWETH THE DAY OR THE HOUR

Many are unaware of the real significance of Jesus' words regarding His return. They believe His return to be God's secret and something no man should ever know. Some believe that God would never reveal this time point so that we might always be prepared. Can we determine the time of His return? Were the year, month, or "The Day of the Lord" ever revealed by God?

The Day of the Lord begins with Rosh Hashanah on the first day of the seventh month. This begins the one-thousand-year reign of the Messiah on earth. This crucial holiday is shown by the New Moon, the exact instant the crescent of the new moon is seen from earth.

The moon is critically important to Israel; all of their feast days are signaled according to the moon's cycles from new to full.

Leviticus 23:4 describes the appointed festivals of the Lord— the holy days celebrated at specific times each year. Rosh Hashanah's beginning—the feast's day and hour—is determined by the New Moon's announcement (Mattityahu 18:18-20). Two witnesses are appointed to watch for the New Moon, explicitly looking for the "crescent," which is a thin sliver of moon. Rosh Hashanah begins when the two designated witnesses first see the sign, marking God's appointed time. No one has the right to set this time; it is determined by God alone. And no one has the authority to change the appointed time of this feast.

The calculations revealed in this book go back 6000 years to creation and point to the exact year the United States of America would be born. They also include the year Mystery Babylon would fall, and America would be reborn. Incredibly, the evidence all converges on Rosh Hashanah, September 2040, as the long-awaited "Appointed Time."

In 2040, will two appointed witnesses be looking for the waxing crescent moon to signify the beginning of Rosh Hashanah? Revelation speaks of those two witnesses.

> And I will give power to my two witnesses, and they will prophesy one thousand two hundred and sixty days, clothed in sackcloth.
>
> Revelation 11:3 NKJV

Also, consider that during the time of the Antichrist, the Bride who was "left" behind in the wilderness—in a safe haven—is devoid of any technology. Therefore, expect the remnant of the Bride of Christ to be looking for that thin sliver of moon in anticipation of The Day of the Lord.

Will the waxing crescent be seen on September 7, 2040, with only 1% illumination? If so, at what time? Or will the waxing crescent be seen on September 8 at 5% illumination? And if so, at what time? Will there be clouds in the sky obstructing visibility on either of these dates?

The waxing crescent will likely be seen by September 9 at 10% illumination. We know that the eyes of the Bride will be looking for the waxing crescent. And it will appear in September, as it has for centuries. But there is no prior knowledge of the exact day or hour the waxing crescent will be seen. This is only known by God, the creator of the cycles of the moon. When Jesus replied to the apostles, saying "No man knows the day or hour" he was telling them indirectly that he will return on Rosh Hashanah. Fascinating!

Even so, when you see all these things,
you know that it is near,
right at the door.

Matthew 24:33 NIV

ABOUT THE AUTHOR

ACCURACY AND SUCCESS have always been a part of Bo Polny's life. A childhood diagnosis of a learning disability led Bo to develop personal strategies to overcome the challenge.

His passion for learning led him to graduate near the top of his class in 1991, when he subsequently moved to California to pursue his career as a chiropractor. Soon after, he established one of the largest multidisciplinary health clinics in the area, and Orange Coast recognized him as one of their "Top Doctors."

A personal family challenge caused Bo to reconsider his life and priorities after spending 20 years in private practice. The focus shifted from self-interests to a burning desire to do more of God's will. Bo's career as a chiropractor ended when he sold his clinic and immersed himself in studying the precious metals market, a passion that deeply resonated within him. As he delved deeper into gold and silver market analysis, he uncovered similarities to timing patterns mentioned in the Bible, particularly in the book of Daniel.

While conducting research, Bo encountered Nostradamus' prediction of the catastrophic events of 9/11, as well as investigating other patterns and events referenced in the Bible. Further reading brought him Ecclesiastes 1:9, which states, "What has been will be again," and he realized that life is full of cycles that create specific patterns on charts. By analyzing these patterns and comparing them to historical time points, some repeat with surprising accuracy. Bo then understood that an event is required to fulfill the expected cycle pattern.

As a result, Bo ended up coining the phrase, *"Cycles precede all events, and then events including price manipulation, natural disasters, and war complete the cycle."* Further research led him to discover the way the timing cycle, described as Daniel's Timeline, dictates certain world circumstances, such as gold's price movement. He began constructing his market analysis using these biblical timing calculations overlaid with cycle-specific historical patterns. One could derive an accurate and captivating glimpse into future market cycles.

As a Christian, Bo believes God has blessed him with the gift of helping others find direction and godly hope, fueled by faith, for a bright future. Through prayer and prophetic dreams, he validates his belief and gains insight into market patterns. Dreams and prayers are always subject to personal interpretation, and perfection in predicting future market movements is impossible. However, Bo's historical accuracy in predicting future market movement has proven to be eerily and shockingly accurate beyond anything of probability or chance.

For example, on February 8, 2020, in an interview on USA Watchdog, Bo Polny forecasted, in advance, the exact top for the U.S. stock markets and warned of a 35% market crash in March 2020. As predicted, a 36% crash followed and only ended with the rapid onset of COVID-19. He predicted the exact top date and the crash percentage beforehand, something rarely accomplished by other analysts and just one of the dozens of verifiable forecasts Bo has made.

In October 2022, Bo stated that Bitcoin would drop below $19,000 on November 8, 2022. And on exactly November 8, it crashed as forecast. On the 8th Bitcoin began spiraling down from $20,000 and within two days later it was trading at $15,600. Later it was discovered that the crash was caused by FTX and noted as "the biggest financial fraud case in U. S. history."

Bo's market timing newsletter has become one of the most popular and successful private market timing circulars in the world. His devotion to God, prayer, Bible knowledge, and memorization of historic chart patterns have led to his successful forecasting of price direction and critical market time points.

He has been given what the Bible refers to as "The Issachar Anointing," or people who understand the times as written in 1 Chronicles 12:32. His goal in founding the *Gold 2020 Forecast* was to reach and awaken more people to the Biblical times we live in. While honored by the gifts God has given him, Bo humbly acknowledges "all the glory to God."

Does Bo get everything right 100% of the time? No. It's not possible because the only perfect One is God. But there are cycle points that are very accurate and follow the timelines of history.

For example, he knew that something significant was going to happen in April 2020. Sure enough, oil went to a negative $38 a barrel, which Bo had forecast three months in advance before the coronavirus became a pandemic. That event was the first time the price fell less than 0.00, since trading began in 1983 for WTI - West Texas Intermediate crude.

Bo also knew something big was going to happen in September 2020 and on September 18, 2020, Ruth Bader Ginsburg died. These incidents were based on calculations that Bo took from the Bible and applied to the present day.

DEFINING ACCURATE TIMEPOINTS

When God gives Bo a revelation or calculation and it doesn't play out like expected, he goes to God and gets down on his knees. And God has anointed Bo to help with understanding. But Bo doesn't want people looking to him or any other human for answers. Only look to God for the truth.

The Lord will reveal answers for where the plan was misunderstood. With the various calendars used throughout history, and God's plan being precise and strategic, it is important to hear from Him regarding dates and times, because it was planned out thousands of years ago. The plans were set out by God's clock and God's clock hasn't changed.

But many kings and popes have manipulated the calendar through the centuries. Because God operates on His time and in His seasons, it would only make sense that the year would begin in the Spring. Winter is death.

Some might argue that the Bible says "But of that *day* and *hour* no one knows, not even the angels of heaven, but My Father only" according to Matthew 24:46 (KJV, Emphasis Added). However, these words are often misunderstood.

Man's calculated dates aren't always exact, but at times they can be very accurate. Where are we in the spectrum of time? We are approaching a multi-thousand-year turning point—the third seal of Revelation which opens in 2025.

The third seal is the fall of Mystery Babylon, and the evil puppet masters can't be ready for that. They will soon realize there is no alternative to God's plan. God is undefeated and will remain that way. And if the prophecy is true, no man can stop it

> *For prophecy never came by the will of man, but holy men of God spoke as they were moved by the Holy Spirit.*
>
> 2 Peter 1:21 NKJV

The final image on page 212 summarizes the three 7-year periods and one year of Jubilee that were discussed in *Revelation The Good News: Jubilee Edition*. It provides the timepoints marking the beginning of each season. One season is complete. A Jubilee and two seven-year periods remain as of the time of this writing.

There is **good news** in the events that are to come. My prayer is that you are blessed as you live and walk in a generation that will defy death and see the glory of the Lord in the days to come.

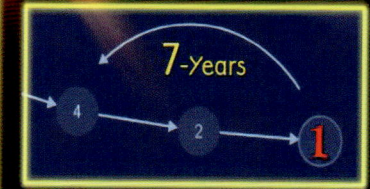

WOMAN AND THE DRAGON

REVELATION 12 SIGN
Starts the Final 3 Seasons

Virgo
Jupiter

FINAL 3 SEASONS
7 | 7 | 7
717

GOD'S CALENDAR: 5800   5801

Tabernacles Ends!

Royal Wedding!
The Day of The Lord

September 28-30, 2040
Shemini Atzeret
Year 1 of 1000
Year 5801

Must Watch!

SEPTEMBER 28, 2040

Tabernacles ENDS

Blessed is the one who waits for and reaches the end of the 1,335 days
- Daniel 12:12

1200-WEEKS (8400-DAYS)

600-WEEKS (4200-DAYS)

Rosh Hashana
September 7-9, 2040

Yom Kippur
September 16-17

Tabernacles FINAL HARVEST
STARTS: September 22

Armageddon
Ezekiel 38-39
WORLD WAR 3
6 Days

September 28
2040

1000 Years Begins

FINAL 3 SEASONS

2025 - REST, JUBILEE

717

EVIL   GOOD   EVIL

2017 - 2024   2026 - 2033   2033 - 2040

"TIME OF DARKNESS"   "TIME OF PLENTY"   "TIME OF TRIBULATION"